T&T Clark Introduction to Spirit Christology

T&T Clark Introduction to Spirit Christology

Leopoldo A. Sánchez M.

LONDON • NEW YORK • OXFORD • NEW DELHI • SYDNEY

T&T CLARK
Bloomsbury Publishing Plc
50 Bedford Square, London, WC1B 3DP, UK
1385 Broadway, New York, NY 10018, USA
29 Earlsfort Terrace, Dublin 2, Ireland

BLOOMSBURY, T&T CLARK and the T&T Clark logo are trademarks
of Bloomsbury Publishing Plc

First published in Great Britain 2022

Copyright © Leopoldo A. Sánchez M., 2022

Leopoldo A. Sánchez M. has asserted his right under the Copyright, Designs
and Patents Act, 1988, to be identified as Author of this work.

For legal purposes the Acknowledgments on p. xix constitute an extension
of this copyright page.

Cover image © Bernardo Ramonfaur/Shutterstock

All rights reserved. No part of this publication may be reproduced or transmitted
in any form or by any means, electronic or mechanical, including photocopying,
recording, or any information storage or retrieval system, without prior permission
in writing from the publishers.

Bloomsbury Publishing Plc does not have any control over, or responsibility for, any
third-party websites referred to or in this book. All internet addresses given in this
book were correct at the time of going to press. The author and publisher regret any
inconvenience caused if addresses have changed or sites have ceased to exist, but can
accept no responsibility for any such changes.

A catalogue record for this book is available from the British Library.

Library of Congress Cataloging-in-Publication Data
Names: Sánchez M., Leopoldo A. (Leopoldo Antonio Sánchez Merino), 1973- author.
Title: T&T Clark introduction to Spirit christology / Leopoldo A. Sánchez M..
Description: London, UK ; New York, NY, USA : Bloomsbury Academic, 2021. |
Includes bibliographical references and index. |
Identifiers: LCCN 2021013498 (print) | LCCN 2021013499 (ebook) |
ISBN 9780567690135 (paperback) | ISBN 9780567690142 (hb) |
ISBN 9780567690159 (epub) | ISBN 9780567690166 (epdf)
Subjects: LCSH: Spirit christology–Textbooks. | Holy Spirit–Textbooks. |
Jesus Christ–Person and offices–Textbooks.
Classification: LCC BT205 .S194 2021 (print) | LCC BT205 (ebook) | DDC 232–dc23
LC record available at https://lccn.loc.gov/2021013498
LC ebook record available at https://lccn.loc.gov/2021013499

ISBN: HB: 978-0-5676-9014-2
PB: 978-0-5676-9013-5
ePDF: 978-0-5676-9016-6
ePUB: 978-0-5676-9015-9

Typeset by Newgen KnowledgeWorks Pvt. Ltd., Chennai, India
Printed and bound in Great Britain

To find out more about our authors and books visit www.bloomsbury.com
and sign up for our newsletters.

To Luis F. Ladaria and Ralph Del Colle† (1954–2012):
For instilling in me, through their works,
an abiding ecumenical appreciation for the depth and joy
of knowing Jesus Christ more deeply through the Holy Spirit,
respectively in Spanish and English.

Contents

Preface ix
Acknowledgments xix
Abbreviations xxi

1 **A Bird's-Eye View of Spirit Christology: Its Burden, Varieties, and Contemporary Revival** 1

2 **The Fullness of the Spirit in and through Jesus: Insights from Biblical Studies** 33

3 **The Spirit Enters the Flesh to Save the Flesh: Building Blocks from Spirit Christology in the Early Church** 57

4 **The Spirit in the Trinity: Spirit and Logos Christologies in Trinitarian Key** 93

5 **Who Do You Say That I Am? The Complementarity of Spirit and Logos Christologies** 115

6 **Christlike Ways of the Spirit: Spirit Christology and Life in the World** 151

Conclusion 173

Glossary 177
Bibliography 183
Author Index 195
Subject Index 197
Scripture Index 201

Preface

"Who do people say that I am?" (Mk 8:27). In Jesus' day, many opinions circulated about him. Is he John the Baptist, Elijah, one of the prophets? (v. 28). Today, the same is true. Is he a special man, a holy man, a man who speaks for God? Is he a contemplative, a man of prayer, or an activist, a man of action? Is he divinelike, a god or deified person, or God himself in the flesh? "He asked them, 'But who do you say that I am?' Peter answered him, 'You are the Messiah'" (Mk 16:29).[1] Jesus' question to his disciples then remains our question now. Ever since Peter took a stab at it, disciples of Christ the world over and across the centuries have followed suit. Theology, the study of God and all things in view of God, invites us to ask ourselves Jesus' question and answer it in every generation in ways that are faithful, intelligible, and compelling. No answer captures everything there is to say or grasp about Jesus. Although Peter speaks right words, "You are the Messiah" (v. 29), he soon finds out he has neither said nor understood what that little word "Messiah" implies. A word so pregnant with meaning. So Jesus helps him out. He identifies the Messiah as "the Son of Man," whose destiny is to "undergo great suffering, and be rejected … and be killed, and after three days rise again" (v. 31). Peter does not associate the Messiah with suffering and the cross, and so he rebukes Jesus (v. 32). He has not grasped the depth of his own words about Jesus, the sense and trajectory of his messianic mission.

The title "Messiah" has various layers of meaning in Scripture, depending on the context in which it is used. Consider the title "Christ," another word for "Messiah," often rendered as "Anointed One." If we look at Jesus' identity through the lens of *anointing* language, a link between Jesus and the Spirit of God emerges. At his baptism, "the Holy Spirit descended upon him" to bring him into his mission as Yahweh's Servant (Lk. 3:22; cf. Isa. 42:1). After his temptation in the desert, where "Jesus, full of the Holy Spirit … was led by the Spirit" (Lk. 4:1), he begins his public ministry in Galilee with these words: "The Spirit of Lord is upon me, because he has *anointed* me to bring good news to the poor" (4:18a, italics mine). In the book of Acts, Peter

---
[1] Unless otherwise noted, all biblical references are taken from NRSV.

sums up the message concerning Jesus Christ, noting "how God *anointed* Jesus of Nazareth with the Holy Spirit and with power; how he went about doing good and healing all who were oppressed by the devil, for God was with him" (Acts 10:38, italics mine). Rich with references to the Spirit, these Lukan texts invite us to associate Jesus' identity as the "Christ" with the Holy Spirit, God's anointing from above, who comes upon him at his baptism and leads him through the desert into the Father's mission to bring good news and deliverance from evil to his people Israel and the nations.

Luke invites us to read Jesus' whole life and work through a Spirit-oriented lens. The Spirit is present with the child from the very first moment of his human existence (Lk. 1:35; cf. Mt. 1:18, 20). Jesus teaches as one "filled with the power of the Spirit" (Lk. 4:14-15; cf. Acts 1:2). He proclaims good news because he is anointed with the Spirit (Lk. 4:18-19). A manifestation of God's gracious kingdom in our midst, Jesus heals and drives out demons "by the Spirit of God" (Mt. 12:28; "the finger of God" in Lk. 11:20). Jesus "rejoiced in the Holy Spirit" in prayer, thanking the Father for revealing the truths of the kingdom to his disciples (Lk. 10:21). As the suffering Servant, his baptism in water at Jordan culminates with his baptism in blood at Golgotha (cf. Lk. 12:50; cf. Mk 10:38). As the risen Lord, he also sends the promise of the Holy Spirit upon his disciples (Lk. 24:49; Acts 1:4-5). The Son pours out the same Holy Spirit with whom the Father anointed him for mission upon the church, sending her on a mission to Israel and the nations. A similar Spirit-oriented reading of Jesus can easily be achieved through the Gospel of John, where the divine Word made flesh (Jn 1:14) is also proclaimed to be the Lamb of God upon whom the Spirit descends and remains, and the one who will baptize others with the Holy Spirit (Jn 1:29-34). The Son who is sent by the Father and bears the Spirit "without measure" to speak "the words of God" (Jn 3:34; cf. Jn 6:63) breathes the same Spirit on his disciples, sending them to the world to forgive and retain sins (Jn 20:21-22). In various places, the gospels portray Jesus as one who is full of God's Spirit and whose life is led and empowered by the same Spirit.

Spirit Christology Today

In the last fifty years or so, a growing international group of scholars working from different disciplines has taken note of the Spirit-oriented aspects of the gospel accounts. They have reflected on Jesus' perennial question from the perspective of a Spirit (or pneumatological) Christology, unpacking who Jesus is in terms of the Spirit's role in his life and mission. To Jesus' question, "who do you say that I am?," a Spirit Christology responds, "the receiver, bearer, and giver of God's Spirit." What are the implications of such a statement for what we say about God, his Messiah's life and work, and how his disciples live in the world? The main impetus for exploring Spirit Christology as a theological framework to answer these questions began in the twentieth century with the revival of Trinitarian theology, the Second Vatican Council's call for a vigorous return to the study of biblical and patristic sources, and the rise of the Pentecostal and charismatic movements as a global phenomenon. As an introduction to this global and interdisciplinary field of study, this introduction surveys some of its key voices and themes. Yet our primary goal is to highlight the main questions or problems raised by a Spirit Christology and some constructive ways theologians have begun to address them. In doing so, it is our hope to show how looking at Jesus' identity from a pneumatological angle can enrich our approach to fundamental theological questions.

Our thesis is twofold. First, a review of literature in Spirit Christology written from biblical, historical, systematic, and practical theology perspectives suggests three types of questions theologians working in the field have pursued and offered proposals for. Second, answers to these questions, except for some important exceptions, are framed and integrated within a biblically informed Nicene logic that allows for a diversity of legitimate proposals within a theological consensus. Such consensus lies in a commitment to understand Christ's identity in dialogue with the Trinitarian and Christological teachings inspired by the Council of Nicaea (AD 325). The three major questions in the field are the following:

(1) *Christology and Soteriology*: How do we describe the activity of the Holy Spirit in the life and mission of Jesus? What is the role of the Holy Spirit in the mystery of the incarnation, in the humanity or human life of the Son, and in his work of salvation?

(2) *Trinitarian Theology*: How do we describe the proper mission (Lat. *proprium*) of the Holy Spirit in God's economy of salvation? How is the Spirit's unique mission distinct from the proper mission of the Son? How do these missions relate to or interact with one another? How do the distinction and relationship between the missions of the Holy Spirit and the Son in God's economy of salvation (economic Trinity) reveal or correspond in some way to their eternal relations in or with one another (immanent Trinity)?

(3) *Life in the Spirit*: How is Jesus' life in the Spirit different from and similar to his disciples' life in the Spirit? What is the degree of discontinuity and continuity between the presence and activity of the Holy Spirit in the Son of God and the adopted sons (and daughters) of God? What are the Christlike ways of the Spirit, or the ways the Spirit shapes Christ in human persons? How do we discern and walk in step with the Spirit in the world?

This work aims to introduce significant authors and themes in the field of Spirit Christology in a way that the aforementioned questions receive proper attention. Along the way, we draw attention to areas of divergence and especially consensus, as well as potential areas for further exploration.

Outline of Chapters

Each of the book's chapters delves into prominent examples of past and present authors' contributions to issues raised when a pneumatological lens is brought to bear on the question of Jesus' identity. The first chapter provides an introduction to the field. Before offering a working definition of Spirit Christology, Chapter 1 discusses the burden every consideration of the Spirit's role in Jesus since the times of the early church has had to wrestle with. The question may be framed as follows: If Jesus is God, does he really need the Spirit? The chapter also introduces readers to three varieties of Spirit Christology, namely, Nicene, pre-Nicene, and post-Nicene (also referred to as Chalcedonian, pre-Chalcedonian, and post-Chalcedonian). Each one has a particular way of defining the reality of "Spirit" and how it operates in relation to some aspect of Christ's identity. Finally, a discussion of major events or movements giving rise to the revival of Spirit Christology in the twentieth century highlights how the field is both a product of and response to a broader interest in the place of theological reflection on the Holy Spirit in church and world. A potpourri of theologians and ideas shaped by these global events brings this introductory chapter to a close by offering a bird's-eye view of the creative output in the field.

Although Spirit Christology has found a special home among systematic theologians, their work has interacted significantly with insights from the fields of biblical studies and historical theology. The next two chapters look at these intersections. Mining insights from biblical studies, Chapter 2 introduces readers to James D. G. Dunn and Gerald F. Hawthorne, whose works explicitly explore the implications of the New Testament's (especially, the gospels') presentation of Jesus from a Spirit-oriented reading of the texts. Each of these authors focuses respectively on the eschatological framework and kenotic dimension of the Spirit's presence and activity in and through Jesus. The chapter ends by highlighting a more recent sample of the deployment of Spirit Christology in the field of the theological interpretation of Scripture. A collaboration of biblical and systematic theologians at an annual meeting of the Society of Biblical Literature led to the publication of a *Journal of Theological Interpretation* themed issue on Spirit Christology and the Theological Interpretation of the Gospels. Showing the international and ecumenical breadth of Spirit Christology, Myk Habets, a Reformed theologian from New Zealand, and myself, a Panamanian-Chilean Lutheran theologian working in the United States, collaborated as editors for the issue. As an example of the articles therein, Michael J. Gorman's brief intertextual study of John's "Spirit Christology" in response to the "Johannine Jesus" thesis shows how biblical studies can both enrich and be enriched by the field of Spirit Christology.

Chapter 3 deals with some patristic insights systematic theologians have at their disposal as they articulate a Spirit Christology. The chapter focuses first on the nascent but foundational contributions of two early church fathers, Irenaeus and Athanasius, to the development of a Spirit Christology. In their responses to the Gnostic and Arian portrayals of Jesus, which used his baptism with the Spirit, respectively, to deny his incarnation and divinity, these fathers stressed the presence of the Holy Spirit in the flesh of the Word as a condition in God's plan for the salvation of the flesh (all humanity). Their insights give us an early look at the possibility and means for thinking about Jesus' identity and work from a bifocal angle, namely, in a way that speaks of him both as divine and human (incarnational aspect), and as the bearer and giver of God's Spirit (pneumatological aspect). In the second part of the chapter, we look at some issues raised by early church fathers that are still relevant for contemporary constructions of Spirit Christology, such as the Spirit's personal identity in the Trinity, the relative ambiguity in the early church's understanding of "Spirit," their interpretations of the anointing of Jesus, and the contrast between Syriac-Antiochene and Alexandrian approaches to the Spirit's role in Christ's humanity. The questions these problems raise provide scholars with further building blocks and some unresolved tensions to work with in their own Spirit Christologies today.

Chapters 4 and 5 delve into the contributions of systematic theologians from various theological traditions to the main Trinitarian and

Christological issues raised by a Spirit Christology. The fourth chapter deals with the integration of Spirit Christology into a broader theological program and Trinitarian scheme. Although there are many theologians who have reflected on the Trinitarian outcomes of the field, this chapter focuses on two major figures. German Protestant theologian Jürgen Moltmann's kenotic and eschatological view of the Spirit arises from an investigation of the Spirit's role in Jesus' death and resurrection, and this pneumatology of the cross (*pneumatologia crucis*) aligns with his view of a Trinity that is open to the world not out of a deficiency of being but out of overflowing love. Australian Catholic theologian David Coffey shows how a study of Jesus as recipient and sender of the Spirit offers a "return" model of the Trinity that serves as a complement to the traditional "procession" model. The latter portrays the Spirit as proceeding from the Father and the Son, and the former depicts the Spirit as the interpersonal love of the Father and the Son. By bringing the procession model into the more comprehensive return model, Coffey offers a synthesis of Logos and Spirit Christologies with the capacity to speak of Jesus' sonship in incarnational and pneumatic terms and of human participation by the grace of adoption in his sonship. The chapter introduces readers to these theologians' insights, as well as to some critiques and extensions of their work.

Chapter 5 deals with Spirit Christology as a complement to Logos Christology. It brings together a trio of Lutheran (Leopoldo Sánchez), Reformed (Myk Habets), and Pentecostal (Skip Jenkins) voices, who exemplify the systematic retrieval of partially forgotten insights on the Holy Spirit from their theological traditions in order to integrate incarnational (Logos) and pneumatological (Spirit) aspects of the mystery of Christ's identity. In their proposals in Spirit Christology, Sánchez, Habets, and Jenkins, respectively, appropriate critically and constructively expand on pneumatic elements from the Christologies of German Lutheran theologian Martin Chemnitz, English Puritan theologian John Owen, and Scottish theologian Edward Irving. My interest in Chemnitz lies in articulating a pneumatological interpretation of his teaching on the supernatural created gifts that inhere in Christ's humanity, making it a suitable instrument for the Logos to work in cooperation with it to bring about his work of salvation. I argue that such gifts can be attributed to the uncreated Spirit's presence and activity in, with, and through the Son's human life and mission. Bringing the Spirit into Lutheran Christology yields a way to speak about the mutual cooperation of the Son and the Spirit in the mystery of the incarnation. Habets explores Owen's idea that, although the Logos alone assumes a human nature as his immediate work, the Spirit is the personal agent who is directly or immediately involved in the rest of his human life and work. Owen's teaching aligns with a Reformed Christology, according to which the Holy Spirit brings the divine and human natures of Christ together in the personal union and thereafter mediates between them. Jenkins finds in Irving's teaching that Christ assumed a sinful flesh sanctified and empowered by the Spirit a viable way to integrate incarnational and pneumatological aspects of Jesus' identity—aspects he feels Pentecostals tend to separate. Although all theologians use their Christological insights to reflect on the place of the Spirit in the Trinitarian life, the chapter focuses more on Christological concerns such as the relation between the Logos' assumption of a human nature and the Spirit's indwelling of it, the role of the Spirit in the Son's human growth in obedience to the Father for our sake, the soteriological implications of the Spirit's presence in Christ, and the degree of continuity between the Spirit's activity in Christ and his disciples.

If the Spirit of Christ dwells in his disciples today, what then does life in the Spirit look like? What are the implications of the relative continuity between the Spirit's presence in Christ and in his followers? In the final chapter, we offer three ways in which systematic theologians explore how a Spirit Christology can inform reflections and foster practices in response to issues in the field of practical theology. These issues include the contextual nature of ministry, especially among the poor and marginalized, the theology and practice of mission in a post-Christian Western context, and the pastoral and missional benefits of a theology of sanctification for spiritual formation today. Mexican American theologian Sammy Alfaro reflects on the affinity of a Spirit Christology with the Pentecostal Fivefold model of Jesus as Savior, Sanctifier, Healer, Baptizer, and Coming King. In order to develop a Christology that speaks to the context of a large US Hispanic Pentecostal demographic, he brings these pneumatic emphases into dialogue with contextual/liberative Latin American/US Hispanic Christologies. English Evangelical theologian Lucy Peppiatt asks how a Spirit Christology can engage in a critical and constructive dialogue with the field of missiology, which can in turn frame the church's theology and practice of mission in the post-Christian and postmodern Western European context. I conclude the chapter with my own reflections on the practical use of a Spirit Christology as an ecumenical framework for articulating a models-based approach to sanctification that depicts and fosters complementary ways of living in the Spirit of Christ. I give particular attention to the usefulness of the models-based approach for engaging North American neighbors who though not interested in institutional religion still hunger for some form of spirituality or meaningful life. The authors' interest in practical contributions come from our close association and work with churches, including the formation of lay and pastoral leaders for service in church and society.

A Final Note to the Reader

Each chapter can be read in sequence or on its own. For example, a reader may choose to focus only on an introduction to the field (Chapter 1) and some of its implications for ministry and mission (Chapter 6). Another reader may be interested in some of the biblical (Chapter 2) and patristic (Chapter 3) sources available to Spirit Christology. Yet others want to delve into the Trinitarian and Christological issues raised by scholars in the field (Chapters 4 and 5). If a matter has been discussed in another chapter, the reader will be alerted to this in the main text or in a footnote. Generally speaking, more technical issues of interest to scholars are discussed in the footnotes. Each chapter concludes with questions for review and reflection. A glossary at the end of the book defines key concepts. Given the vast and ongoing contributions to the field, this introduction is not meant to be exhaustive, and it is likely that some may feel some topics, issues, and authors could have been covered more deeply or extensively. This is inevitable in a work of this nature. Having said that, the book is comprehensive enough to get students, teachers, and scholars at various levels a taste of key voices and issues to guide their own research.

Over twenty years ago, I myself began to savor the beauty of Spirit Christology. Its insights have nourished my life and ministry, strengthening my teaching, preaching, and scholarship. Spirit Christology is a remarkably comprehensive and productive field of study that demands us to wrestle with profound questions in all areas of theology. Either directly or indirectly, some of my own doctoral students have now looked into the implications of the field for investigating social models of the Trinity, the theology of Scripture, accounts of spiritual warfare in dialogue with the Global South, post-Constantinian accounts of the church, and the theology of the Lord's Supper. Happily, teaching in this area has brought me into generative encounters with students, pastors, missionaries, and laity in the field, who over the years have gently encouraged me to look at the practical implications of the field for faith and life. Last but not least, Spirit Christology has given me the opportunity to learn from and work with theologians of various ecclesial traditions working in the field from across the globe, reminding me once again of the gifts of the church catholic.

As we begin this journey together, let us call upon the Holy Spirit, who is called the "sweet anointing from above" in the medieval hymn *Veni Creator Spiritus* (Come, Holy Spirit), to help us speak and grasp the depth and breadth of the Father's love in his Son for us: "Oh, may Thy grace on us bestow the Father and the Son to know; and Thee, through endless times confessed, of both the eternal Spirit blest."

St. Louis, Missouri

Acknowledgments

Over the years, the classroom has been my garden and playground. God has made me a steward of his gifts among students at Concordia Seminary, where I have taught in English and Spanish for almost twenty years, communicating ideas that shape minds and hearts for service to Christ in church and world. Conducting course electives and graduate seminars in pneumatology, Trinitarian theology, and Spirit Christology has become fertile ground for exploring, honing, and consolidating themes, arguments, and proposals in this book. I thank my students for joining me in the playground with their curiosity, hunger for learning, challenging questions, and gifts.

The field of Spirit Christology has given me the great joy of entering a multilingual and international conversation with friends and colleagues across theological traditions. Traveling to Rome as a graduate student to meet with Luis F. Ladaria, John O'Donnell, and Philip Rosato at the Gregorian University made me aware of the ecumenical promise of a Spirit Christology. Although I never had the pleasure of meeting him in person, Catholic theologian Ralph Del Colle's work instilled in me a desire to articulate a Spirit Christology within my own Lutheran tradition. In recent years, Myk Habets has been a generous encourager, conversation partner, and collaborator in the field. My colleagues in the faculty of Concordia Seminary have always been enthusiastically supportive of my work. My gratitude to all these kindred spirits, and others I do not have the space to mention here, for their friendship and scholarship.

A word of thanks to my editor, Anna Turton, for reaching out to me with this project idea and for guiding me through its completion. And finally, a word of thanksgiving to God for my dear Tracy, fellow companion on the pilgrimage of life in the Spirit, and for our children Lucas and Ana, the garden and playground God gave us to care for and rejoice in his lavish gifts.

From *Sculptor Spirit* by Leopoldo A. Sánchez M. Copyright © 2019 by Leopoldo A. Sánchez M. Used by permission of InterVarsity Press, P. O. Box 1400, Downers Grove, IL 60515. www.ivpress.com.

Abbreviations

ANF   *The Ante-Nicene Fathers: Translations of the Fathers down to A.D. 325*. Edited by Alexander Roberts and James Donaldson. 10 vols. Peabody, MA: Hendrickson, 1994

CCC   Catechism of the Catholic Church

Credo   *Credo in Spiritum Sanctum: Atti del Congresso Teologico Internazionale di Pneumatologia*. Edited by R. P. José Saraiva Martins. 2 vols. Vatican City: Libreria Editrice Vaticana, 1983

Greg   *Gregorianum*

HeyJ   *Heythrop Journal*

JPT   *Journal of Pentecostal Theology*

JTI   *Journal of Theological Interpretation*

LG   Lumen Gentium (Dogmatic Constitution on the Church)

NPNF   *The Nicene and Post-Nicene Fathers*. Edited by Philip Schaff. 28 vols. in two series. 1886–90. Reprint, Grand Rapids, MI: Eerdmans, 1983–87

NRSV   New Revised Standard Version

SJT   *Scottish Journal of Theology*

ST   Thomas Aquinas, *Summa Theologiae*

TAT   Myk Habets (ed.), *Third Article Theology: A Pneumatological Dogmatics* (Minneapolis, MN: Fortress, 2015)

TDNT   Gerhard Kittel and Gerhard Friedrich (eds.), *Theological Dictionary of the New Testament* (trans. Geoffrey W. Bromiley; 10 vols.; Grand Rapids, MI: Eerdmans, 1964–)

TS   *Theological Studies*

1

A Bird's-Eye View of Spirit Christology: Its Burden, Varieties, and Contemporary Revival

Imagine approaching all of theology through a Holy Spirit lens. What would that look like? How might theology done through the third article of the creed enrich our grasp of Christian faith and life? And where should we look first to put to the test the productivity of such a pneumatic reading or perspective? Since Christian faith and life is, at its very core, a way of confessing Christ and living as his disciple in the world, it makes sense for a pneumatic angle on theology to start with an exploration of Jesus' identity and mission. This type of study brings us right into the heart of Spirit Christology, which is an account of the Spirit's role in the life and work of Jesus. In his introduction to *Third Article Theology* (TAT), Myk Habets argues that "Spirit Christology is the area of most study and the first theological *loci* [sic] to find an articulation of a TAT ... given that even in a TAT Christology occupies the center."[1] He adds that TAT "is both a consequence of and a stimulus for Spirit Christology, given that TAT is birthed out of such a Christology."[2] It is now common for scholars from all church traditions to agree that, when it comes to theology, one cannot see reality through the Spirit apart from Jesus Christ, who is the definitive receiver, bearer, and giver of God's Spirit.

---

[1] Myk Habets, "Prolegomenon: On Starting with the Spirit," in *TAT*, 13.
[2] Ibid., 17; cf. Myk Habets, *The Anointed Son: A Trinitarian Spirit Christology* (Eugene, OR: Pickwick, 2010), 228–5; for an earlier outline of Spirit Christology, see Myk Habets, "Spirit Christology: Seeing in Stereo," *JPT* 11, no. 2 (2003): 199–234.

As Yves Congar once put it in succinct yet profound terms: "No Christology without pneumatology and no pneumatology without Christology."[3]

In this chapter, we offer a bird's-eye view of Spirit Christology that includes a historic burden every theologian reflecting on the Spirit in Jesus' life needs to deal with, an understanding of the different varieties of Spirit Christology, and a taste of contemporary voices in the field and the broader movements in Christianity generally giving rise to or informing their works. First, we highlight a classic instructive example of uneasiness about the proposition that Jesus, who is God, in some way needs the Holy Spirit. This uneasiness among theologians in the early church goes back to Justin Martyr (AD 100–165), but still lies in the background of various proposals in the field today. Second, we introduce readers to three major types of Spirit Christology, which assume distinct views of the reality of "Spirit" in an account of Christ. We label them Nicene, pre-Nicene, and post-Nicene (at times, referred to as Chalcedonian, pre-Chalcedonian, and post-Chalcedonian). Finally, we locate today's interest in Spirit Christology in three major twentieth-century events or movements, namely, the revival of Trinitarian theology, the Second Vatican Council, and the global rise of Pentecostalism and Charismatic churches. Although briefly, we highlight some important contributions of theologians whose works in most cases are best appreciated within the framework of these major events.

Justin's Old Burden: Does Jesus Really Need the Spirit?

When asked who Jesus Christ is, most Christians almost instinctively recognize that he is both like us and unlike us. They confess Jesus to be truly human and truly divine. In language inspired by the ecumenical creeds, Jesus is consubstantial with us according to his humanity and consubstantial with God according to his divinity. Because of the early church's struggles in the fourth century with the Arians, a group that taught Jesus was a special creature of God in whom the Spirit dwelt, theologians spent a considerable amount of time defending Jesus' special divine status as the divine Word (Logos) made flesh. Italian patristic scholar Raniero Cantalamessa has

---

[3] Yves Congar, *The Word and the Spirit*, trans. David Smith (San Francisco, CA: Harper & Row, 1986), 1.

argued that the church's response to the Arian view of Jesus especially led theologians from that point forward to favor in their language a "strong tendency towards ontologization," which means they focused on Jesus' divine being (ontology)—his "metaphysical constitution" or "essence"—more than on his "becoming and history."[4] Arians interpreted events like Jesus' baptism (anointing) and resurrection (exaltation) to deny his divinity by arguing that, unlike God who is by nature unchangeable, Jesus became something in time he was not before. Arianism paints Jesus as a creature who shares in the grace of the Spirit as a prize or reward from God for his virtues or works on earth. In such a climate, speaking of Jesus' becoming in history by the action of the Spirit in him becomes a hot potato that needs careful handling. As Cantalamessa rightly notes, "the question naturally arises: how can the Word incarnate become at baptism something new, which he was not already at the moment of the incarnation?"[5] If Jesus is already God in the flesh, does he really *need* the Holy Spirit?

In Chapter 3, we will lay out and assess how the church handled the Arian view of Jesus. In the meantime, we should note that the question about the Spirit's role in the life and mission of Jesus precedes the Arian controversy. It is an old burden laid upon Christian apologists as far back as the second century. Consider Justin Martyr, who in his *Dialogue with Trypho* gets the following question from him: If Christ is "pre-existent God" and "incarnate," how can he be said to be "filled with the powers of the Holy Ghost, which the Scripture by Isaiah enumerates [cf. Isa. 11:1–3], as if He were in lack of them?"[6] Justin rightly acknowledges the seeming difficulty of upholding Christ's identity as the incarnate God and, at the same time, as one filled with the Spirit and its gifts.[7] He explains that Jesus did not really need this Spirit's power since, as the Magi demonstrated by worshipping him at birth, he already possessed his own power from the time of his incarnation.[8] The Spirit does not rest on Jesus at his baptism to accomplish something new in him, but rather to reveal to others that he brings to fulfillment the prophets and their promises of a future outpouring of the Spirit upon all

---

[4] Raniero Cantalamessa, *The Holy Spirit in the Life of Jesus: The Mystery of Christ's Baptism*, trans. Alan Neame (Collegeville, MN: Liturgical Press, 1994), 8.
[5] Ibid.
[6] Justin, *Dialogue with Trypho* 87, in ANF 1:243.
[7] To distinguish between the persons of the Son and the Spirit, I use neuter pronouns for the Spirit. I understand the potential danger of depersonalizing the Spirit. The Spirit's personalizing descriptions in Scripture and the Christian tradition mitigate against this potential risk.
[8] Justin, *Dialogue with Trypho* 87, in ANF 1:243.

flesh. The Spirit now rests upon Jesus to reveal to the world that he will give the promised Spirit and its gifts to those who believe in him. Like a fire from above, the Spirit comes on Jesus at his baptism not "because He stood in need of baptism, or of the descent of the Spirit" but "because of the human race" and to give others "proof, that they might know who is Christ."[9] Accordingly, the voice of the Father at the Jordan, "Thou art My Son: this day have I begotten Thee" (cf. Ps. 2:7), does not mean that Christ undergoes a new birth of some sort, but rather that "His generation would take place for men, at the time when they would become acquainted with Him."[10] Given Justin's commitment to the revelatory character of the Jordan event due to his being "hesitant to fully exploit the pouring out of the Spirit on Jesus at the Jordan lest it place the divinity of the pre-existent Logos in peril," Kilian McDonnell describes the apologist as "committed but uneasy."[11] The Spirit does not bring about something in Jesus, like an empowerment for his mission, but reveals something to us about him already established beforehand (namely, his divinity). McDonnell explains the sense in which the Son, according to Justin's use of Ps. 2:7 in the baptism narrative, is said to be "begotten" at the Jordan: "When he is recognized by us as the Son of God, at that moment he, in some mysterious fashion, is born Son of God for us, for the Church. To be known is to be born."[12] Like other events of Christ's life and mission, his baptism does not tell us something about him as much as something about us.

Ever since the days of Justin Martyr, theologians have taken on the burden of finding an answer to Trypho's question: How can the preexistent God made flesh be said to be filled with the Spirit as if he needed its power? Since a Spirit Christology deals with the role of the Holy Spirit in, with, and through Christ, it is quite legitimate to ask how his life in the Spirit relates to his identity as the incarnate Word (Logos). Justin's response to Trypho already illustrates the importance of interpreting biblical statements about the Spirit in the life of Christ in such a way that they account for the proper distinction and relation between the Logos and the Spirit. The apologist's response also shows us a way to link the power Christ possesses from his incarnation to the gifts of the Spirit he pours out on the church. Interestingly, Justin does

---

[9] Ibid., 1:243–4.
[10] Ibid., 1:244.
[11] Kilian McDonnell, *The Baptism of Jesus in the Jordan: The Trinitarian and Cosmic Order of Salvation* (Collegeville, MN: Liturgical Press, 1996), 111–12.
[12] Ibid., 92–3. Baptism texts in the gospels including the entirety of Ps. 2:7 come from the Western (D) variant of the manuscript.

not place the anointing of Jesus with the Spirit at the moment of his baptism. Instead, on the basis of Ps. 45:7, which reads "Therefore God, your God, has *anointed* you with the oil of gladness beyond your companions (italics mine)," Justin speaks of the Son's begetting from the Father in view of his ordering of the world as his eternal and cosmic anointing.[13] As the apologist puts it, the Son "who also was with Him [i.e., the Father] and was begotten before the works ... is called Christ, in reference to His being anointed and God's ordering all things through him."[14] In other words, Christ has the fullness of Spirit in his humanity by virtue of his prior being anointed as God from eternity and as creator of the cosmos. The descent of the Spirit at the Jordan reveals his already established identity as the divine Christ to others. Justin does add, however, that the Jordan shows Christ will anoint the church with the Holy Spirit and endow her with its gifts upon completion of his work of salvation. Regardless of how satisfactory we think Justin's answer to Trypho is, we can appreciate his attempt to account for Christ's divine preexistence and role as creator, his possession of the Spirit's powers already from the time of his incarnation, and his pouring out of the Spirit who descended on him at Jordan on others. Still today theologians working in Spirit Christology bear Justin's old burden and continue to propose ways of integrating all these aspects of Christ's identity into a coherent, comprehensive, and compelling systematic approach.

What's in a Name? Varieties of Spirit Christology

Spirit Christology (also known as pneumatological Christology) explores the role of the "Spirit" (Gk. *pneuma*, Lat. *spiritus*) in Christ, his life and mission. But what exactly does "Spirit" mean? Answering that question alone reveals a variety of answers. Is "Spirit" a divine person distinct from the Son? Or is "Spirit" the Son's divine substance or preexistent being? Or is it a way of speaking more generally about God's presence in and activity through the Son and others? Each of these interpretations aligns

---

[13] Irenaeus held a similar view. On the cosmic anointing in Justin and Irenaeus, see Antonio Orbe, *La unción del Verbo*, vol. 3 of *Estudios valentinianos* (Roma: Università Gregoriana, 1961), 61–72, 521–7; cf. McDonnell, *The Baptism of Jesus in the Jordan*, 57–60, 112–13, 122–3, 243–4.
[14] Justin, *Second Apology* 6, in ANF 1:190.

respectively with a Nicene, pre-Nicene, and post-Nicene view of "Spirit" in Christology. Although the designations "pre" (before) and "post" (after) refer to Trinitarian and Christological formulations proposed before and after the Council of Nicaea (AD 325), we use these terms not mainly temporally but in a *theological* sense. This qualification is important because there are instances of pre-Nicene uses of "Spirit" in statements about Christ even after the fourth century. Moreover, in our discussion, post-Nicene approaches to "Spirit" do not refer to further elaborations of Spirit Christology in the spirit of Nicaea and subsequent ecumenical councils but rather to completely alternative proposals for understanding God and Jesus. The term "Nicene," therefore, means "the faith of Nicaea," the teaching that elaborates on while remaining in continuity with the Council of Nicaea. This inclusive view of the significance of Nicaea for subsequent theological formulations emerges more formally in the Definition of the Council of Chalcedon (AD 451), which affirms that the teachings of the fathers at the Council of Constantinople (AD 381)—particularly, their elaborations or clarifications on the theology of the Holy Spirit—were in continuity with the "faith of the fathers" at Nicaea, so that they "set their seal to the same faith."[15] The Definition is a statement of faith that sums up and builds on the Trinitarian logic of the creed of Nicaea, especially in a more Christological direction.

J. N. D. Kelly has shown how the Chalcedonian consensus on the value of Nicaea includes both continuity in and clarification of the teachings received.[16] By adopting such faith as their own, and clarifying it in response to theological extremes in the teachings of Apollinaris (c. AD 310–c. 390), Nestorius (died c. AD 451), and Eutyches (c. AD 375–454), the fathers of Chalcedon viewed their Christological Definition as an expression of Nicaea with applicability to their particular situation. By confessing the Lord Jesus Christ to be "consubstantial" with and "begotten" from the Father before the ages, Chalcedon joins the Council of Nicaea's rejection of Arianism. In their affirmation that the Son is truly God, but also truly man of "a rational soul" and body, Chalcedon joins the fathers of Constantinople in their rejection of Apollinaris' teaching that the Logos took the place of the human soul of Christ in the incarnation. In response to the Nestorian error, and implicitly appealing to the letters of Cyril of Alexandria (c. AD 375–444) refuting Nestorius (c. AD 386–451) adopted at the Council of Ephesus (AD 431),

---

[15] Cited in J. N. D. Kelly, *Early Christian Creeds*, 3rd ed. (New York: Longman, 1972), 330.
[16] Ibid., 331.

the Definition asserts that the Son is one and the same person, whose two natures undergo "no division, no separation." Against Eutyches, on the other hand, Chalcedon affirms that the Son's two natures undergo "no confusion, no change."

In the spirit of Chalcedon, our theological use of the term "Nicene" Spirit Christology includes the teachings of the ecumenical councils subsequent to but also inspired and guided by the basic Trinitarian and Christological logic first laid out at Nicaea. With Lewis Ayres, we can speak of a "pro-Nicene theology" or "pro-Nicene theological culture," which develops in the period between the 360s and 380s, and allows for a diversity of legitimate expressions of the Trinitarian logic of Nicaea in the East and the West.[17] A key question defining a Nicene logic concerns the nature of the generation of the Logos/Son from God the Father and the ensuing implications for the theology of the Son's incarnation and salvation in him. Despite differences in language or terminology, Ayres argues that on this question one finds a "continuity in fourth-century accounts of God," namely, "the insistence that one must speak of the Son's incomprehensible generation from the Father as a sharing of the Father's very being."[18] More specifically, Ayres identifies "three central principles" that characterize a pro-Nicene theology:

1. a clear version of the person and nature distinction, entailing the principle that whatever is predicated of the divine nature is predicated of the three persons equally and understood to be one;
2. clear expression that the eternal generation of the Son occurs within the unitary and incomprehensible divine being;
3. clear expression of the doctrine that the persons work inseparably.[19]

---

[17] Lewis Ayres, *Nicaea and Its Legacy: An Approach to Fourth-Century Trinitarian Theology* (New York: Oxford University Press, 2004), 1, 6, 80–1 (cf. 434). Ayres explains that

> the creed of Nicaea was not used directly for catechetical purposes or in worship: the theology for which the creed was a cipher rather came to shape the interpretation and presentation of local baptismal creeds—at times by the insertion into existing creeds of phraseology from Nicaea. In this context faithfulness to Nicaea still did not rule out a certain flexibility of how one formally stated the "Nicene" faith. (256)

[18] Ayres, *Nicaea and Its Legacy*, 4. This principle is shared by theologians such as Athanasius, Basil of Ancyra, and Hilary of Poitiers (186).

[19] Ibid., 236; for another account of elements contributing to a retrieval of Nicene theology, see Khaled Anatolios, *Retrieving Nicaea: The Development and Meaning of Trinitarian Doctrine* (Grand Rapids, MI: Baker Academic, 2011), 281–92.

Once again, Ayres notes that there are differences in how these principles are articulated among fourth-century theologians. For instance, he agrees with Michael Barnes that earlier on "the Father/Son relationship is used to show continuity of nature," but in later usage "the Father/Son relationship is used only to show that the persons are distinct because now the eternal generation occurs a priori within the unitary and simple Godhead."[20] Thus the Son's generation from the Father shows both his unity with and distinction from the Father. For instance, if one thinks of how Athanasius speaks of the generation of the Son from the Father against the Arians, he does so to show the *unity* of the divine nature of the Son with the Father. But later theologians such as the Cappadocian fathers,[21] a group of theologians in the East, begin to speak of the Son's generation from the Father as a way to think about the *distinction* between the persons (Gk. *hypostases*) without harming their one divine nature (Gk. *ousia*). This contrast should not be seen, however, as a hard-and-fast rule, since these church fathers still share in common the aforementioned pro-Nicene themes.

Nicene Spirit Christology

Due to the influence of a host of fourth-century authors defending the divine rank of the Holy Spirit with the Father and the Son, and the ensuing ecumenical councils of the church beginning with the Council of Nicaea, church theologians today often confess the Holy Spirit as "the Lord and giver of life, who proceeds from the Father [and the Son], who with the Father and the Son together is worshipped and glorified." Except for the later addition of the phrase "and the Son" (Lat. *filioque*), the words above come from the Council of Constantinople (AD 381) and express some key theological convictions about the Holy Spirit. The beginning of the third article of the Niceno-Constantinopolitan Creed lays out an outline of the Holy Spirit's identity in relation to creation and to the Father and the Son. In relation to creation, the Holy Spirit is sovereign Lord over all of it and the life-giving creator of all things. In relation to the Father and the Son, the Holy Spirit is both distinct from and equal to them. The Holy Spirit proceeds from the Father (and the Son) in the unity of the divine essence, while being distinct from them. Moreover, the Holy Spirit is neither the Father nor the

---

[20] Ayres, *Nicaea and Its Legacy*, 236.
[21] Basil of Caesarea (AD 330–379), his brother Gregory of Nyssa (AD 335–394), and their friend Gregory of Nazianzus (AD 329–389).

Son, and yet is equal to them because it receives worship and glorification together with them. By the fourth century, language to describe the Holy Spirit as a distinct *hypostasis* or *person* of the Godhead had emerged in the church. The Cappadocian fathers in the East and Tertullian (*c.* AD 160–225), a church father in the West, contributed such language respectively in Greek (*hypostasis*) and Latin (*persona*) to express the Holy Spirit's distinctiveness or uniqueness in the Trinity. They did so without doing harm to the unity of the Holy Spirit with the Father and the Son in the one divine being (Gk. *ousia*, Lat. *substantia*) and in their common works. Like the generation of the Son, the procession of the Spirit from the Father is understood within the incomprehensible unity of the Trinity. All the aforementioned themes of Nicene pneumatology align with Ayres' description of the three central principles of pro-Nicene theology described earlier.[22]

Since individual theologians and the Council of Chalcedon described Trinitarian and Christological formulations subsequent to Nicaea as elaborations of its faith, we can also speak for convenience's sake of a Nicene interpretation of the identity of the Son and the Holy Spirit. When we describe the Son and the Holy Spirit respectively as the second and third persons (or hypostases) of the Trinity, we are speaking in Nicene terms. Applied to a Spirit Christology, such hypostatic interpretation of "Spirit" will frame what we say about its role in the life of Jesus in terms of how their distinct persons relate to one another and the person of God the Father (immanent Trinity) and to us (economic Trinity). In this introduction to Spirit Christology, we will be working with a Nicene understanding of the Holy Spirit, and therefore from a Nicene understanding of God as Triune and of the person of Jesus Christ as true God and true man (or as the Word or Logos made the flesh). As we will see in other chapters, a Nicene Spirit Christology is most congenial to a complementary approach that seeks to integrate Chalcedonian Logos (two natures) and Spirit Christologies. There are, of course, other understandings of Spirit Christology that we must be aware of, describe, and interact with. Given our Nicene definition, we can now proceed to describe two other types of Spirit Christology as "pre-Nicene" and "post-Nicene."[23] Generally speaking, pre-Nicene Spirit Christologies

---

[22] On pro-Nicene pneumatology, see Ayres, *Nicaea and Its Legacy*, 211–18. In Chapter 3, we discuss Athanasius' pneumatology.

[23] Ralph Del Colle correctly speaks of "Pre-Chalcedonian" and "Post-Chalcedonian" Spirit Christologies. See Del Colle, *Christ and the Spirit: Spirit-Christology in Trinitarian Perspective* (New York: Oxford University Press, 1994), 157–69. I see the terms pre-Nicene and post-Nicene as interchangeable with Del Colle's categories.

are most commonly seen through the middle of the fourth century among orthodox church fathers who hold to a Trinitarian understanding of God. Post-Nicene Spirit Christologies are most commonly seen in the twentieth century among theologians who seek to reflect on the significance of the Spirit in Jesus outside of a Nicene framework and thus without committing to a Trinitarian understanding of God.

Pre-Nicene Spirit Christology

In the East and the West, we find pre-Nicene theologians who at times identify "Spirit" not with the third hypostasis or person of the Trinity but more generally with "divinity." When they do so, instead of a personal or hypostatic view of the Spirit, they operate with a *substantial* view of Spirit— that is to say, Spirit is a synonym for divine nature or substance. Applied to a Spirit Christology, Spirit means the divine aspect of Christ in distinction from his human aspect. Two examples of pre-Nicene theologians will suffice. In the East, Ignatius of Antioch (c. AD 35–107) describes Jesus Christ as "possessed both of *flesh* and *spirit*; both made and not made; God existing in flesh; true in life in death; both of Mary and of God; first possible and then impossible" (italics mine).[24] Using the contrast *flesh-spirit* (see Rom. 1:3-4) in the framework of an incarnational theology that confesses Christ as "God existing in flesh," Ignatius interprets "flesh" as the human aspect of Christ, which is "of Mary" and undergoes "death," and thus reads "spirit" as his being "of God." In the West, Tertullian refers to Christ as possessing "the two substances, both of flesh and of the Spirit," which respectively signify his "being generated in the flesh as man" and his being "born of God" (i.e., of the Spirit).[25] Tertullian operates with a flesh-spirit paradigm; but unlike Ignatius, he speaks more explicitly of "flesh" and "spirit" as "two substances," describing respectively his being born of Mary "as man" and his being begotten of God the Father. These examples illustrate what we call a pre-Nicene *substantial* view of "Spirit."

There are other versions of this view of "Spirit" among some church fathers. One of the most interesting (and strange) ones comes from an identification of "the Holy Spirit ... the power of the Most High," who comes

---

[24] Ignatius, *Letter to the Ephesians* 7 (shorter version), in ANF 1:52; cf. Hermas, *Similitude Fifth* 6, in ANF 2:35–6.
[25] Tertullian, *On the Flesh of Christ* 18, in ANF 3:537.

upon Mary at the Annunciation in Lk. 1:35, with the divine preexistent Christ. To pick on Tertullian again, he suggests that "Spirit" in this text refers to "that portion of the Godhead" named "the Son," and thus argues that "the Spirit of God in this passage must be the same as the Word. ... For both the Spirit is the substance of the Word, and the Word is the operation of the Spirit, and the Two are One (and the same)."[26] Adopting a view of Spirit as the divine "substance of the Word," the theologian reads in the text not a descent of the Holy Spirit on Mary but a descent of the Son or Word (Logos) on her for the sake of bringing about the incarnation. Although the aforementioned views of Spirit as the divinity of Christ lead to a certain binitarian expression, which partially eclipses the uniqueness of the Holy Spirit and therefore a fully Trinitarian presentation of the mystery of God, it is also the case that these pre-Nicene theologians ultimately held to a Trinitarian theology accounting for the incarnation of the divine Son and the unique role of the Holy Spirit in God's plan of salvation.[27] For instance, in the same source cited above, Ignatius, referring to Jn 16:13-15, teaches that "the Holy Spirit does not speak His own things, but those of Christ, and that not from himself but from the Lord; even as the Lord also announced to us the things that he received from the Father."[28] Ignatius clearly shows awareness of the Trinitarian structure of biblical narrative. In opposition to Praxeas and his followers, who "contend that Father, Son and Spirit are the same person," Tertullian explains that according to God's "economy" of salvation "the Father is one, the Son another, and the Spirit another."[29] Even before Nicaea in the East, Tertullian in the West explicitly highlights the distinction between three persons in the unity of the Trinity. In short, these theologians' sporadic substantial use of the term Spirit, though peculiar in view of subsequent and more precise Nicene formulations, did not finally get in the way of their interpreting the Spirit in other texts in a more personal or hypostatic manner that distinguished the Spirit from and related it to the Son.

---

[26] Tertullian, *Against Praxeas* 26, in ANF 3:622; cf. *On the Flesh of Christ* 14, in ANF 3:534.
[27] See Manlio Simonetti, "Note di cristologia pneumatica," *Augustinianum* 12 (1972): 226–32; and Antonio Peñamaría de Llano, "'Espíritu' en la Cristología de los Padres: ¿Binitarismo o Trinitarismo?," *Recherches Augustiniennes* 21 (1986): 55–84; for other Western examples of pre-Nicene Spirit Christology, see Luis F. Ladaria, "El Espíritu Santo en San Hilario de Poitiers," *Credo* 1 (1983), 243–53; and Paul McGukin, "Spirit Christology: Lactantius and His Sources," *HeyJ* 24 (1983): 141–8.
[28] Ignatius, *Letter to the Ephesians* 9 (longer version), in ANF 1:53.
[29] Tertullian, *Against Praxeas* 9, in ANF 3:46.

Post-Nicene Spirit Christology

In contemporary Spirit Christologies, post-Nicene proposals seek to move the discussion of the Spirit's presence and activity in Jesus beyond the Trinitarian and Christological categories of the Council of Chalcedon (AD 451). The Council identifies the Lord Jesus Christ as the person or hypostasis of the Son (Word/Logos), who is consubstantial with the Father in his divinity and consubstantial with us in his humanity except for sin. Theologians such as G. W. H. Lampe, Paul Newman, and Roger Haight have questioned the viability of this Logos Christology and its Trinitarian tenets and have offered instead an alternative Spirit Christology to replace it.[30] As an example, Roger Haight, a Catholic theologian, has proposed that, in our historically grounded rather than metaphysically oriented age, "Spirit" rather than "Logos" serves as the most viable biblical metaphor or symbol to explain how God is present in Jesus.[31] A metaphysical orientation means an interest in defining how Jesus is God using ontological categories, emphasizing his *divine* nature (or person) before moving on to his human nature. But today, Haight argues, people are more historically conscious and thus more likely to ask how the *human* Jesus is divine, how God saves in and through this human being, and finally how Jesus is relatable to other humans so as to empower a Christian spirituality.[32] To make Jesus intelligible to people today, we must find a language that gives modern ears a sense that the human being Jesus is both God beyond us and God near us at once, both transcendent and immanent. The language of "symbol" helps us see how a biblical metaphor, such as Spirit, Logos (Word), or Wisdom, can convey "the same generalized experience of God outside God's self and immanent

---

[30] See Roger Haight, *Jesus: Symbol of God* (Maryknoll, NY: Orbis, 1999); Paul W. Newman, *A Spirit Christology: Recovering the Biblical Paradigm of Christian Faith* (Lanham, MD: University Press of America, 1987); G. W. H. Lampe, *God as Spirit* (Oxford: Clarendon Press, 1977). Other works include: Hendrikus Berkhof, *The Doctrine of the Holy Spirit* (Richmond, VR: Knox, 1964); Marcus J. Borg, *Jesus, A New Vision: Spirit, Culture, and the Life of Discipleship* (San Francisco, CA: Harper & Row, 1987); Michael E. Lodahl, *Shekinah/Spirit: Divine Presence in Jewish and Christian Traditions* (Eugene, OR: Wipf & Stock, 1992); and Norman Hook, "A Spirit Christology," *Theology* 75, no. 623 (1972): 226–32. Among Dutch theologians, Cornelis van der Kooi includes Gerrit van de Kamp and Gijs Dingemans. J. D. G. Dunn (discussed in Chapter 2) could partly be included here.

[31] Roger Haight, "The Case for Spirit Christology," *TS* 53 (1992): 157; for a similar proposal, see G. W. H. Lampe, "The Holy Spirit and the Person of Christ," in S. W. Sykes and J. P. Clayton, eds., *Christ, Faith, and History* (London: Cambridge University Press, 1972), 111–30; for a summary of Lampe, see Leopoldo A. Sánchez M., *Sculptor Spirit: Models of Sanctification from Spirit Christology* (Downers Grove, IL: IVP Academic, 2019), 17–20; cf. David A. Dorman, "The Spirit Christology of Geoffrey Lampe: A Critical Analysis" (PhD diss., Fuller Theological Seminary, 1992).

[32] See Haight, "Spirit Christology," 260–2.

in the world in presence and active power."³³ When thought of as a person or hypostasis, the author claims that symbols like Logos or Wisdom "tend to connote someone or something distinct from and less than God that was incarnate in Jesus even though it is called divine or of God."³⁴ But what if instead of saying that Jesus is the "Logos" incarnate—a way of speaking that, according to Haight, made more sense when people thought in ontological terms—there was another symbol to communicate what it means for Jesus to be God? Haight proposes "Spirit" as a better option.

What is meant by "Spirit" in this case is not a person or hypostasis of the Trinity—as in "the Holy Spirit." More generally, "Spirit" stands for "God" present and active—what Haight calls "God as Spirit."³⁵ As he puts it, "God as Spirit is not a personification of God but refers directly to God."³⁶ This view of Spirit redefines the meaning of the incarnation, so that instead of saying that Jesus is the Word (Logos) made flesh, Haight's Spirit Christology presents Jesus as "an embodiment of God as Spirit."³⁷ However, to avoid an adoptionist view of Jesus, Haight notes that Spirit is not present in Jesus as an "impersonal power that takes over and controls" his genuine humanity but as God who "works within human freedom" in cooperation with him.³⁸ Like other post-Nicene Spirit Christologies, the author sees his proposal as an attempt to recover a stronger sense of Jesus' consubstantiality with us as a human subject, over against the traditional teaching of the councils that the divine Logos is the personal subject of his human actions.³⁹ If Jesus were not truly human, he could neither save other human beings nor be followed by them. Therefore, as an embodiment of

---

³³ Ibid., 267.
³⁴ Haight, "Spirit Christology," 272.
³⁵ See ibid., 266–8; cf. Lampe: "In speaking of God as Spirit we are not referring to an impersonal influence, an energy transmitted by God but distinct from himself. Nor are we indicating a divine entity or hypostasis which is a third person of the Godhead. We are speaking of God himself, his personal presence, as active and related." Lampe, *God as Spirit*, 208.
³⁶ Haight, "Spirit Christology," 272.
³⁷ Ibid., 276.
³⁸ Ibid.; similarly, against calling Jesus "substantivally" God, Lampe states:

> An interpretation of the union of Jesus with God in terms of his total possession by God's Spirit makes it possible, rather, to acknowledge him to be God "adverbially." By the mutual interaction of the Spirit's influence and the free response of the human spirit such a unity of will and operation was established that in all his actions the human Jesus acted divinely. (Lampe, "The Holy Spirit and the Person of Christ," 124)

³⁹ Similarly, Lampe sees as problematic "the idea that human thoughts and feelings are thought and felt by a divine subject" because "it implies an excessively anthromorphic picture of God … it almost inevitably suggests that Christ's manhood is no more than an outward form, like a suit of

Spirit, Jesus must be different from us but also like us. He is different from us not according to essence but rather by degree: "God as Spirit was present to Jesus in a superlative degree and this is sufficient to convey all that was intended by a qualitative difference."[40] Haight's proposal highlights the role of God as Spirit working in cooperation with the human Jesus in a way that makes Jesus unique from but also relatable to other humans in whom such Spirit is at work. Like the pre-Nicene type of Spirit Christology, the post-Nicene kind uses "Spirit" as a replacement for "Logos." But unlike the pre-Nicene type, whose authors generally ascribed the incarnation to the Son (as opposed to the Spirit) and held to a basic Trinitarian view of God, the post-Nicene type redefines the incarnation as the presence of "Spirit" in Jesus—in contrast to the traditional view of Jesus as the Word made flesh, which holds to the personal identity of Jesus and the Logos.[41] Post-Nicene Spirit Christology essentially replaces Nicene (Trinitarian, Chalcedonian) Logos Christology. Admittedly, the post-Nicene view speaks of an economic account of divine agency in which God as Spirit is powerfully present in and saves through Jesus, but in doing so revises the Nicene logic for speaking about the Trinity as three distinct persons who relate to and work with one another in order to save us. Salvation has more to do with the human imitation of Jesus' life as one who embodies "Spirit" than with the divine Son's saving deeds on behalf of humans by the power of the Holy Spirit.[42]

The main criticisms leveled against Spirit Christologies designed as an alternative to Logos Christology are Christological, Trinitarian, and

---

clothes in which God the Son has dressed up as a man." Lampe, "The Holy Spirit and the Person of Christ," 118.

[40] Haight, "Spirit Christology," 279–80; cf. Lampe:

> The Christian saint is really "Christlike," and a difference in kind between Christ and all other men seems to be incompatible either with his true humanity or with the faith and hope of Christians that they are indwelt by his Spirit. … It may be enough to acknowledge that Christ is unique in being wholly possessed and inspired by God's Spirit and in being, therefore, the unique agent of God's atoning or reconciling work. (Lampe, "The Holy Spirit and the Person of Christ," 126)

[41] Thus Lampe argues that "the concept of the pre-existent personal Son, or pre-existent Christ, would have to be re-expressed in terms of the eternal Spirit who was manifested at a particular point in history operating humanly in the person of Jesus Christ." Lampe, "The Holy Spirit and the Person of Christ," 129.

[42] "Jesus saves by being the revealer of God and God's salvation which God as Spirit has effected from the beginning, the revelation of what human life should be, and the empowering example of life for disciples." Haight, "Spirit Christology," 181.

pneumatological.[43] In short, Jesus is not simply divine because he is a man in whom Spirit dwells in a special way (which sounds like a form of adoptionism), but rather because he is God the Son (Logos) who is the subject of his divine-human (theandric) actions. Moreover, "Spirit" and "Logos" are not basically two equal ways of speaking about the one God (which sounds like a form of modalism) but rather two distinct persons who relate in different ways to the Father and to the man Jesus (or Christ's humanity). Jesus is personally the Logos (Son), not the Spirit; yet, Jesus, who is personally the Logos (Son) incarnate is acted upon by the Holy Spirit in distinct moments of his existence.[44] In terms of pneumatology, the Nicene response to the post-Nicene proposal accents that, by not properly distinguishing the Son and the Holy Spirit in an account of the incarnation, one ends not only with a less than satisfactory view of the uniqueness of the Logos but also a less robust theology of the Holy Spirit.[45] As to responses to Haight's specific proposal, John H. Wright, a fellow Jesuit, observes that Haight does not give proper attention in his Christology to the Johannine identification of Jesus as the incarnate creator Logos and only-begotten Son, whose preexistence and divine lordship are testified to in the Gospel by Jesus himself before his critics and in prayer, and by his disciple Thomas (cf. Jn 1:1-3, 14; 8:58; 17:5; 20:28).[46] Thomas Weinandy adds that, by speaking of "Spirit" as a general description of the transcendent God embodied in Jesus, Haight finally renders biblical language about God impersonal. For instance, in Haight's proposal, "Jesus is not the eternal Son who as man relates to the Father in love and obedience. ... The Holy Spirit is not a divine subject who anoints Jesus and sanctifies his followers."[47] Consequently, the biblical dynamic of persons relating to one another and bringing us into communion with them is also lost.[48] Without a strong incarnational Logos

---

[43] For critiques of the post-Nicene model, see Colle, *Christ and the Spirit*, 141–94; Habets, *The Anointed Son*, 193–200; Harold Hunter, "Spirit Christology: Dilemma and Promise (1)," *HeyJ* 24 (1983): 127–40; and "Spirit Christology: Dilemma and Promise (2)," *HeyJ* 24 (1983): 266–77; Olaf Hansen, "Spirit-Christology: A Way Out of Our Dilemma?," in Paul D. Opsahl, ed., *The Holy Spirit in the Life of the Church: From Biblical Times to the Present* (Minneapolis, MN: Augsburg, 1978), 172–203.
[44] See Ladaria, "Cristología del Logos y cristología del Espíritu," 355–6.
[45] On the Trinitarian principle of identity (Jesus is the Logos) and nonidentity (Jesus is not the Holy Spirit), see Leopoldo A. Sánchez M., *Receiver, Bearer, and Giver of God's Spirit: Jesus' Life in the Spirit as a Lens for Theology and Life* (Eugene, OR: Pickwick, 2015), 149–57.
[46] John H. Wright, "Roger Haight's Spirit Christology," *TS* 53 (1992): 730–1.
[47] Thomas Weinandy, "The Case for Spirit Christology: Some Reflections," *The Thomist* 59, no. 2 (1995): 180–1.
[48] Ibid., 185–6 (cf. 178).

Christology, the overall effect of a Christology built entirely on "a strict monotheism on the one hand and a theology of grace on the other" is—as in the case of early adoptionist Christologies—reducing "the Messiah to the model of man's own relationship to God, to the paradigm of man's own adoption as son of God."[49] The most public critical reaction against Haight came from the Vatican's Congregation for the Doctrine of the Faith, which prevented him from teaching Catholic theology.[50] In US Catholic circles, a mixed reaction took place, with some praising Haight's work and others questioning its proposals even if not agreeing with Rome's silencing or formal way of handling dissent.[51] The incident shows that discussions about Spirit Christology have the potential to become a hot potato issue in the church today.

On the Protestant camp, Cornelis van der Kooi has observed that Haight's view of the symbolic or metaphorical nature of language does not allow him to speak to Jesus' being as the Word (ontology) but only to our knowledge of his grace (epistemology). In other words, Haight's symbolic theory of knowledge does not allow for "personifying the concept of the Word," which stresses the uniqueness of God's revelation in Christ, with the result that "the divinity of Jesus Christ can mean only that people have encountered grace from God in Jesus."[52] Since Jesus as an embodiment of "Spirit" represents a special case but not the unique revelation of God for the world, other divine revelations or incarnations of "Spirit" in the world can be (at least, potentially) apprehended as expressions of his grace. But van der Kooi sees Haight's assertion, "There is no hard reason why God could not approach humanity in a variety of ways and in more than one medium,"[53] as problematic because

> the uniqueness of the revelation in Jesus Christ is hereby questioned ... the divinity of Jesus Christ [according to Haight] ... should not mean that the person of Jesus is somehow unique, for grace can be found in many places.

---

[49] Philip J. Rosato, "Spirit Christology: Ambiguity and Promise," *TS* 38 (1977): 435.

[50] Congregation for the Doctrine of the Faith, "Notification on the Book 'Jesus Symbol of God' by Father Roger Haight D.J.," December 13, 2004, www.vatican.va/roman_curia/congregations/cfaith/ documents/rc_con_cfaith_ doc_20041213_notification-fr-haight_en.html.

[51] Haight's *Jesus: Symbol of God* received the 1999 top prize in theology from the US Catholic Press Association.

[52] Cornelis van der Kooi, *This Incredible Benevolent Force: The Holy Spirit in Reformed Theology and Spirituality* (Grand Rapids, MI: Eerdmans, 2018), 49.

[53] Cited in ibid., 48–9.

However, exactly that element of the identity of Jesus was pivotal in the decisions of the church in the fourth century.[54]

The aforementioned Catholic and Protestant critiques have been offered as examples of standard, contemporary analyses of post-Nicene Spirit Christology. However, these criticisms are not interested in preserving a Logos Christology merely on the grounds of the tradition of the councils, but because such tradition reflects a biblical basis for grounding Jesus' identity and redemptive work in his unique sonship.[55] The criticism of the post-Nicene paradigm incorporates the biblical activity of the Holy Spirit in Christological reflection, particularly in the humanity of Christ. Therefore, as we will see in various chapters, the point of a complementary approach that seeks to integrate Logos and Spirit Christologies, as opposed to an alternative one where the latter replaces the former, is not simply to affirm a Logos Christology but to fully elaborate its pneumatic dimensions for the sake of enriching our view of Jesus, the Spirit, the Trinity, salvation, and the Christian life.

A Bird's-Eye View of the Field: The Contemporary Renewal of Spirit Christology

In contemporary theology, the field of Spirit Christology owes its growth to a variety of factors. Let us consider three of them: the revival of Trinitarian studies across theological traditions, the call in the Western Catholic Church for a vibrant return to the patristic and biblical sources of the church's faith (especially, in dialogue with Orthodox and Protestant churches), and the rise of the Pentecostal and Charismatic churches and theologians.

The Revival of Trinitarian Theology

The revival of Trinitarian theology in Protestant and Catholic circles, ushered in respectively by Reformed theologian Karl Barth's *Church Dogmatics* (1932–68) and Catholic theologian Karl Rahner's *The Trinity* (1967), raised

---

[54] Ibid., 49.
[55] See ibid., 28–34.

questions about the specific place of the Holy Spirit in a Trinitarian account of God's salvation in Christ. It is commonplace among theologians to point out how Karl Barth (1886–1968), toward the end of his life, envisioned the need for a Christian theology framed from the perspective of the third person of the Trinity.[56] His vision implied a pneumatological deficit in his own theology. Eugene Rogers Jr., an Anglican theologian, for instance, feels that Barth's demotion of the Spirit as the "power" of Christ made one wonder whether there was some work "the Spirit can do that Christ can't do better."[57] In response, he proposes that the Spirit can indeed do something unique to its person that neither the Father nor the Son can do, namely, rest in bodies—the body of Jesus, "his body the Church," and "the bodies of his members."[58] The Spirit's uniqueness does not lie in its being above the flesh but in entering the flesh in order to sanctify it for God's purposes. Because the Spirit "rests" on the Son's body, the Spirit also rests on the creature to inhabit human nature "in excess of nature, or 'paraphysically' … in a way that redeems, transfigures, elevates, and exceeds" human nature to bring it into communion with God."[59] Although the Spirit is God and distinct from creation, there is a certain materiality that defines its work. The Spirit rests on the waters of creation, Mary's womb, and baptism.[60] Rogers rightly observes that Barth offers no significant place to the acts of the Holy Spirit in the events of Christ's life.[61] Grounding his material pneumatology in a Spirit Christology becomes Rogers's way to move beyond Barth's deficit.

Karl Rahner (1904–1984) is known for his theology of divine revelation as "divine self-communication," by which he means that, in the mysteries of the incarnation and grace, the triune God does not merely reveal to us something *about* himself but actually communicates God's own *self* or his

---

[56] In his "Nachwort, or Concluding Unscientific Postscript on Schleiermacher," Barth wonders about

> the possibility of a theology of the third article … predominantly and decisively of the Holy Spirit. Everything which needs to be said, considered, and believed about God the Father and God the Son in an understanding of the first and second articles might be shown and illuminated in its foundations through God the Holy Spirit, the *vinculum pacis inter Patrem et Filium*. (Cited in Habets, "Prolegomenon," in *TAT*, 4)

[57] Eugene F. Rogers Jr., *After the Spirit: A Constructive Pneumatology from Resources outside the Modern West* (Grand Rapids, MI: Eerdmans, 2005), 20.

[58] Ibid., 14.

[59] Ibid., 14–15.

[60] Ibid., 15.

[61] Ibid., 23; for a summary of Rogers's "narrative approach" to Spirit Christology, see Sánchez, *Sculptor Spirit*, 23–9.

own divine life to the human creature. In divine self-communication, the one God does not relate to human reality in a merely monotheistic way, but in a Trinitarian or threefold way so that each divine person has a unique way of touching human life.[62] In the economy of salvation, there are two ways or modalities in which the one God communicates his own life to created reality, namely, in Christ and in the Holy Spirit.[63] In the first one, the divine Son (Logos) of God the Father communicates his divine life to the human nature he assumes in the incarnation (hypostatic or personal union). In the second one, the divine persons come to dwell in the graced creature, although such communication can be especially ascribed or appropriated to the Holy Spirit. Catholic theologian Walter Kasper builds on Rahner's anthropological view of the incarnation of the Son (personal union) as the highest instance of God's self-giving (or divine self-communication) to a human creature and the human creature's acceptance by grace of such self-giving. In speaking of the Son as receiving and responding to God's self-giving in and through his humanity, Rahner speaks mainly in terms of the Son's divine-human identity without giving much attention to the role of the Holy Spirit in the incarnation. Kasper remedies this deficit by placing Rahner's Christology in a pneumatological framework. He does so by ascribing to the Holy Spirit the unique work of sanctifying the humanity of the Son so that "it can freely and wholly constitute a mould and receptacle for God's self-communication ... in such a way as to enable him, to be the incarnate response to God's self-communication."[64] The Spirit's sanctification of the Son, which does not only take place at his conception but also allows his human response of obedience to the Father during his entire human *history*, becomes the presupposition for asserting the personal union of the Son to his human *nature*. The Son does assume not only a human nature (incarnation) but also a human history in which the Spirit plays a defining role.[65] Moreover, Kasper notes that the Spirit who sanctifies the humanity of Christ, the head of the church, also sanctifies the members of his body so that they too might partake of Christ's grace.[66] Rahner portrayed the personal union (incarnation) of the Son as

---

[62] For Rahner's critique of "mere monotheism" in Western theology, see Karl Rahner, *The Trinity*, trans. Joseph Donceel (New York: Herder & Herder, 1970), 10–15.
[63] Rahner, *The Trinity*, 46–8.
[64] Walter Kasper, *Jesus the Christ*, trans. V. Green (New York: Paulist Press, 1976), 251.
[65] See Kasper, *Jesus the Christ*, 37. For summaries of Kasper, see Gary D. Badcock, *Light of Truth and Fire of Love: A Theology of the Holy Spirit* (Grand Rapids, MI: Eerdmans, 1997), 153–9; and Sánchez, *Receiver, Bearer, and Giver*, 126–8.
[66] Kasper, *Jesus the Christ*, 253.

the highest instance of communion between God and human nature, but also as a communion human persons could participate in—not through an incarnation (only the Word became flesh) but through the indwelling of the Trinity in them. Kasper's contribution lies in showing that our participation in the divine life or in Christ by grace (also known as deification) is only possible through the indwelling in the graced person of the same Spirit in whom the incarnate Son became the bearer and giver of the Spirit.

In the aforementioned reflections, we see how Rogers's and Kasper's Spirit Christologies arise from a desire to extend and enrich the Trinitarian theology of the two Karls in a more explicit pneumatological direction that links the presence and activity of the Spirit in Christ to its resting on or sanctifying of the church. Rogers and Kasper give us a glimpse of the robust theological contributions of Spirit Christology to the revival of Trinitarian studies in Protestant and Catholic circles.[67] Other notable writers such as Catholic theologian Hans Urs von Balthasar (1905–1988) and Protestant theologian Jürgen Moltmann have contributed to the field of pneumatology as part of their broader systematic theologies, with particular reference to the place of the cross in Trinitarian theology.[68] In Chapter 4, we will explore Moltmann's attempt to locate a Spirit Christology in his proposal for a Trinitarian kenosis grounded in a pneumatology of the cross.

The Second Vatican Council

A second impetus for studies in Spirit Christology comes from the Roman Catholic Church's Second Vatican Council (October 11, 1962–December 8, 1965). In the biblical exposition of the Council's Dogmatic Constitution on the Church (Lat. *Lumen Gentium*, meaning "Light of the Nations"), one sees statements that highlight the joint mission of the Son and the Spirit in God's economy of salvation. The Holy Spirit is "one and the same" in Christ the

---

[67] Nevertheless, Petriano argues that Kasper's Spirit Christology is surpassed in his later work by a Son Christology and thus remains underdeveloped. See Thomas I. Petriano, "Spirit Christology or Son Christology? An Analysis of the Tension between the Two in the Theology of Walter Kasper" (PhD diss., Fordham University, 1998).

[68] Among Spirit Christologists, von Balthasar's proposal for an inversion Father-Spirit-Son in Trinitarian theology is well known. See John J. O'Donnell, "In Him and Over Him: The Holy Spirit in the Life of Jesus," *Greg* 70, no. 1 (1989): 25–45; Luis F. Ladaria, *La Trinidad, misterio de comunión* (Salamanca: Secretariado Trinitario, 2002), 189–202; and Adrian Davis Day, "The Spirit in the Drama: Balthasar's 'Theo-Drama' and the Relationship between the Son and the Spirit" (PhD diss., Marquette University, 2001); for Moltmann, see especially *The Way of Jesus Christ: Christology in Messianic Dimensions*, trans. Margaret Kohl (Minneapolis, MN: Fortress, 1993).

head and in the members of his body.⁶⁹ By sharing his Spirit with them, Christ enlivens, unifies, and moves the whole body, in a similar way to how "the principle of life, the soul" enlivens the human body.⁷⁰ An analogy is drawn between the Son's assumption of a human nature (incarnation) and the Holy Spirit's life-giving role in the Church: "As the assumed nature, inseparably united to him, serves the divine Word as a living organ of salvation, so, in a somewhat similar way, does the social structure of the Church serve the Spirit of Christ who vivifies it, in the building up of the body (cf. Eph. 4:15)."⁷¹ The human nature of Christ and his humanly constituted body, the Church, are respectively the Son's and the Holy Spirit's created instruments of salvation in the world. Not only the priests in the hierarchical Church but all "the baptized," the people of God, "by the anointing of the Holy Spirit … each in its own proper way shares in the one priesthood of Christ."⁷² The people of God also share in "Christ's prophetic office" to bear witness to him in faith and love; and because they have received "an anointing that comes from the holy one (cf. 1 Jn 2:20 and 27)," they are preserved in the true faith and "cannot err in matters of belief."⁷³ This preservation from error is attributed to the people of God's "supernatural appreciation of the faith (*sensus fidei*)," which is "aroused and sustained by the Spirit of truth" and "guided by the sacred teaching authority (magisterium)" of the Church.⁷⁴ It is the teaching on the Church's derivative participation by the Holy Spirit in the life and work of Christ that comes through most clearly in Lumen Gentium's ecclesiology.

In its instruction on the second article of the Creed, the Catechism of the Catholic Church expands upon the relationship between the Son and the Holy Spirit. Already from the time of his conception, "the mission of the Holy Spirit is always conjoined and ordered to that of the Son."⁷⁵ The name "Christ" points to the Son's being "anointed by the Holy Spirit, from the beginning of his human existence" and signals that "the whole life of Jesus Christ will make manifest 'how God anointed Jesus of Nazareth with the Holy Spirit and with power' [citing Acts 10:38]."⁷⁶ The Catechism grounds

---

[69] LG 7.
[70] Ibid.
[71] LG 8.
[72] LG 10.
[73] LG 12.
[74] Ibid.
[75] CCC, 485.
[76] CCC, 486; "The Son of God was consecrated as Christ (Messiah) by the anointing of the Holy Spirit at his Incarnation (cf. *Ps* 2:6–7)." CCC, 745.

Christ's giving of grace to the Church as her head in his own human bearing of the Spirit in all fullness: "From the moment of conception, Christ's humanity is filled with the Holy Spirit, for God 'gives him the Spirit without measure' [citing Jn 3:34]. From 'his fullness' as the head of redeemed humanity 'we have all received, grace upon grace' [citing Jn 1:16]."[77] Along with the Father's voice from heaven, the Holy Spirit's descent upon Jesus at his baptism signifies "the manifestation ('Epiphany') of Jesus as Messiah of Israel and Son of God."[78] Even though Jesus has the fullness of the Spirit from conception, the Spirit "comes to 'rest on him'" at his baptism (citing Jn 1:32-33), signifying that "Jesus will be the source of the Spirit for all mankind."[79] In the Catechism's exposition of the third article of the Creed, the Spirit is portrayed as being "inseparable" from the Father and the Son, "in both the inner life of the Trinity and his gift of love for the world."[80] Just as the Father's "Word" is inseparable from his "Breath," so also the Son and the Spirit work in a "joint mission" in which they are "distinct but inseparable."[81] The identity of Jesus is linked to the Spirit's presence in him throughout his whole ministry: "Jesus is Christ, 'anointed,' because the Spirit is his anointing, and everything that occurs from the Incarnation on derives from this fullness."[82] Upon his glorification, Jesus will also "send the Spirit from his place with the Father to those who believe in him: he communicates to them his glory, that is, the Holy Spirit who glorifies him."[83] Finally, the "joint mission" manifested in the Spirit's anointing of Christ's humanity "will be manifested in the children adopted by the Father in the

---

[77] CCC, 504.

> By his Death and his Resurrection, Jesus is constituted in glory as Lord and Christ (cf. *Acts* 2:36). From his fullness, he poured out the Holy Spirit on the apostles and the Church. The Holy Spirit, whom Christ the head pours out on his members, builds, animates, and sanctifies the Church. She is the sacrament of the Holy Trinity's communion with men. (CCC, 746–7 (cf. LG 7))

[78] CCC, 535.
[79] CCC, 536.
[80] CCC, 689.
[81] Ibid.; "From the beginning to the end of time, whenever God sends his Son, he always sends his Spirit: their mission is conjoined and inseparable" (CCC, 743).
[82] CCC, 690;

> The entire mission of the Son and the Holy Spirit, in the fullness of time, is contained in this: that the Son is the one anointed by the Father's Spirit since his Incarnation—Jesus is the Christ, the Messiah. Everything in the second chapter of the Creed is to be read in this light. Christ's whole work is in fact a joint mission of the Son and the Holy Spirit. (CCC, 727)

[83] CCC, 690.

Body of his Son: the mission of the Spirit of adoption is to unite them to Christ and make them live in him."[84] The seven gifts of the Spirit from Isa. 11:1-2 (wisdom, understanding, counsel, fortitude, knowledge, piety, and fear of the Lord) "belong in their fullness to Christ, the Son of David"[85] but are also "bestowed upon Christians."[86]

It is not the intention of Lumen Gentium or the Catechism to lay out a full Spirit Christology. Yet many of its statements on the Father's anointing of the Son's humanity in view of his work of salvation and giving of the Spirit to the Church illustrate the Catholic Church's interest in framing the mysteries of Christ's life in a Trinitarian framework and invite further reflection on the pneumatic dimensions of Christology in relation to ecclesiology. Among those accepting the invitation, Heribert Mühlen (1927–2006) is well-known for drawing out the implications of the anointing of Jesus for an ecclesiology and theology of the Trinity. Although Mühlen sees the anointing of the Son's humanity with the Holy Spirit as a consequence of his being the incarnate Word (personal union), he also wants to show how the presence of the Spirit revealed not at the incarnation but in his anointing at the Jordan makes it possible for others to be anointed with his Spirit.[87] He correctly observes that Jesus' perfect Spirit-led life of obedience to the Father in his messianic mission, spanning from his baptism to his glorification, allows for the extension of his habitual grace (related to his human growth in holiness) to the church.[88] The Holy Spirit orients Christ's personal grace (Lat. *gratia personalis*) toward a plurality of persons, making him the source of grace for others as head of the church (Lat. *gratia capitis*). Making the anointing at Jordan a condition for Christ's giving of the Spirit to his mystical body, Mühlen defines the church as one person (i.e., the Holy Spirit) in many persons (i.e., Christ and Christians).[89] Just as the Holy Spirit is oriented toward a plurality of persons (Christ and Christians) in the incarnation and the church, so also in proceeding from the Father and the Son, the Holy Spirit

---

[84] Ibid.
[85] CCC, 1831.
[86] CCC, 1845.
[87] See Heribert Mühlen, *Una Mystica Persona: Die Kirche als das Mysterium der Identität des Heiligen Geistes in Christus und die Christen: Eine Person in Vielen Personen*, 2nd ed. (Münich: Schöningh, 1967); for summaries of Mühlen in English, see Badcock, *Light of Truth and Fire of Love*, 145–53; and Congar, *I Believe in the Holy Spirit*, trans. David Smith, vol. 1 (New York: Crossroad, 1997), 22–5; in Spanish, see Ángel Antón, "El Espíritu Santo y la Iglesia: En busca de una fórmula para el misterio de la Iglesia," *Greg* 47, no. 1 (1966): 101–13.
[88] See Mühlen, "El acontecimiento Cristo como acción del Espíritu Santo," in J. Feiner and M. Löhrer, eds., *Mysterium Salutis*, vol. 3 (Madrid: Cristiandad, 1992): 960–84.
[89] Mühlen, *Una Mystica Persona*, 196–200.

is the bond of love between the "I" (Father) and the "Thou" (Son), namely, their "We-union" (Ger. *Wir-Vereiningung*).[90] Mühlen uses interpersonal language to restate Augustine's conception of the Spirit as a certain bond of love between the Father and the Son. By way of a marital/family analogy, the Holy Spirit is like a child who, being the fruit of the common love between his father and mother, does not cease to be distinct from them.[91] As the "We-union" of the Father ("I") and the Son ("Thou"), the Holy Spirit can be described as one person in two persons.

Vatican II's call for *ressourcement*, which means a return to the sources, especially led to a renewed interest in and appreciation for the study of patristic writers, particularly from the East. Significantly, in addition to expected authoritative citations from Western church fathers such as St. Augustine (AD 354–430) and Thomas Aquinas (1225–1274), Vatican II documents such as Lumen Gentium, as well as the Catechism, cite many Eastern fathers. This return to the rich fountains of the church's theological heritage has led to greater ecumenical engagement in the West with contemporary Orthodox theology. Theologians such as John D. Zizioulas, Boris Bobrinskoy (1925–2020), and Sergius Bulgakov (1871–1944) explore to various degrees the Trinitarian and ecclesial dimensions of a pneumatologically informed Christology.[92] Some insights from Bobrinskoy will be shared in Chapter 3 on patristics. Here we will briefly note some contributions from Zizioulas and Bulgakov before discussing Catholic theologians. Within the framework of his theology of being (divine and human) as communion, Zizioulas shows how pneumatology brings together Christology and ecclesiology because both Christ's person and his body (the church) are *"formed in the Spirit."*[93] The Holy Spirit is not a mere aid who "bridges" the distance between Christ and us after Christ's work is done, but already constitutes the One Christ as a relational (personal) being for our sake in his incarnation and baptism, so that the Many might enter into communion with his body in the church

---

[90] Mühlen, *Der Heilige Geist als Person: In der Trinität, bei der Inkarnation und im Gnadenbund: Ich–Du–Wir*, 2nd ed. (Münster: Aschendorff, 1966), 195–7 (cf. 157, 164).
[91] Ibid., 76.
[92] See John D. Zizioulas, *Being as Communion: Studies in Personhood and the Church* (Crestwood, NY: St. Vladimir's Seminary Press, 1997); Boris Bobrinskoy, *The Mystery of the Trinity: Trinitarian Experience and Vision in the Biblical and Patristic Tradition*, trans. Anthony P. Gythiel (Crestwood, NY: St. Vladimir's Press, 1999); and Sergius Bulgakov, *The Comforter*, trans. Boris Jakim (Grand Rapids, MI: Eerdmans, 2004).
[93] Zizioulas, *Being as Communion*, 110. See also John D. Zizioulas, *Communion and Otherness: Further Studies in Personhood and the Church* (London: T&T Clark, 2006).

through a new birth in baptism.⁹⁴ By giving the individual Christ an ecclesial "corporate personality," a pneumatologically constituted Christology makes possible an ecclesiology of communion.⁹⁵ Constituted by the Spirit of Christ, his ecclesial body becomes one church in a communion of many local churches—a reality that finds its basis in God's own being as a communion of persons.⁹⁶ As an example, in the church and in any church act (e.g., baptism, ordination), there can be no bishop (representing unity) without the laity (representing multiplicity).⁹⁷ Zizioulas suggests that such an ecclesiology of communion in which the gifts of all members of the church are equally needed moves beyond a "pyramidal" view of the church and proposes that the Catholic Church consider adopting this Orthodox insight in a future "Vatican III" ecumenical council so that the ministry of the pope might be seen more positively and not as a stumbling block to unity.⁹⁸ Pneumatology also contributes an eschatological trajectory to both Christology and ecclesiology. While Christ alone *"becomes history"* in the incarnation, the Holy Spirit is the *"beyond* history" who makes Christ "an eschatological being, the 'last Adam'" through the resurrection.⁹⁹ Such a perspective reminds the church not to become entrenched in an institutional mindset reduced to the present historical moment but to depend on the Holy Spirit in prayer as she fulfills her mission to bring people into the kingdom of God through her sacramental life and ministry.¹⁰⁰

Bulgakov reflects on the Spirit's place in Christ's condescension (kenosis) on the cross. He argues that because of its close association with Christ, the Spirit undergoes a certain kenosis of its own. The Spirit reposes on the Son throughout his life, especially at his baptism (i.e., his "personal Pentecost") where he "becomes *Christ*" or "the Spirit-bearer" for his "entire ministry."¹⁰¹ There are events in Christ's life, such as his exorcisms and healings, and especially his Transfiguration, which show he is filled with the Spirit and manifest the Spirit's glory to others through his humanity.¹⁰² Yet there are

---

⁹⁴Zizioulas, *Being as Communion*, 110–12 (cf. 127–8).
⁹⁵Ibid., 130–1.
⁹⁶Ibid., 136–7.
⁹⁷Ibid., 136–8.
⁹⁸Ibid., 139, 141–2.
⁹⁹Ibid., 130.
¹⁰⁰Ibid., 138; cf. Nikos A. Nissiotis, "Pneumatological Christology as a Presupposition of Ecclesiology," in Friedrich Wilhelm Kantzenbach and Vilmos Vajta, eds., *Oecumenica: An Annual Symposium of Ecumenical Research* (Minneapolis, MN: Augsburg, 1967), 235–52.
¹⁰¹Bulgakov, *The Comforter*, 249–50.
¹⁰²Ibid., 250–1.

also times, such as Christ's infancy and youth, his prayer at Gethsemane, and especially his death on the cross, in which the Spirit's own "kenosis" comes through. When the Son is forsaken by the Father on the cross (Mt. 26:38), Bulgakov asserts that "the palpable action of the Holy Spirit is diminished … although it is not abolished" because the Spirit still reposes or "abides permanently" on the Son in his forsakenness.[103] There is no division in the Trinity, but the event affects the Son in the flesh in that he dies. The Spirit undergoes a kenosis of its own on the cross, since at that time "the power of life from the Life-giving Spirit is diminished" in Christ.[104] Yet the same Spirit kept Christ's body from corruption and raised him from the dead.[105] At the resurrection, "the Holy Spirit spiritualized the matter of Christ's flesh, which spiritualization corresponds to the victory over death and to the state of the *spiritual* body in its glorification."[106] Bulgakov sees the Spirit's kenosis most intensely in Jesus' cry of dereliction on the cross but also in Christ's giving of the Spirit of Pentecost to the church. He sees Pentecost as an ongoing descent, whereby the Spirit limits its power by deifying or sanctifying people in such a way that the human response to God's love, which the Spirit enables by grace, is not denied. It is by the Spirit's kenotic and glorifying activity, respectively in Christ's death and resurrection, that he deifies fallen human beings to participate in Christ's glory.

The Second Vatical Council inspired Catholic theologians of various nations such as Heribert Mühlen (German), Yves Congar (French, 1904–1995), Bruno Forte (Italian), Piet J. A. M. Schoonenberg (Denmark, 1911–1999), and Luis F. Ladaria and Xabier Pikaza (Spanish)—to name only a few—to write studies in Christology and the Trinity informed by pneumatology.[107] In North America, Kilian McDonnell is a prominent

---

[103]Ibid., 252.
[104]Ibid., 253.
[105]Ibid., 253–4.
[106]Ibid., 346–7.
[107]For an analysis of significant post-Vatican II Catholic authors, see Veronika Gašpar, *Cristologia Pneumatologica in alcuni autori postconciliari (1965-1995): Status quaestionis e prospettive* (Roma: Gregoriana, 2000). The Croatian Catholic author discusses the following theologians: H. Mühlen, K. Rahner, and W. Kasper (German); C. Duquoc, F. X. Durrwell, and Y. Congar (French); and B. Forte, F. Lambiasi, and M. Bordoni (Italian); see also Piet J. A. M. Schoonenberg, "Spirit Christology and Logos Christology," *Bijdragen* 38 (1977): 350–75; and *El Espíritu, la Palabra y el Hijo* (Salamanca: Ediciones Sígueme, 1998); Luis F. Ladaria, "Cristología del Logos y cristología del Espíritu," *Greg* 61 (1980): 353–60; and "La unción de Jesús y el don del Espíritu," *Greg* 71 (1990): 547–70; Xabier Pikaza, *El Espíritu Santo y Jesús* (Salamanca: Secretariado Trinitario, 1982); and Nicolò Madonia, *Cristo siempre vivo en el Espíritu: Fundamentos de cristología pneumática*, trans. Fernando Torres Antoñazas (Salamanca: Secretariado Trinitario, 2006); for articles, see Luiz

pneumatologist.[108] In the English-speaking world, Catholic scholars such as Thomas Weinandy, Ralph Del Colle (1954–2012), and David Coffey deserve special mention for their studies on the Trinitarian implications of a Spirit Christology. Considering the traditional models of the Trinity in the East and the West, Weinandy observes that the Greek focus on the Spirit's proceeding from the Father "through the Son" (Lat. *per filium*) and the Latin emphasis on the Spirit's proceeding from the Father "and the Son" (Lat. *filioque*) tend to portray the third person in passive terms and thus are inadequate to ascribe the Spirit a more active personhood.[109] The monarchical and processional views tend to put the persons in a philosophically conceived sequence that suggests an ontological priority of the Father and the Son in relation to the Holy Spirit. To stress the equality of the persons, and their reciprocal simultaneous relations, Weinandy proposes another model of conceiving the Trinity. He argues that the Father's raising of Jesus in the power of the Spirit and the saints' participation in his sonship by the same Spirit through resurrection (see Rom. 8:14-17) are icons in history of an eternal Trinitarian reality, namely, that "the Father begets the Son in the Spirit."[110] By arguing for a begetting of the Son "in or by the Holy Spirit," Weinandy assigns the Holy Spirit a more active personhood than the one given by the Eastern emphasis on the monarchy of the Father or the Western focus on the Holy Spirit's procession from the Father "and the Son" (*filioque*). By raising the Spirit's profile in an articulation of the Trinitarian life, the author hopes to arrive at a more perichoretic or social view of Trinitarian relations. Moreover, linking the mystery of God to the mystery of salvation, Weinandy shows how the Spirit's relationship to Jesus in history (economic Trinity) corresponds to the Spirit's relationship to the Son in eternity (immanent Trinity). In Chapter 4, we will focus on how Moltmann and Coffey deal with the *filioque* issue in their Trinitarian theologies.

Del Colle wants to make room for a proper work (Lat. *proprium*) of the Holy Spirit in the Trinity that distinguishes its person from that of the Son and the Father. He argues that the language of "anointing" and "spiration"

Fernando Ribeiro Santana, "O Espírito Santo na vida de Jesus: Por uma Cristologia Pneumática," *Atualidade Teológica* 14, no. 36 (2010): 265–92; and Robert P. Imbelli, "The New Adam and Life-Giving Spirit: The Paschal Pattern of Spirit Christology," *Communio* 25 (1998): 233–52.

[108] See Kilian McDonnell, *The Baptism of Jesus in the Jordan*; *The Other Hand of God: The Holy Spirit as the Universal Tough and Goal* (Collegeville, MN: Liturgical Press, 2003); "The Determinative Doctrine of the Holy Spirit," *Theology Today* 39 (1982): 142–61.

[109] Thomas G. Weinandy, *The Father's Spirit of Sonship: Reconceiving the Trinity* (Edinburgh: T&T Clark, 1995), 6–9.

[110] Ibid., 25.

used by neo-scholastic Catholic theologians such as Matthias Scheeben (1835–1888), Emile Mersch (1890–1940), and others prepared the way for thinking about the unique sanctifying work of the Spirit in both the Son's humanity and the adopted sons' human lives.[111] According to Coffey, an influence in Del Colle's own work, the Holy Spirit creates and sanctifies the human nature that the divine Son (or Logos) assumes (incarnation), and this work of the Spirit allows for the sanctification of human persons by adoption as children of God through union with the Son.[112] This formative work of the Holy Spirit in the incarnation and grace reveals that the third person does not only proceed from the Father and the Son. Inspired by Augustine and his image of the Spirit as a certain bond of love between the Father and the Son, Coffey points out that the Holy Spirit is also "the mutual love of the Father and the Son" and, therefore, the personal (hypostatic) love in whom the Father and the Son exist in eternity and incorporate humans by the grace of adoption into this mutual love.[113] Weinandy, Del Colle, and Coffey share an interest in the implications of a Spirit Christology for seeing Jesus' life through a pneumatological lens, ascertaining the Holy Spirit's special role in the incarnation and the Trinity, and accounting for our human sharing in Christ's life by the Spirit.[114] As a way to deepen our discussion of the issues raised by these Catholic theologians, Chapter 4 will delve into David Coffey's use of Spirit Christology in Trinitarian theology.

The Global Rise of Pentecostal and Charismatic Churches

The global rise of Pentecostalism and Pentecostal scholarship has contributed to the field of Spirit Christology. A brief summary of contributions by Sammy Alfaro, Andréa Snavely, Frank Macchia, and Skip Jenkins gives us a sense of their distinct questions and approaches. Although ecumenical in character,

---

[111]Colle, *Christ and the Spirit*, 57–8.

[112]David Coffey, "The Method of Third Article Theology," in *TAT*, 27; for a summary of Del Colle's "historical approach" to Spirit Christology, see Sánchez, *Sculptor Spirit*, 29–37.

[113]David Coffey develops his proposal in *Deus Trinitas: The Doctrine of the Triune God* (New York: Oxford University Press, 1999); and *"Did You Receive the Holy Spirit When You Believed?": Some Basic Questions for Pneumatology* (Milwaukee, WI: Marquette University Press, 2005); cf. Declan J. O'Byrne, "Spirit Christology and the Trinity in the Theology of David Coffey" (PhD diss., Dublin City University, 2009); and Gerrit van de Kamp, "De pneumatologische christologie van David Coffey," *Australian Catholic Record* 92, no. 1 (2015): 67–80.

[114]On Peppiatt's use of these theologians for articulating a theology of mission, see Chapter 6.

their works clearly seek to ground a Spirit Christology in Pentecostal theological categories and practices. Alfaro and Snavely are especially concerned with reaping the benefits of the field for calling their own churches to bold discipleship in a broken world. In conversation with Latin American and US Latino/a Christologies, Alfaro argues that a Spirit Christology offers an intelligible way to account for the fivefold Pentecostal presentation of Jesus' identity (namely, Jesus as Savior, Sanctifier, Spirit Baptizer, Healer, and Coming King) in a way that fosters a practice of accompaniment or solidarity with suffering and marginalized neighbors.[115] Although Snavely agrees with the post-Constantinian theologians' critique of the church's cultural accommodation to North American culture, he proposes that only a Spirit Christology can provide the church with the energy to be a countercultural force for nonviolence, contentment and sharing, and racial reconciliation in the world.[116] These authors have a keen sense of the need for thinking through a Spirit Christology from the perspective of communal practices of solidarity, such as the singing of *coritos* in Mexican churches (Alfaro) and multiethnic worship in the spirit of the Azusa Street revival (Snavely), which can engender an ethically responsible vision of life in the Spirit. The last chapter offers a more in-depth look at Alfaro's work.

Macchia develops a full Christology from the perspective of Pentecost, which constitutes a central event in Pentecostal theology and practice. Seeing Jesus' giving of the Spirit on Pentecost as "the decisive disclosure of Christ's identity … the experiential beginning for those called to follow him," Macchia has argued that Pentecost manifests Christ's divine identity in unity with the Father, his human identity in unity with humanity, and the incorporation of humanity into God's life.[117] A former student of Ralph Del Colle, Jenkins has shown that a Spirit Christology offers a productive Trinitarian framework for bringing together into one systematic Pentecostal theology what he sees as disjointed Pentecostal emphases on holiness and power, or as the lack of integration between the fivefold presentation of Jesus and the experience of Spirit Baptism.[118] In dialogue with James D. G. Dunn (1939–2020) and Karl Barth, and inspired by Scottish theologian Edward Irving (1792–1834), Jenkins proposes that at his incarnation the Son

---

[115]Sammy Alfaro, *Divino Compañero: Toward a Hispanic Pentecostal Christology* (Eugene, OR: Pickwick, 2010).

[116]Andréa Snavely, *Life in the Spirit: A Post-Constantinian and Trinitarian Account of the Christian Life* (Eugene, OR: Pickwick, 2015).

[117]Frank Macchia, *Jesus the Baptizer: Christology in Light of Pentecost* (Grand Rapids, MI: Eerdmans, 2010), 5 (cf. 64).

[118]Skip Jenkins, *A Spirit Christology* (New York: Peter Lang, 2018).

assumed a fallen humanity, which he sanctified together with the Spirit so that fallen humans can be made holy and empowered by the same Spirit.[119] All the aforementioned Pentecostal scholars test the usefulness of a Spirit Christology to discuss how the Spirit's presence in Christ informs a theology of God, salvation in Christ, and life in the Spirit. Among his conversation partners, it is noteworthy that, in a section of his last chapter, Jenkins engages the Spirit Christologies of New Zealand Reformed theologian Myk Habets and Panamanian-Chilean Lutheran theologian Leopoldo Sánchez.[120] Chapter 5 offers a more in-depth ecumenical discussion of Sánchez, Habets, and Jenkins, as it relates especially to the retrieval of historical voices within their own ecclesial traditions in the development of a Spirit Christology that complements the Logos Christology of the ecumenical councils.

Although not a Pentecostal, we end this section with Clark Pinnock (1937–2010), a broadly Evangelical theologian whose interest in the Holy Spirit was influenced by his interaction with Pentecostal and Charismatic theologies—including contributions to *The Journal of Pentecostal Studies*.[121] In *Flame of Love*, a systematic theology written from the perspective of the Holy Spirit, Pinnock includes a section on Spirit Christology that reflects on the anointing of Jesus with the Spirit for his mission.[122] Pinnock also shows how a soteriology of the cross informed by pneumatology fosters both "a representative and participatory model of atonement."[123] Echoing Irenaeus' image of the Son and the Spirit as God's "two hands" in creation, Pinnock locates both atonement models in a view of salvation as "recapitulation."[124] God gives the history of humanity "a new start" through Christ, the last Adam, who lived "in obedience to God and dependence on the Spirit, so that the effect of Adam's sin is reversed … creation restored," and humans might receive "incorporation into him through faith by the Spirit."[125] The Holy Spirit has a role in Christ's journey of death and resurrection in the place of Adam, and in humanity's union with

---

[119] Ibid., 182.
[120] Ibid., 319–29.
[121] For example, see Clark H. Pinnock, "The Recovery of the Holy Spirit in Evangelical Theology," *JPS* 13, no. 1 (October 2004): 3–18; and "The Work of the Spirit in the Interpretation of Holy Scripture from the Perspective of a Charismatic Biblical Theologian," *JPS* 18, no. 2 (April 2009): 157–71.
[122] In a constructive critique of Pinnock, Studebaker, following Coffey, argues for the Spirit's defining role not only in the anointing of the Son's humanity but in preparing his humanity for union with the Logos. See Steven M. Studebaker, "Integrating Pneumatology and Christology: A Trinitarian Modification of Clark H. Pinnock's Spirit Christology," *Pneuma* 28, no. 1 (Spring 2006): 5–20.
[123] Clark H. Pinnock, *Flame of Love: A Theology of the Holy Spirit* (Downers Grove, IL: InterVarsity Press, 1996), 103.
[124] Ibid., 92–3.
[125] Ibid., 95.

Christ through conformity to his death and resurrection. A Spirit Christology best "helps us to take seriously the motif of the last Adam's tracing of our human path and directs our attention to a participatory model of atonement, in which the central motif is union with Christ."[126] In a representative model, which focuses on Christ's objective work of redeeming humanity from sin through his self-surrender to the Father (cf. Heb. 9:14), the Spirit "enabled Jesus to make a perfect offering for us" in solidarity with sinners.[127] In a participatory account, the work of the Spirit who raised Jesus from the dead (cf. Rom. 8:11) is to make us into a new creation, "to form Christ in us and change us into his likeness. The task is to reverse the power of sin in us until death itself is overcome and we can share in the glory of God."[128]

Christ's vicarious work on the cross is not as an independent event but the culmination of his Spirit-led journey of obedience to the Father. The cross can also be seen from the side of the Spirit's raising of the Son from the dead and the Son's sending of the Spirit upon humanity on Pentecost to share in his sufferings and glory. Although Pinnock agrees that there is a "legal" or "penal" aspect to the atonement in Scripture (cf. Rom. 3:25), whereby the Son's sacrifice appeases God's wrath against sinners, he warns against seeing such aspect in a way that "pits the Father against the Son and construes forgiveness as something that God finds difficult to give," or fails to see that ultimately God's "love provided the incarnation and the atonement, not wrath."[129] The problem is not God's wrath per se but its association with retribution as part of God's own character. Departing from John Calvin's retributive emphasis, according to which "God's vengeance struck out against Christ" (*Institutes* 2.16.1–5), Pinnock notes that "love for sinners, not anger, brought Jesus into the world."[130] Jesus' cry of dereliction, "My God, my God, why have you forsaken me?" (Mk 15:34), does not mean that God rejected the Son in an ontological sense or that the Father did not love him, but that God's wrath "blazed against sinners in the person of their representative."[131] The cross shows that God's wrath is not "the dark side of God that frustrates grace" but rather "the other side of God's saving action, and it serves grace. … The cross reflects not God's thirst for retribution but his determination to overcome alienation and enslavement."[132] Pinnock's contribution lies

---

[126] Ibid., 97.
[127] Ibid., 104.
[128] Ibid., 106.
[129] Ibid., 106–7.
[130] Ibid., 107.
[131] Ibid., 108.
[132] Ibid., 109.

in showing how a Spirit Christology facilitates an account of salvation (atonement) that links the Spirit's action in Christ as our representative Adam, who frees us from the guilt of sin, to the Spirit's ongoing formation of Christians after his likeness to free us from the recurrent power of sin.

Questions

(1) You are speaking to a friend about the Holy Spirit in the life of Jesus. After a few minutes, your friend, a bit confused and concerned, asks you: "You are not saying that Jesus *needed* the Holy Spirit. Are you?" How would you answer her question?

(2) Three theologians—a pre-Nicene, a Nicene, and a post-Nicene one—read the text from the Annunciation of Mary: "The angel said to her, 'The Holy *Spirit* will come upon you, and the power of the Most High will overshadow you; therefore the child to be born will be holy; he will be called Son of God'" (Lk. 1:35). How would their distinct views of "Spirit" shape their interpretations of this text?

(3) A number of theologians working in Spirit Christology connect the Spirit's activity in the life of Christ with the Spirit's activity in the life of the Christian or the church. Choose one or two theologians or texts discussed in this chapter and show the ways they make this connection.

2

The Fullness of the Spirit in and through Jesus: Insights from Biblical Studies

In an often cited study of the anointing of Jesus, French exegete Ignace de la Potterie argues that, contrary to a common patristic identification of the anointing of Christ with his incarnation or hypostatic union, the New Testament only knows of one anointing of Jesus taking place at his baptism in the Jordan.[1] In Chapter 3, we will discuss a peculiar interpretation of the anointing of Jesus among some church fathers, according to which the Word (Logos) anoints his human flesh with his Spirit (or his own divinity) at the moment of the incarnation. Although the reasons for this interpretation could be understood as a way of dealing with Justin's burden as described in the previous chapter, some early church theologians were able to account more compellingly for the uniqueness of Jesus' anointing with the Spirit at his baptism without doing harm to the confession of his divinity and incarnation. De la Potterie observes that in biblical narrative the baptism of Jesus does not function as an outward manifestation of a prior consecration of his human nature at the incarnation, but as his anointing with the Holy Spirit for his prophetic mission.[2] The author speaks of the event as "a real communication of the Holy Spirit, an illumination, an impulse" that launches Christ into his public mission, inaugurating the eschatological age of salvation leading to the outpouring of the Spirit upon others.[3] Rather than

---

[1] Ignace de la Potterie, "L'onction du Christ. Étude de théologie biblique," *Nouvelle revue théologique* 80, no. 3 (1958): 225–52.
[2] Ibid., 251–2.
[3] Ibid., 252.

looking at the anointing of Jesus through later theological concepts in the church's tradition, such as its interpretation as the Logos' consecration of his humanity with his own divinity (at times called "spirit" according to a pre-Nicene interpretation discussed in the previous chapter), de la Potterie's classic study remains a useful reminder for theologians to engage in a careful reading of the biblical texts themselves in all their specificity for the sake of enriching our understanding of the various moments of Jesus' life.[4] Although Spirit Christology is often thought of as a systematic theologian's wheelhouse, the field is interdisciplinary, using insights from biblical studies, historical theology (including patristics), and practical theology.

In this chapter, we focus on the contributions of exegetes to the field of Spirit Christology. Biblical scholars play an important role in theological studies by keeping systematic theologians honest in their use of biblical texts. Similar to de la Potterie, A. Vanhoye offers an example of an approach to biblical interpretation that hones in on the richness of a pneumatological text in all its specificity for understanding Jesus' mission. Consider his study of the Spirit's role in Christ's passion according to Hebrews. Focusing on a text's reference to "the blood of Christ, who through the eternal Spirit offered himself without blemish to God" (Heb. 9:14), Vanhoye identifies "the eternal Spirit" as the "inspirer" (*ispiratore*) or "power" (*potenza*) who moves Christ and gives eternal value to his self-offering to the Father.[5] The expression "through the eternal Spirit" (Gk. *dia pneumatos aiōniou*) does not signify an internal disposition in Christ, his divine nature, or his human spirit (soul). Referring to the disposition of Christ's heart or soul (*disposizione d'animo*) as "eternal spirit" seems ambivalent, and identifying "spirit" with his divine nature reads a later patristic use of *spiritus* into the text.[6] Moreover, Vanhoye submits that it makes little sense to speak of Christ's death as an offering of his human "spirit" to the Father apart from his body (cf. Heb. 10:10)! Although atypical, the expression "eternal spirit" refers to the Holy Spirit. The "value" (*valore*) of Christ's blood lies in its power to effect an "eternal redemption" (Heb. 9:12) and offer an "eternal inheritance" (v. 15). The Spirit's role is to "communicate to Christ the needed strength to effect an offer of such extraordinary efficacy."[7] Through the Spirit's sanctifying presence in Christ, his sacrifice is transformed into an unblemished offering

---

[4] Ibid., 251–2.
[5] A. Vanhoye S. J., "L'azione dello Spirito Santo nella passione di Cristo secondo l'epistola agli Ebrei," *Credo*, vol. 1, 760, 762 (cf. 764).
[6] Ibid., 761. We discuss this patristic use of spirit in Chapters 1 and 3.
[7] Ibid., 762 (translation mine).

that is efficacious before God in heaven (cf. Heb. 9:24).[8] The Spirit leads Christ to align perfectly his will to the Father's (cf. Heb. 10:4-10) and thus be in solidarity with his brothers and sisters (cf. Heb. 2:17; 4:15).[9] Christ's life in the Spirit is a life of prayer and obedience to God for our sake. By its association with Christ's blood, the Spirit "transformed the death [of Christ] into a covenantal act" before God on behalf of humans.[10] The result of the new covenant, as the Spirit testifies, is the creation of a new heart (cf. Heb. 10:14-16).[11]

The aforementioned Catholic exegetes' call for careful exegesis embodies the spirit of the Second Vatican Council's appreciation for a *ressourcement* or return to the sources of the church's tradition, including the Scriptures.[12] Although their intent is not to develop a systematic Spirit Christology, we can appreciate how helpful their reading of texts speaking to the Spirit's role in Jesus' anointing (de la Potterie) and passion (Vanhoye) can be for articulating such a Christology. They offer key pieces in a larger puzzle. But there are also biblical theologians who have offered a deeper and more extensive look at the pneumatic identity of Jesus, and to various degrees have done so in dialogue with biblical, historical, systematic, and practical theologies. In this chapter, we introduce readers to some of those voices and their contributions to reflection on the fullness of the Spirit in Jesus. We will first discuss British New Testament scholar James D. G. Dunn's eschatological perspective on the experience of Jesus and his disciples—a perspective in which the Spirit of God plays a foundational role in establishing the kingdom of God among us. Then, we look at US Evangelical exegete Gerald F. Hawthorne's kenotic approach to Christ's life in the presence and power of the Spirit, which highlights the Son's receptivity to the Spirit's influence and empowerment in his life and mission. The final section deals with the field known as the theological interpretation of Scripture, highlighting ways in which a Spirit Christology can make more explicit the interpretation of texts that are only implicitly pneumatological, and assist in the interpretation of texts which though explicitly pneumatological are difficult to interpret. After briefly looking at examples of two systematic theologians' work in this area (B. Laytham and L. Sánchez), we focus on American Methodist New Testament scholar Michael J. Gorman's brief intertextual study of the Spirit

---

[8] Ibid., 764-5.
[9] Ibid., 767.
[10] Ibid., 771 (translation mine).
[11] Ibid., 773.
[12] On the Second Vatican Council and Spirit Christology, see Chapter 1.

in Jesus according to John's Gospel as a critical and constructive response to the "Johannine Jesus" thesis in biblical studies. All the authors' arguments in this chapter illustrate how insights from biblical scholars can potentially enrich and be enriched by interacting with theological insights from the field of Spirit Christology.

The Experience of the Spirit: James D. G. Dunn's Eschatological Perspective

Few theologians have devoted so much time to the study of the experience of the Spirit in the life of Jesus and the first generation of Christians than James D. G. Dunn. In *Jesus and the Spirit*, the author places his studies in the broader context of a major shift in biblical studies from a nineteenth-century Liberal Protestant portrayal of Jesus as a moral paradigm of sonship—what Adolf von Harnack (1851-1930) called Jesus' consciousness of the fatherhood of God—to the twentieth-century eschatological presentation of Jesus ushered in by scholars like Johanness Weiss (1863-1914) and Albert Schweitzer (1875-1965), which portrays him as a figure with a consciousness of his Spirit-empowered end-time role in history.[13] Although Harnack's focus on Jesus' self-consciousness of sonship holds promise to describe his unique relationship with God as Father, Dunn argues that such focus needs to be grounded in gospel narratives describing Jesus' Abba (a familiar term for "father") prayer life (e.g., Mk 14:32-42) and knowledge of the Father (e.g., Mt. 11:27) and, moreover, must be linked more clearly to his disciples' sharing in his life and knowledge.[14] More importantly, such a discussion of sonship—Jesus' and ours—must be located in the eschatological story of the Spirit's role in the inbreaking of God's kingdom on earth.

---

[13] "*How shall we pursue our quest?* Two avenues immediately commend themselves. The first may be called the nineteenth-century way of Liberal Protestantism … the second, the twentieth-century way of eschatology. The first focuses on Jesus' consciousness of sonship; the second on his consciousness of Spirit." James D. G. Dunn, *Jesus and the Spirit: A Study of the Religious and Charismatic Experience of Jesus and the First Christians as Reflected in the New Testament* (Grand Rapids, MI: Eerdmans, 1997), 14 (cf. 41–3).

[14] Ibid., 37–8.

Jesus' Consciousness of Sonship and Eschatological Power

Religious experience becomes the broader category Dunn uses to describe the contours of Jesus' sense of sonship in ways that are both distinct from and similar to his disciples'. Thus a key issue for the author is the degree of discontinuity and continuity between Jesus' sense of being son and that of his disciples. Consider how Paul's description of Christians crying out "Abba! Father!" by the leading of "the Spirit of his [God's] Son" in their hearts suggests a link to Jesus' own Abba prayer at Gethsemane (Rom. 8:14-17; Gal. 4:6). The Spirit shapes the prayer life of Jesus in the church, giving his disciples access to the same Father. According to Dunn, Jesus' Abba prayer shows he "*experienced an intimate relation of sonship in prayer ... sensed this relationship with God to be something distinctive ... encouraged his disciples to pray in the same way, but even then he seems to have thought of their relationship as somehow dependent on his own, as somehow a consequence of his own*" (emphasis in the original).[15] Jesus remains son in that he relates to God in a distinctive way, but also in a way that others can participate in his identity as son derivatively through the Spirit.[16] Similarly, consider how Matthew notes that "no one knows the Father except the Son and anyone to whom the Son chooses to reveal him" (Mt. 11:27). Here the Son's relationship to the Father is like none other, yet also open for others to share in through the mediation of the Son. Dunn explains that Jesus "knows God as no man ever has; the mutual relation he experiences with God is without parallel. At the same time, that unique knowledge of God can be shared by others ... just as others address God as 'Abba.'"[17] Jesus' special identity as son of God sets him apart from and marks the early Christians' identity as adopted sons (and daughters) of God.

To Jesus' unique sense of sonship Dunn adds his "*consciousness of eschatological power, of God's Spirit upon him and working through him*," which Jesus displays in his "work as an exorcist" and in his "conviction" that he is the inspired end-time prophet of God.[18] A key text that highlights

---

[15] Ibid., 26.
[16] "Moreover, it is clearly implied in Rom. 8.15 and Gal. 4.6 that *the early Christians' experience of sonship was understood as an echo and reproduction of Jesus' own experience*; it is precisely *the Spirit of the Son* who cries 'Abba.'" Ibid., 22.
[17] Ibid., 34.
[18] Ibid., 43; see also James D. G. Dunn, "Spirit and Holy Spirit in the New Testament," in *The Christ and the Spirit*, vol. 2, *Pneumatology* (Grand Rapids, MI: Eerdmans, 1998), 6–7; emphasis in the original.

Jesus' empowering by the Spirit in his exorcisms reads: "But if it is by the Spirit of God that I cast out demons, then the kingdom of God has come to you" (Mt. 12:28). Unlike other Jewish exorcists, Jesus claimed his exorcisms were distinct in that they "were performed by the *Spirit/finger of God*" (see Lk. 11:20) and achieved "that binding of the powers of evil which was looked for at the end of the age" (emphasis in the original).[19] In his discussion of Jesus' binding of the strong man (Satan) in Mt. 12, Dunn emphasizes Jesus' dependence on the Spirit for his works, so that the incident "was not so much a case of 'Where *I* am there is the kingdom', as, 'Where the *Spirit* is there is the kingdom' ... Jesus saw in his experience of power to cast out demons a manifestation of God, and of God acting through him in a decisive new and final way."[20] Furthermore, Jesus speaks of his ministry of proclamation as the fulfillment of Old Testament prophecy: "The Spirit of the Lord is upon me, because he has anointed me to bring good news to the poor. He has sent me to proclaim release to captives ... to proclaim the year of the Lord's favor" (Lk. 4:18-19; Isa. 61:1-2). As in the case of Jesus' exorcisms, Dunn sees in this text evidence that Jesus' consciousness of his authority to proclaim the kingdom as God's end-time prophet was informed by "His awareness of being uniquely possessed and used by the divine Spirit" to accomplish God's mission.[21] Jesus had a keen sense of "*divine power and inspiration*" (emphasis in the original) of his possession of "the eschatological Spirit operating in and through him" as the power of God at work in his healings and proclamation of God's forgiveness.[22] Jesus is the preeminent bearer of the Spirit, who empowers and inspires his eschatological mission.

The Holy Spirit's descent upon Jesus at the Jordan becomes the event at which Jesus most likely becomes aware of his unique sonship and possession of the Spirit for his end-time mission. Dunn sees Jesus' baptism as the "most probable" occasion in which "these convictions must have crystallized."[23] Like his baptism, Jesus' temptation in the desert brings together "as two sides of one coin" his sense of being God's son and Spirit-anointed: "The son obeys the Father's will. The Spirit drives forth. The two statements describe the same inward compulsion, which could not be denied, which had to find

---

[19] Dunn, *Jesus and the Spirit*, 48–9.
[20] Ibid., 49; Dunn highlights that "during Jesus' earthly life the Spirit was the dominant partner." See Dunn, "Spirit and Kingdom," in *Pneumatology*, 138.
[21] Dunn, *Jesus and the Spirit*, 54.
[22] Ibid., 61.
[23] Ibid., 63 (cf. 38).

expression in word and deed."²⁴ Dunn sums up his eschatological perspective on Jesus' pneumatic identity as follows:

> Jesus thought of himself as God's son and as anointed by the eschatological Spirit, because in prayer he experienced God as Father and in ministry he experienced a power to heal which he could only understand as the power of the end-time and an inspiration to proclaim a message which he could only understand as the gospel of the end-time.²⁵

In this perspective, the baptism at Jordan becomes a key moment for Jesus' understanding of himself in relationship to his Father and his Spirit-led mission.

Jesus' Sonship in the Spirit, Christology of Inspiration, and the Christness of the Spirit

Working with tools of modern biblical exegesis, Dunn looks for the most reliable early sources of the tradition of interpretation concerning Jesus, asks what those biblical texts reveal about Jesus' experiences of God, and then sees how these experiences relate to those of the early Christians. Regardless of how one feels about Dunn's method, his study of the power of the Spirit of God in and through Jesus remains an important contribution to Spirit Christology today. His work raises key questions for the field and offers frameworks for addressing them. First, Dunn offers a history of interpretation framework for thinking through the issue of the degree of continuity between Jesus' and the early Christians' experiences of sonship and Spirit. Jesus' experience of God can be reduced neither to the Liberal Protestant focus on the ethical dimension of sonship as a paradigm of obedience to God nor to a "charismatic" eschatological overemphasis on Jesus as a prophet inspired by the Spirit. Instead, both perspectives are incorporated within the gospels' broader eschatological outlook. As Dunn puts it, "Jesus can be presented neither simply as a moralist not simply as an ecstatic. *It is the interaction of sonship and Spirit that gives Jesus' ministry its distinctive character*" (emphasis in the original).²⁶

---

[24] Ibid., 66.
[25] Ibid., 67.
[26] Ibid., 90.

Second, Dunn's efforts to show the degree of continuity between Jesus' experiences of sonship and Spirit and those of other sons (children) of God anointed with the Spirit lead the author to ask what type of Christology best accounts for Jesus' identity. Although the author acknowledges that traditional "Logos Christology" (the Word becomes flesh) or "Chalcedonian Christology" (Christ's two natures) wrestles with the question of "Jesus' relation to God," he ultimately sees it as "an abstraction from the NT material" and feels the synoptic gospels offer "a check on traditional formulations."[27] In the synoptic gospels, Jesus' sonship is "an existential relationship, not a metaphysical relationship ... Jesus' consciousness of an intimate relationship with God, not of awareness of metaphysical sonship, nor of a 'divine consciousness', (far less consciousness of being 'second Person of the Trinity'!)."[28] Dunn sees in certain NT references to divine titles for Jesus and especially in the Johannine account of Jesus the roots for the later articulation of his sonship in terms of "essence and substance, 'begotten from the Father before the ages."[29] However, preferring a "Christology from below," the author initially proposed a historical view of Jesus' "divinity" in terms not of his divine nature but "*his relationship with the Father as son and the Spirit of God in him*" (emphasis in the original).[30] In an article preceding the publication of *Jesus and the Spirit*, Dunn concluded that "Jesus' possession and experience of the Spirit is that which later dogma has called his divinity. The 'deity' of the Jesus of history is a function of the Spirit—is, in fact, no more and no less than the Spirit."[31] Later on, Dunn changed this position, sensing that it had become a one-sided Christological assertion grounded in a legitimate but insufficient view of "the relation between the earthly Jesus and the Spirit ... in terms of inspiration and empowering."[32] Dunn's change of heart leads him to

---

[27] Ibid., 12.
[28] Ibid., 38.
[29] Ibid., 38–9.
[30] Ibid., 92.
[31] James D. G. Dunn, "Rediscovering the Spirit (1)," in *The Christ and the Spirit*, vol. 2, *Pneumatology* (Grand Rapids, MI: Eerdmans, 1998), 50; see also James D. G. Dunn, "Jesus—Flesh and Spirit: An Exposition of Romans 1:3-4," in *The Christ and the Spirit*, vol. 1, *Christology* (Grand Rapids, MI: Eerdmans, 1998), 143.
[32] Dunn, "Rediscovering the Spirit (2)," in *Pneumatology*, 75. Dunn specifically states: "The Spirit cannot be simply identified with the divinity or deity of Christ" (74); similarly, Dunn's preface to his *Pneumatology* volume of collected essays in *The Christ and the Spirit* includes this clarification:

> Probably the most striking feature where I would want to plead change of perception is in the overemphasis on the Spirit ... I would no longer want to identify the Spirit with experience quite so crudely ... The Spirit-christology ... (the Spirit as the 'divinity' or 'deity' of Jesus) was more a reflection of 'the rediscovery of the Spirit' than balanced theology. (ix)

identify a "Spirit Christology" with a "christology of inspiration" and contrasts it to a "christology of incarnation."[33] More importantly, he acknowledges the need to account for these "distinct christologies ... in any dogmatic synthesis which claims canonical authority."[34] Such an integration would both preclude a Spirit Christology from assuming "the whole weight" of reflection on Christ and see it instead as a "bridge" between Logos (incarnation) and Adam/Lord (resurrection) accounts of Christ.[35] Although the author does not offer such a synthesis, his studies commend further work on the relationship between Logos and Spirit Christologies.

Finally, Dunn shows that the same Spirit who anoints Jesus as God's son for his mission belongs to the Christian community whose experience takes on the form of the Spirit of Jesus. The author pairs the Pauline corpus' focus on "the *Jesus-character* of Christian experience" with various marks of the Spirit's works in the community.[36] Thus the Spirit delineates the experience of inspiration in the community in terms of the proclamation of Jesus' lordship (1 Cor. 12:3), the life of sonship as the "impress" of Jesus' own "Abba" relationship with God (Rom. 8:14-15; Gal. 4:6), the "goal" of being conformed to Christ's image in accordance with its eschatological form in a resurrected spiritual body (1 Cor. 15:49), and the fruit of the Spirit in line with the "'character sketches' of Christ" (1 Cor. 13:4-7; Gal. 5:22).[37] In the life of believers, the risen Christ and the Spirit of life are two sides of the same coin. One cannot experience one without the other. For this reason, Dunn interprets the expression "the last Adam became life-giving Spirit" (1 Cor. 15:45) to mean that Paul is equating the resurrected Lord with the Holy Spirit functionally or "in existential rather than in ontological terms."[38] The point is not to deny that Jesus has his own "personal existence," but to show that "only that experience which embodies the character of Christ is experience of the Spirit."[39] Likewise, the Spirit is not ontologically Jesus, yet functionally Jesus is "the personality of the Spirit" since he is "the archetype which the eschatological Spirit filled, the 'shape' which the Spirit took on as a mould, the shape which the Spirit in turn stamps upon believers. ... In Paul then *the*

---

[33] Dunn, "Rediscovering the Spirit (2)," in *Pneumatology*, 76–7.
[34] Ibid., 77.
[35] Ibid., 79–80.
[36] Dunn, *Jesus and the Spirit*, 319.
[37] Ibid., 319–21.
[38] Ibid., 322; see also Dunn, "1 Corinthians 15:45—Last Adam, Life-Giving Spirit," in *Christology*, 165–6; and Dunn, "2 Corinthians 3:17—The Lord Is the Spirit," in *Christology*, 124–5.
[39] Dunn, *Jesus and the Spirit*, 322–3.

distinctive mark of the Spirit becomes his Christness."[40] Dunn shows how the Spirit in Jesus shapes Jesus in the believer. A pneumatic Christology flows seamlessly into a Christological pneumatology: "In brief, the dynamic of the relationship between the Spirit and Jesus can be expressed epigrammatically thus: *as the Spirit was the 'divinity' of Jesus … so Jesus became the personality of the Spirit*" (emphasis in the original).[41] By linking Jesus' life in the Spirit to the early Christian's description of life in the Spirit, Dunn offers an exegetical case for articulating the pneumatological link between Christ and Christians—an important task in a Spirit Christology today.

Dependent on the Spirit's Power: Gerald F. Hawthorne's Kenotic Perspective

Gerald F. Hawthorne explores the Spirit's role in the conception and birth, boyhood and youth, baptism, temptation, ministry, death, and resurrection of Jesus. Similar to Dunn's pneumatic description of Jesus' identity, Hawthorne points out that the evangelists "agree that Jesus was dependent upon the Spirit for the successful completion of the work God had given him to do in this world throughout the whole of his life."[42] Dunn's work leaves room for integrating pneumatological and incarnational Christologies. Hawthorne is conscious of this challenge and wants to show how the Spirit's presence in Jesus does not replace but enriches an incarnational Christology. He does so by consistently applying a kenotic principle to his reading of the gospels, according to which Jesus in his condescension (kenosis) shows a dependence on the Spirit in his life and ministry.

The Spirit in the Incarnate Son's Holiness, Infancy, Baptism, and Temptation

In describing the proper works of the Spirit and the Son, Hawthorne indicates that "the Holy Spirit created the humanity that the Eternal

---

[40] Ibid., 324–5.
[41] Ibid., 325. As noted earlier, Dunn later retracts from speaking of the Spirit's presence in Jesus as his "divinity."
[42] Gerald F. Hawthorne, *The Presence & The Power: The Significance of the Holy Spirit in the Life and Mission of Jesus* (Eugene, OR: Wipf & Stock, 1991), 179.

Son made his very own, within which he completely immersed himself. As a result, then, of the creative work of the Holy Spirit in combination with the condescension of the divine Son, the son of Mary is the Son of God!"[43] Only the eternal Son becomes incarnate, not the Spirit; but the Spirit creates the humanity the Son assumes in Mary's womb. The incarnation highlights both the Spirit's work as creator and the divine Son's condescension or kenosis. Jesus is portrayed mainly as the recipient of the Spirit's activity upon him and, to a lesser extent, as the divine agent of his own actions. For instance, speaking about the holiness of the child from birth, the author argues that the Spirit's work "was to provide him with a human nature that was initially unstained by sin."[44] Yet it was still up to Jesus to choose not to sin from then on by his obedience to the Father: "Jesus was holy, but not perfected in holiness. The former was the result of the creative work of the Spirit. The latter was something that only Jesus himself could achieve by the choices he made throughout his life."[45] Jesus is made holy and becomes holy. The former is the Spirit's special doing, and the latter the Son's special doing. By his obedience, the Son becomes a new Adam, giving sinful humanity a fresh start, disentangling it from the ongoing effects of Adam's disobedience.[46] Although more intuitively than explicitly, Hawthorne's reflections on the Christ child's holiness begin to integrate what Dunn calls Spirit-oriented, incarnational, and new Adam Christologies.

The Spirit is not only involved at the beginning of the Son's human existence. In all the events of the Son's life, including his boyhood and youth, the Spirit became "the divine influence ever present with him, the one nudging him always in the direction of the fear of God."[47] Here too the author applies the same kenotic principle of interpretation to his pneumatic readings of the gospels, namely, that the Son in his kenosis or condescension makes himself dependent on the Spirit without losing his own personal identity and will. The Spirit nudges, illumines, and draws Jesus toward a life of wisdom, in favor toward God and humans, without making decisions for him: "The Spirit was not, however, the one to make choices for him or determine the direction his life would take. Those

---

[43] Ibid., 79.
[44] Ibid., 84.
[45] Ibid., 85 (cf. 102).
[46] Ibid., 85–8. Hawthorne compares this view with Irenaeus' theory of recapitulation, namely, "the summing up or restoration of fallen humanity to communion with God through the obedience of Jesus, the Son of God incarnate" (87).
[47] Ibid., 102.

things Jesus must do for himself."[48] When Hawthorne states that "the divine Son limited himself to the confines of the man Jesus" or that "in this person God the Son looked at the world through the eyes of Jesus," he highlights the Son's kenosis in the strongest possible way—although, if pressed too hard, these expressions could sound as if the Son and Jesus are two distinct agents.[49] Be that as it may, Hawthorne's main concern lies in highlighting how the divine Son is acted upon by the Spirit in his humanity, so that the events of his life truly affect him in a human way. Accordingly, his baptism at the Jordan does not merely reveal to others that Jesus is the Son of God, but that the Spirit descends into him to fill, anoint, or equip him in a special way for his messianic commissioning as Yahweh's Servant.[50] The Father's voice from heaven, directed at Jesus, makes him more humanly aware of his unique power and authority for this mission.[51] In the temptation account, where Jesus is led by the Spirit into the desert, the Spirit's influence upon him and the Son's passivity or receptivity in yielding to God's will through the Spirit also come forth strongly: "But although he [i.e., Jesus] remains the master of his will and consciousness, he, nevertheless, elects to subject himself to the guiding influence of the Spirit. He chooses to substitute the will of God, made known to him through the Spirit, for his own will."[52] The assertion that the Son substitutes God's will for his own Spirit-influenced human will suggests an alignment of wills, as it were, in the divine plan—with the human will always under but cooperating with the divine one. The Spirit guides the Son according to the Father's will, and the Son wills the Spirit to guide him, thus making his will one with the Father's. Hawthorne indirectly raises issues of systematic integration related to the proper way to speak about the Holy Spirit in the framework of the communion of Christ's divine and human natures and works in his person—an issue we deal with in depth in Chapter 5.

---

[48] Ibid.
[49] Ibid., 119. Throughout this introduction, the reader will note that some theologians working in the field of Spirit Christology tend to speak of the divine Son (Logos) and the man Jesus (or human person Jesus) in this way. Others speak of the divine Son (Logos) and his humanity (flesh) or human life. Others speak in both ways.
[50] Ibid., 132.
[51] Ibid., 132–3.
[52] Ibid., 138.

The Spirit in the Ministry, Death, and Resurrection of Jesus and in the Life of His Followers

The kenotic principle of interpretation applies to Jesus' ministry of proclamation, healings, and exorcism: "The Spirit so fully motivated Jesus' speech and actions that the miracles he performed and the words he spoke and performed, not by virtue of his own power, the power of his own divine personality, but by virtue of the power of the Holy Spirit at work within him and through him."[53] It is within this framework, according to which the power of Jesus' speech and deeds "lay not in the strength of his own person, but … in the power of God mediated to him through the Spirit,"[54] that Hawthorne inquires about the Spirit's role in other events. He asks whether the Spirit "aided" Jesus in his self-giving unto death on the cross or whether Jesus accomplished atonement "solely by himself," and furthermore, whether the Spirit is "*the* power" through which Jesus was raised from the dead or whether Jesus raised himself "of his own intrinsic divine power."[55] Bearing his own version of Justin's burden (see Chapter 1), the author is uneasy about reducing Jesus to a mere instrument of the Spirit (because Jesus is the Son of God!). But he finally stresses the Spirit's identity as the power of God that moves Jesus to accomplish his mission. Reflecting on Jesus' death, Hawthorne sees the expression "through the eternal Spirit" in Heb. 9:14 as referring to the Holy Spirit. Like Vanhoye, whose view we rehearsed earlier, Hawthorne discards interpretations of "eternal spirit" as synonyms for "Jesus' own eternal spiritual nature," or spiritual "disposition" to do his work.[56] The Spirit's presence with Jesus on the cross follows from its ongoing presence with him during his whole ministry.[57] Without systematically reconciling Christ's preexistence and genuine humanity, the author of Hebrews articulates both "a most exalted view of Jesus, describing him as Son, Divine, God even" and a view in which "Jesus faced life *and death* as a person of flesh and blood … not as a person who by virtue of his divine

---

[53] Ibid., 145–6; Hawthorne stresses the Spirit's power to the point of saying that "Jesus did not begin to preach, to teach, or to perform miracles, nor did he continue to do such things … on his own initiative or by virtue of his own skills or because he possessed inherently some power for healing or exorcising" (148).
[54] Ibid., 170 (cf. 179).
[55] Ibid., 179–80.
[56] Ibid., 180–2.
[57] Ibid., 182.

nature had a distinct and unparalleled advantage over all other persons."[58] The divine Son is at work, but he limits himself to the man Jesus whom the Spirit leads.[59] How then does the Spirit influence Jesus on the cross? Hawthorne argues that, as in the rest of Jesus' life and mission, the Spirit's role was "to help him make the right moral choices … he was strengthened by the Spirit so that he was able to choose for God … it was by the aid of, through the morally strengthening support of, by the power of the Spirit that Jesus offered himself as the perfect sacrifice to God."[60]

As expected, in his discussion of Christ's resurrection, Hawthorne asks: "Did he rise from the grave by virtue of his own inherent power, or was it the power of another that released him from death and raised him to life again?"[61] Admittedly, John shows Jesus can raise his body ("this temple") from the dead (Jn 2:19-21; cf. 10:17-18). Yet Hawthorne notes how John's use of the passive voice (Jn 2:22: "when he *had been raised* from the dead" (emphasis in the original)) and Jesus' explanation that he is doing God's command (Jn 10:18b) "indicates that in the final analysis a power other than Jesus' own power brought about his resurrection."[62] Moreover, a number of Pauline texts such as Rom. 1:1-4 and 8:11, 1 Cor. 6:14, and 1 Tim. 3:16 strongly suggest that the Spirit is the Father's means or agent of Jesus' resurrection.[63] Consistently, Hawthorne reads all events in Jesus' life through a kenotic Spirit Christology, which offers a synthesis of preexistence and incarnation mediated by the Spirit's presence in the humanity of the divine Son. The author distances himself from nineteenth-century kenotic Christologies that claimed the Son divested himself of his divine attributes in the incarnation.[64] Rather, along with later modified kenotic approaches, Hawthorne holds that, although the Son possesses his divine attributes (i.e., omnipresence, omnipotence, omniscience), these are latent but not exercised or operative in his condescension.[65] Instead of exercising those attributes, the Son makes a decision to become dependent on the Spirit to complete his mission.

---

[58] Ibid., 183.
[59] "The divine Son limited himself to the confines of the man Jesus. … The eternal Son of God and Jesus were one Person as the result of the incarnation. But … the divine did not swamp the human or even diminish it in the process. Rather, in this gracious act of humility, God fully experienced for himself what it meant to be truly human." Ibid., 119.
[60] Ibid., 183.
[61] Ibid., 184.
[62] Ibid., 185.
[63] Ibid., 188-94.
[64] Ibid., 206-7.
[65] Ibid., 208, 211-12.

Jesus possessed the power himself, but … by a preincarnate deliberate decision the eternal Son of God chose that all his intrinsic powers, all his attributes, would remain latent within him during the days of his flesh and that he would become truly human and limit himself to the abilities and powers common to all other human beings. Therefore, he depended upon the Holy Spirit for wisdom and knowledge and for power to perform the signs and wonders that marked the days of his years.[66]

Like Dunn, Hawthorne begins to explore the implications of a Spirit Christology for the life of Jesus' disciples in the world. Because Dunn sees Jesus as the "mold," "shape," and "archetype" of the eschatological Spirit, he accents the "Jesus-character" of the Christian experience of the Spirit and speaks of the fruit of the Spirit as "character sketches" of Christ. By focusing on the Spirit-filled humanity of Christ, which believers share with him, Hawthorne reflects on the Christlike ways the Spirit shapes in the lives of his followers. Although Jesus is distinct from his followers in that he alone is "their Savior because of who he was and because of his own complete obedience to the Father's will," he is also "the supreme example for them of what is possible in a human life because of his own total dependence upon the Spirit of God."[67] Just as Jesus is led by the Spirit in a way that the Spirit "did not force him to do what he might choose not to do," so also is the Spirit given to his followers as a gift in a way that "he does not infringe upon their freedom nor does he overpower their wills."[68] Behind these assertions lies the thrust of the author's argument throughout his book: The divine Son in his kenosis assumes a genuinely true humanity, which by his own choices is dependent on and cooperates with the Holy Spirit. Because Christ's disciples share with him a Spirit-anointed humanity, they too become "christs" or anointed ones in a way that they, like "*the* Christ par excellence," are "set apart to serve God, authorized to act in his behalf."[69] The same Spirit who accompanied Jesus to the cross and raised him from the dead will do the same for his disciples.[70] A key contribution of Hawthorne's exegetically informed pneumatic reading of Jesus' work lies in his ability to frame such reading in dialogue with kenotic Christologies and think through its implications for

---

[66] Ibid., 218.
[67] Ibid., 234.
[68] Ibid., 236.
[69] Ibid., 237; "And as it was true of Jesus, so it is true of his followers: 'As the Father has sent me, even so I send you' (John 20:21b). As Jesus was filled and equipped by the Spirit, so those who belong to Jesus are filled and equipped by the Spirit (Acts 2:4), or at least potentially so (Eph. 5:18)" (238).
[70] Ibid., 241–2.

the lives of Christ's followers who receive and live by his Spirit. He shows the possibility of engaging the field of Spirit Christology from a biblical studies angle in a way that shows its potential organic links with the disciplines of systematic and practical theology.

Spirit Christology as a Lens for Biblical Interpretation

As an interdisciplinary field of study, Spirit Christology interacts with all the theological disciplines, including biblical studies. As we gathered from the exegetical studies of de la Potterie and Vanhoye, the Second Vatican Council's call for a more robust incorporation of the study of Scripture in what has been historically a dogmatically oriented Catholic tradition significantly raised the profile of the work of Catholic biblical scholars in commending the careful interpretation of Spirit texts employed in the formulation of Christological statements. Among Protestants, Dunn works out a pneumatologically informed reading of Jesus' and his disciples' experiences of sonship and Spirit in the New Testament by offering an interpretative lens that adopts significantly the eschatological interest and shift in the field of biblical studies since the turn of the nineteenth century. In Hawthorne's work, we see an exegete's more explicit attempt to account for prominent Spirit texts in the gospels in a way that integrates them into a broader Christological perspective—a kenotic approach in which the pneumatic identity of Jesus does not compete with his divine sonship or incarnation.

Spirit Christology and the Theological Interpretation of Scripture

In the aforementioned examples, we see not only how biblical scholars offer systematic theologians important insights into the biblical texts (de la Potterie, Vanhoye, Dunn) but also how the work of biblical scholars can benefit from the theological interpretation of those texts (Hawthorne). More recent studies adopt this twofold, interactive approach. Consider, as an example, how the editors of a special issue of the *Journal of Theological Interpretation* on "Spirit Christology and the Theological Interpretation of Scripture" describe the mutually informing work of biblical scholars and theologians afforded by the field. On the one hand, the articles originally presented at sessions of the 2016 annual meeting of the Society of Biblical Literature seek "to examine particular moments presented in the gospels (Jesus' conception, baptism, temptation, ministry, passion, resurrection, and the giving of the Spirit) in order to develop fruitful ways of understanding the identity of Jesus by means of his relationship with the Holy Spirit."[71] The focus lies on exegesis informing theology. On the other hand, the articles aim at "bringing this theological paradigm [Spirit Christology] to bear upon the reading of Gospel texts."[72] Here the emphasis is on theology informing exegesis. The hermeneutical cycle at work is further defined by the editors as follows: "Proponents of Spirit Christology contend that the resultant view of Jesus is soundly grounded in a reading of the Gospels and that it, in turn, provides an account of Christ through which to read other texts in a christological way. Spirit Christology thus offers one way of interpreting texts theologically."[73]

Not only pneumatologically explicit texts but even "texts which seemingly contain no Spirit-saturated talk, or texts which are difficult to interpret despite there being mention of the Spirit" might yield deeper and richer dimensions with the aid of a Spirit Christology. Consider how a text such as the Lord's Prayer in Matthew's Gospel, though not pneumatologically explicit, can nevertheless invite us to think of Jesus as "the Father's Son who prays *and lives* this prayer *in the Spirit*, and thus opens it for our participation" (emphasis in the original).[74] D. Brent Laytham, a US Methodist theologian, has argued, for instance, that the proleptic victory of Jesus over the evil one at his wilderness temptation in Mt. 4 and in his exorcisms (see especially Mt. 12:28, where Jesus is said to drive out demons "by the Spirit of God") makes Jesus "both the human petition and the divine answer" to the petition "deliver us from the evil one" in the Lord's Prayer.[75] By giving us the same

---

[71] Myk Habets and Leopoldo A. Sánchez M., "Introduction: Spirit Christology and the Theological Interpretation of Scripture," *JTI* 12, no. 1 (2018): 1. The special issue includes: D. Brent Laytham, "'But if ... by the Spirit of God': Reading Matthew's Lord's Prayer as Spirit Christology" (24–38); Habets, "Jesus, the Spirit, and the Unforgivable Sin: A Contribution from Spirit Christology" (39–57); Andy Johnson, "'You Wonder Where the Spirit Went': The Spirit and the Resurrection of the Son in Matthew and John" (58–75); and Leopoldo A. Sánchez M., "The Holy Spirit and the Son's Glorification: Spirit Christology as a Theological Lens for Interpreting John 7:37–39" (76–89).
[72] Habets and Sánchez, "Introduction: Spirit Christology," 1.
[73] Ibid., 2.
[74] Laytham, "'But if ... by the Spirit of God,'" 26; "Put simply, Jesus prays in our place by the power of the Holy Spirit so that *by the power of that same Spirit* we can pray in and through Jesus" (emphasis in the original) (29).
[75] Ibid., 36.

Spirit by whom he is led to the desert and casts out demons, those who pray "deliver us from evil" share in Jesus' gift of the Spirit and, therefore, in his victory over the devil and thus in God's kingdom of power and glory.[76] Placing the Lord's Prayer in the broader Trinitarian context of human participation in the life of Jesus through the Spirit, Laytham's intratextual reading of the prayer within Matthew's Gospel through the lens of a Spirit Christology makes more theologically explicit what is only exegetically implicit in the text.

Furthermore, consider a text such as Jn 7:38-39, which, though explicitly mentioning the Spirit, is difficult to interpret without the aid of a Spirit Christology. In this text, Jesus promises "rivers of living water" to those who believe in him and explains that this is a reference to the gift of "the Spirit" whom the Son would give at his glorification. In the history of exegesis, the text has puzzled interpreters. Two interpretations of the text emerge, depending on how one answers the question, "*who* does the living water flow from—Jesus or the believer?"[77] While Latin interpreters in the West, with the notable exception of Augustine, have generally seen Jesus as the source of the rivers of living waters, Greek interpreters in the East have seen the rivers as flowing from the believer.[78] Who is correct? Joseph Greene's intertextual proposal for the ecumenical complementarity of both readings shows that, in the context of the Feast of Tabernacles, John portrays Jesus as the Temple from which the eschatological Spirit-waters flow (in fulfillment of Zech. 14 and Ezek. 47) and depicts Israel's renewal in the covenant as a joyful drawing of water from the springs of salvation (Isa. 12).[79] In my article for the special issue of the *Journal of Theological Interpretation*, I argue that a Spirit Christology offers a theological basis for Greene's reading of Jn 7:38-39. It does so by drawing attention to the Gospel of John's broader witness to Jesus' identity as the bearer of the Spirit and giver of his Spirit to others (see Jn 1:33; 4:14; 19:30, 34; 20:21-22), which suggests that "the pericope functions *theologically* as an *inclusio* featuring both Christ's pneumatic-eschatological identity and our human sharing in God's Spirit through Christ."[80] Otherwise stated, given the pneumatic trajectory of the Gospel from Jesus' bearing to his giving of the Spirit to others who, through him, become bearers of his Spirit, the text can become inclusive of both textual interpretations. In short,

---

[76] Ibid., 38.
[77] Sánchez, "The Holy Spirit and the Son's Glorification," 76.
[78] Ibid., 79.
[79] Cited in ibid., 79–80.
[80] Ibid., 80.

the examples above illustrate some ways in which a Spirit Christology can assist in the theological interpretation of texts that may not be explicitly pneumatological but lend themselves to such a reading (B. Laytham), or texts that refer to the Spirit directly but are difficult to interpret (L. Sánchez), by placing them in a broader textual matrix or narrative.

Testing the Framework: John's "Spirit Christology" and the Problem of the "Johannine Jesus"

To appreciate further the promise of Spirit Christology as a framework for reading Scripture theologically and thus interpreting texts in conversation with biblical scholars and systematic theologians, let us look a bit more in depth at an article written by a biblical scholar on the Gospel of John's "Spirit Christology." Michael J. Gorman, the Raymond E. Brown Professor of Biblical Studies and Theology at St. Mary's Seminary and University, offers an exegetical and theological response to the "Johannine Jesus" thesis assumed or advanced by some New Testament scholars. Accordingly, the claim is made that in contrast to the synoptic gospels' more humanizing portrayal of the historical Jesus and his concern for the physical restoration of God's creatures, John's Gospel offers a more metaphysical and spiritualizing picture of Jesus and his works—one in which, as M. Eugene Boring starkly puts it, "Jesus is portrayed as without compassion, as divinely aloof."[81] In Gorman's estimation, the "Johannine Jesus" ends up being not merely different from the synoptics' Jesus but de facto "an *inferior* Jesus."[82] The negative ethical implications of such a "Johannine" view are laid out by Jack T. Sanders, who argues that "Johannine Christianity is interested only in whether he [the Christian] believes. 'Are you saved, brother?' the Johannine Christian asks the man bleeding to death on the side of the road."[83] Gorman observes that in the final analysis "*the narrow Johannine Jesus leads inevitably to the narrow Johannine Christian*" (emphasis in the original).[84] The "Johannine Jesus" thesis assumes an exaggerated contrast between the synoptics and

---

[81] Michael J. Gorman, "The Spirit, the Prophets, and the End of the 'Johannine Jesus,'" *JTI* 12, no. 1 (2018): 4. He cites Boring's *Introduction to the New Testament* (668).
[82] Ibid., 4.
[83] Ibid., 5. He cites Sanders' *Ethics in the New Testament* (99–100).
[84] Gorman, "The Spirit," 5.

John, which includes the common assumption that the Spirit's defining role in Jesus' messianic mission is more at home in the synoptics (particularly, Luke's Gospel) than in the Fourth Gospel. Aided by a Spirit Christology lens, Gorman shows how the "Johannine Jesus" thesis does not account adequately for "the Spirit as the determinative reality in Jesus' own ministry and in that of his disciples" and contends for a more unified account of the Spirit in the gospels that clarifies how "the Spirit is powerfully present with Jesus in John, as in the Synoptics—and even in ways not explored in the Synoptics."[85] By drawing attention to "John's 'Spirit Christology,'" including its echoes from and allusions to the Old Testament, the author illustrates how a careful study of biblical texts using the framework of a Spirit Christology can unpack rich dimensions of Jesus' messianic identity that go unnoticed by proponents of the so-called "Johannine Jesus." Rather than an aloof spiritual Jesus and Christian ethic, John's Spirit Christology testifies to "the Spirit's physical (material) as well as spiritual activity" in the prophetic mission of Jesus and his disciples.[86]

Gorman offers four arguments in support of a Johannine Spirit Christology that locates and anticipates eternal life in the materiality of Jesus' life-giving words and works, and in the holistic mission of his disciples in the world. First, on the basis of three texts (Jn 1:25-27, 29-36; 3:34; and 14:16-17), he argues that the Spirit does not only descend upon Jesus for a moment, but in contrast to the prophets remains on or abides with him permanently and abundantly throughout his entire messianic ministry. This pneumatic basis is to be assumed as one reads the entirety of the Gospel. Moreover, because Jesus has received the Spirit from the Father, Jesus is able to give the Spirit generously to his disciples, so that the same Spirit who abides in Jesus and empowers him will abide with and be in them after his glorification (death and resurrection).[87] Second, by showing how John echoes the Spirit-anointed Servant's holistic mission in Isa. 61:1-3 throughout his Gospel (e.g., his healing of the blind in Jn 9), and themes from Ezek. 34–39 describing God's life-giving work of restoring a covenant relationship with his people through his Davidic shepherd-king and Spirit-breath, Gorman demonstrates that the Spirit who is upon Jesus in the Gospel is the Spirit promised by the Old Testament prophets.[88] Against the "Johannine Jesus" portrayal of "*a gnostic*

---

[85] Ibid., 6.
[86] Ibid., 7.
[87] See ibid., 7–11.
[88] See ibid., 11–16, 18.

Jesus offering a gnostic salvation to potential gnostic believers who will then engage in a gnostic mission" (emphasis in the original), John's depictions of Jesus as the Spirit-anointed Messiah who heals the blind and the Good Shepherd who lays down his life to give abundant life (cf. Jn 9, 10) align with Isaiah's and Ezekiel's material images of restoration.[89] When placed in an intertextual matrix, John's Spirit Christology yields a holistic view of eternal life in the Son: "This implies, then, that the abundant life Jesus has come to bring according to John 10 is earthly, physical, tangible—as well as spiritual and relational."[90] The author's third argument expands on the notion that in John's Gospel, much like in the prophets and the synoptics, "*the spiritual and the physical hang together*" (emphasis in the original).[91] When John describes Jesus' work of healing the blind, quenching the thirsty, feeding the hungry, or raising the dead, he is simply "dealing in prophetic mode," by which God's spokespersons can speak metaphorically and symbolically about God's salvation without minimizing its connection to a material, bodily, or fleshly restoration.[92] Significantly, a Spirit Christology further clarifies the materiality of the Spirit's agency in and through Jesus, since "it is the Spirit-enabled figure of Isaiah 61—who is, for John, embodied in Jesus—who gives sight, comforts, and heals."[93]

Gorman's use of John's Spirit Christology, which argues for a Spirit-bearing Jesus whose work attends to both spiritual/relational and physical/material needs, speaks to the disciples' sharing in this Christlike life and mission. His final argument is that "*at his glorification, Jesus hands over his Spirit to his disciples to continue in a similar mission*" (emphasis in the original).[94] Jesus' breathing of the Spirit on the disciples in Jn 20 fulfills the promise in Jn 1 that Jesus will baptize with the Spirit—a promise anticipated throughout the Gospel (cf. the Paraclete passages in Jn 14–16) and fulfilled at the moment of Jesus' glorification (7:38-39).[95] The author draws attention to John's use of "breath" as a reference to the Spirit's "inpouring" in Jesus' disciples for mission—a depiction that echoes material images of God's life bestowed upon Adam in Gen. 2:7 and of God's new life bestowed upon Israel's dry bones in Ezek. 37:9-10.[96] Accordingly, Gorman suggests that

---

[89] Ibid., 17.
[90] Ibid., 16.
[91] Ibid., 17.
[92] Ibid., 18.
[93] Ibid., 19.
[94] Ibid.
[95] Ibid.
[96] Ibid., 20.

the disciples' Spirit-empowered participation in the mission of the "Spirit-endued" Jesus cannot be reduced to a merely spiritual concern for the soul apart from the body.

> The disciples' mission will therefore be one of Spirit-empowered practices of forgiveness—so chapter 20—and, more generally, will be life-giving and cross-shaped in every way. ... Thus the disciples' mission will not be limited to the taking away of sins because, like Jesus, they will also be channels of the gift of the Spirit and of the abundant divine life through their cross-shaped ministry.[97]

Sharing in the Spirit of Jesus entails a sacrificial or cruciform mission that bestows on persons the forgiveness of sins, as well as the inpouring of the Spirit itself on them and the abundant life the Spirit brings to them even now. In contrast to the "Johannine Jesus" theory, Gorman illustrates how a Spirit Christology in Johannine key leads to an engaged and not an aloof discipleship in the world. In his exegetical method, the author demonstrates how a Spirit Christology matrix informs an exegetical Christological interpretation of the Gospel of John that privileges the Spirit's resting on and embodiment in the human life and mission of the incarnate and glorified Son, and consequently, the Spirit's inpouring in and empowerment of his disciples in the world. In this way, the theological interpretation of John's Gospel serves as a corrective to claims in biblical studies about the aims or consequences of the Gospel's presentation of Jesus and his disciples (such as the "Johannine Jesus" thesis). Moreover, the intertextual study of John's Spirit Christology opens up new biblical vistas for understanding the pneumatic identity of Jesus in the New Testament in continuity with the prophetic writings of the Old Testament's witness to the work of the Spirit of God in the eschatological restoration of God's people. In the process, the systematic theologian learns to appreciate meaning-producing dimensions of the biblical texts and the potential productivity of their concomitant narratives for engaging contemporary issues. Theology informs exegesis and vice versa.

From the perspective of systematic theology, Gorman's study of Jesus' identity in John's Gospel in pneumatic key yields important trajectories for understanding divine identity, agency, and generosity. First, an intertextual reading of Jesus' life in the Spirit suggests a "triadic confluence of characters that effect salvation."[98] The narratives invite reflection on the Trinitarian

---

[97] Ibid., 22.
[98] Ibid., 17.

shape of divine activity in the world. As the author observes in his description of Ezekiel's echoes in John, "the restoration and revivification of God's people in Ezekiel will be the work of three dramatic persons: God as the good shepherd, God's anointed one (the Davidic messiah-figure) as the good shepherd, and God's life-giving Spirit."[99] Second, John's depiction of the Spirit's work of restoration in the Gospel suggests not a spiritualizing view of Jesus and his work but a material view of life in the Spirit as embodied in the Word made flesh upon whom the Spirit of God rests and remains. This insight aligns with an incarnational and cross-shaped view of the Spirit—one in which the Spirit does not fly above the Son or flee from his human life and death but is intimately linked to the flesh of the Son, his words, and cross. Seeing Jn 19:34 as the fulfillment of Jn 7:38-39, Gorman notes in passing how John invites us to think of a pneumatology of the cross (*pneumatologia crucis*), according to which, paradoxically, it is through death that the glorified Son gives us eternal life.[100] It is also through the glorified Son's self-giving on the cross that he gives such life to others. Lifted on the cross, "he gave up [his] the spirit" (Jn 19:30)—that is, the Holy Spirit—to his disciples so that the same Spirit who remains on the Son might also remain in them.[101] The Son who bears the Spirit in all fullness gives his Spirit generously to his disciples. This participation in the Spirit of the Son is a sharing in his Spirit-empowered mission to share his abundant life with the world: "Spirit-Christology leads to Spirit-discipleship and Spirit-mission."[102] These insights on the Christlike shape of life in the Spirit are productive for reflecting on the continuity between Jesus' bearing of the Spirit and the lives of others who are indwelt by his Spirit. Gorman's study presents not only a compelling example of the promise of Spirit Christology for the theological interpretation of the gospels but also the contribution of insights from biblical studies for theological reflection on the Trinitarian, incarnational, soteriological, and ecclesial trajectories of Spirit Christology.

---

[99] Ibid.
[100] Ibid., 22.
[101] Ibid., 21.
[102] Ibid., 22.

Questions

(1) Describe how Dunn understands the relationship between Jesus' experiences of sonship and Spirit in his life and mission. Explain how these experiences make Jesus unlike us and like us.

(2) Define Hawthorne's kenotic principle of interpretation and illustrate how he applies it to one or two events of Jesus' life and ministry.

(3) List one or two insights or questions that biblical scholars studying the Spirit in New Testament accounts of Jesus bring to the attention of systematic theologians working in Spirit Christology. Explain the theological significance of these insights or questions.

3

The Spirit Enters the Flesh to Save the Flesh: Building Blocks from Spirit Christology in the Early Church

A Spirit Christology explores the place of the Spirit in Jesus, which begs the question: What exactly do we mean by "Spirit" and how does it relate to Jesus? When we look at the history of the early church, it turns out the answer to this question was honed significantly in response to heterodox views of Jesus' baptism and the Spirit's role in the event. In this chapter, we will first argue that in their respective responses to Gnostic and Arian views of the Spirit in Jesus, Irenaeus of Lyons (c. AD 130–202) and Athanasius of Alexandria (c. AD 296–373) offer theologians today important building blocks for articulating a Spirit Christology. By interpreting Spirit texts such as the anointing of Jesus at his baptism through the principle that the Spirit enters the flesh of Christ in order to save the flesh (humanity), these theologians raised important questions about the identity of Jesus and his work, as well as his relationship to the Spirit, God, and human persons— questions of great interest to theologians working in Spirit Christology today. We will see how Spirit Christology has roots going back to the early church, where answers to the above questions were already being considered.

When we speak of a Spirit Christology in the early church fathers, we refer to an incipient reality. We do not mean that they thought of such Christology in the way theologians think of it today, namely, as a systematic paradigm for answering some issues raised by Christology in response to contemporary concerns—much less as a discrete or unified field of study. Even by early church standards, we see a diversity of approaches to the Spirit in accounts of Jesus—in particular, in reference to Jesus' "anointing" at the incarnation or at his baptism. In his historical survey of Spirit Christology in the patristic period, Herschel Odell Bryant has identified three Spirit Christology "paradigms," which he labels "pneumatic inspiration, incarnation, and mediation."[1] The notion of pneumatic incarnation essentially aligns with our discussion of pre-Nicene Spirit Christology in Chapter 1, to which we will return a bit later. In this view, church fathers at times use the term "Spirit" to signify that "God is one undivided divine substance;" when applied to Christ, "Spirit" then means his divine substance, resulting in a definition of the incarnation as "the union of preexistent Spirit and flesh."[2] Bryant places Gnostics and Arians in the "pneumatic inspiration" camp. The Gnostics asserted that "at the Jordan the Spirit, the impersonal power of deity, descended into Jesus, anointing his life and ministry and identifying him as the Christ," but at the same time "devalued Christ's flesh, emphasizing instead the salvific gnosis available through the Spirit" in Jesus.[3] In the case of Arius, the Logos is incarnate but not God (with the Father), "so through pneumatic inspiration during the salvific mission the Spirit's anointing advanced Christ in grace and deified him."[4] The problem with the "pneumatic inspiration" focus lies in its being "incompatible and incapable of developing alongside the Logos Christology that appeared and unfolded in the central christological tradition."[5]

Irenaeus and Athanasius inhabit a theological world in which, to a significant degree, they have to respond to proponents of the "pneumatic inspiration" paradigm. In doing so, they start to lay out building blocks of a pneumatic approach to Jesus' identity that works with rather than against the Logos Christological tradition. These church fathers best fit in what Bryant calls the "pneumatic mediation" paradigm, whose main characteristic is "compatibility with Logos Christology" and assumes a commitment to basic tenets such as the Logos' preexistence, his unity with and distinction from

---

[1] Herschel Odell Bryant, *Spirit Christology in the Christian Tradition: From the Patristic Period to the Rise of Pentecostalism in the Twentieth Century* (Cleveland, TN: CPT Press, 2014), 269, 514.
[2] Ibid., 270.
[3] Ibid., 270–1.
[4] Ibid., 198.
[5] Ibid., 270.

the Father, his becoming flesh (and thus the distinction between divine and human natures) for our salvation, and the Holy Spirit's role as a mediating agent in bringing about his incarnation and anointing.[6] In their answers to Gnostics and Arians, respectively, Irenaeus and Athanasius offer their own pneumatic picture of Christ, thus influencing the development of an incarnational pneumatology. Upon close examination of texts dealing with the anointing of Jesus, we will demonstrate how these theologians' responses to problems raised by the heterodox align in some ways with current questions asked in contemporary Spirit Christology proposals. Such questions include how best to integrate Logos and Spirit aspects of Christology and how Christ's human life in the Spirit makes possible human participation in his Spirit. It may be too much to say with Bryant that "Spirit Christological issues were integral" to the development of a Nicene Trinitarian theology, but we can definitely show that they were a significant factor.[7] In the first section of this chapter, we turn to the incipient Spirit Christologies in Irenaeus' and Athanasius' apologetic writings as a way to illustrate how the systematic field of Spirit Christology today can benefit from interaction with historical theology. In the second part, we look at some Christological issues and tensions raised by early church fathers in the fourth and fifth centuries, dealing with the Spirit's identity, the interpretation of the anointing of Jesus, and the contrast between Antiochene and Alexandrian approaches to the Spirit in Christ. Coming to us in the form of questions, unresolved tensions, and partial solutions, their contributions provide us with further building blocks for articulating a Spirit Christology today.

Word and Spirit, God's Two Hands: Irenaeus Responds to the Gnostics

When used to describe the church's teaching, the word "orthodox" can be rendered as "right opinion." By contrast, "heterodox" means "other opinion,"

---

[6] Ibid., 271; "The paradigm of pneumatic mediation appears more useful than the paradigms of pneumatic inspiration and incarnation because it can account for certain essential aspects of these two modalist paradigms—the Spirit's anointing inspiring and empowering Christ's humanity, affirmation of the incarnation of the divine Logos or Spirit, while maintaining a monotheistic view of deity—within a triune framework" (515).
[7] Ibid., 513.

a teaching that is deemed different from what is considered as the standard teaching. In his study of the baptism of Jesus, Raniero Cantalamessa describes various heterodox interpretations of this event that the church opposed because of their unorthodox views of Jesus. For our purposes, we focus on his description of the Gnostic and Arian interpretations:

> In the Gnostic view, Jesus was one person and the Christ another: Jesus denoted the man born of Mary, whereas Christ denoted the deity that descended on Jesus at the moment of baptism. Thus the baptism came to negate the reality of the incarnation and this could not but give rise to a strong reaction on the part of the Church. Other heresies came later to reinforce the reasons for "discrediting" the baptism of Jesus: Arianism used Jesus' baptism as a pretext for asserting that if any change occurred in Jesus at the moment of baptism, this meant that he was subject to change and therefore not a changeless God like the Father.[8]

From these comments, we gather some problems in the Gnostic and Arian views of the baptism of Jesus. The former denied the incarnation of the Son, the latter his divinity. What may not be obvious is that both views assumed a position of what (who) the "Spirit" is and does in Jesus. Gnostics and Arians operated with their implicit versions of "Spirit Christology."

The Gnostics (from Gk. *gnōsis*, meaning knowledge) constitute a second-century movement that, although quite diverse in its teachings, held in common the idea that "matter is incapable of salvation" and espoused instead a "spiritual" (immaterial) salvation through special or "perfect knowledge."[9] Spanish patristic scholar Antonio Orbe (1917–2003) has given us an invaluable insight into the teachings of the Gnostics and the church's response in the person of Irenaeus. For instance, a group of Gnostics saw the dove descending upon Jesus at the Jordan as a dyad from the region above (Gk. *plērōma*) called "Christ/Sophia," which denoted a spiritual preexistent consort of two beings (or "eons" in Gnostic language)—a sort of marriage made in heaven, as it were.[10] The spiritual "Christ" signified the preexistent Savior who entered into communion with the man Jesus to sanctify or deify him, so that Jesus might then deify others by communicating to them a special "knowledge" from the Father above.[11] "Sophia" designated the Holy

---

[8] Cantalamessa, *The Holy Spirit in the Life of Jesus*, 7.
[9] Irenaeus, *Against Heresies* 1.6.1–2, in ANF 1:324.
[10] Antonio Orbe, "El Espíritu Santo en el bautismo de Jesús (*en torno a San Ireneo*)," *Greg* 76, no. 4 (1995): 681–2.
[11] Ibid., 682–3.

Spirit, which by descending upon the deified Jesus, could as a mother beget children of the Father into a "spiritual" church.[12] For the Gnostics, there was a kind of union that took place between the spiritual Christ/Sophia and the man Jesus at the Jordan. Such union made the man Jesus a deified or divine-like Son of God, giving him knowledge of the Father above and making him aware of his spiritual mission, until the moment when Christ/Sophia eventually departed from him at his death.[13] The purpose of the baptism at Jordan lay in uniting Christ with Jesus in order to unite people with the Father through perfect knowledge, and in uniting Sophia with the same Jesus in order to gather Gnostics or "knowledgeable ones" into a special spiritual church. This emphasis on a temporary union of Christ/Sophia with Jesus at the Jordan raised a number of problems. First, how should we interpret who the Spirit is and what it is doing in the events of Jesus' life? Second, how should we properly distinguish and relate the works of the Spirit and the Son? Third, how do the Spirit and the Son relate to the Father above? Fourth, how do the Spirit and the Son relate to human persons? Irenaeus offered a response to these questions.

The Anointing of the Incarnate Word in God's Work of Recapitulation

Working from a dualistic view of reality in which "spirit" is above "flesh," Gnostics taught a "spiritual" salvation and thus rejected that God could work through creation, incarnation, and resurrection to save humanity from its bondage to sin and death. By contrast, the driving force of Irenaeus' theology is incarnational. Above all, he is interested in how the Son takes on the flesh to save the flesh. As Irenaeus puts it, "The Word of God ... dwelt in man, and became Son of man, that He might accustom man to receive God, and God to dwell in man, according to the good pleasure of the Father."[14] It is through this incarnational lens that Irenaeus interprets events in the life of Jesus, including his baptism. In the first creation, Adam lost the Spirit of holiness by disobeying God.[15] To restore his creation, the Father above

---

[12] Ibid.

[13] See Orbe, *La unción del Verbo*, 348–9.

[14] Irenaeus, *Against Heresies* 3.20.2, in ANF 1:450; "God recapitulated in Himself the ancient formation of man, that He might kill sin, deprive death of its power, and vivify man." *Against Heresies* 3.18.7, in ANF 1:448.

[15] "I have by disobedience lost that robe of sanctity which I had from the Spirit." Ibid., 3.23.5, in ANF 1:457.

uses his two "hands," the Word and the Spirit, to recapitulate or do over the failed history of Adam for the sake of saving all flesh, all humanity.[16] In a new creation, Jesus, the eschatological Adam, will restore the likeness of God in humans by returning the Spirit to them. For this to happen, the Word will take upon himself the nature of Adam in the incarnation, but also be anointed at his baptism with the Spirit lost by Adam. By descending upon the humanity of the Son, the prototypical Adam after whose image all humans are made, the Spirit returns to dwell once again with the race of Adam (humanity) in order to restore it to its original Christlike image.

> Wherefore He [i.e., the Spirit] did also descend upon the Son of God, made the Son of man, becoming accustomed with Him to dwell in the human race, to rest with human beings, and to dwell in the workmanship of God, working the will of the Father in them, and renewing them from their old habits into the newness of Christ.[17]

In God's plan of salvation, there is no union of a preexistent "Christ/Sophia" or "Christ" (= Spirit) and a man Jesus at the Jordan, but a union of the divine Word and human flesh at the incarnation.[18] Then, at the Jordan, the Word made flesh is anointed by the Father with the Holy Spirit, making the Word "Jesus Christ" for the sake of his mission. Citing Mt. 3:16, Irenaeus explains what took place at Jesus' baptism as follows: "For Christ did not at that time descend upon Jesus, neither was Christ one and Jesus another: but the Word of God ... who did also take upon Him flesh, and anointed by the Spirit from the Father ... was made Jesus Christ."[19] Irenaeus draws a key distinction between the incarnation as the work of the Son (Word) and his anointing at the Jordan as the work of the Father through the Holy Spirit. Reading Isa. 61:1-2 in light of the baptism of Jesus, Irenaeus portrays the anointing at Jordan as a common Trinitarian act of salvation, while distinguishing among three: "For in the name of Christ is implied, He that anoints, He that is anointed, and the unction itself with which

---

[16] The Word of the Father and the Spirit of God, having become united with the ancient substance of Adam's formation, rendered man living and perfect, receptive of the perfect Father, in order that as in the natural [Adam] we all were dead, so in the spiritual we may all be made alive. For never at any time did Adam escape the *hands* of God, to whom the Father speaking, said, "Let us make man in Our image, after Our likeness." And for this reason in the last times (fine), not by the will of the flesh, nor by the will of man, but by the good pleasure of the Father, His hands formed a living man, in order that Adam might be created [again] after the image and likeness of God. (Ibid., 5.1.3, in ANF 1:527)

[17] Ibid., 3.17.1, in ANF 1:444.

[18] For Gnostic interpretations of Jesus' baptism, see Orbe, *La unción del Verbo*, 115–68.

[19] *Against Heresies* 3.9.3, in ANF 1:423.

He is anointed. And it is the Father who anoints, but the Son who is anointed by the Spirit, who is the unction."[20] The anointing of Jesus at the Jordan reveals a Trinitarian pattern of divine activity in the mystery of salvation.

Although Irenaeus can speak of the Father's cosmic anointing of the Word with the Spirit in view of the creation, preservation, and ordering of the world,[21] Irenaeus does not reflect further on the eternal generation of the Son or the place of the Holy Spirit in the intradivine life.[22] Given the Gnostics' focus on spiritual beings (or eons) emanating from God and descending on Jesus, Irenaeus focuses instead on the Trinitarian economy of salvation which includes the anointing of the enfleshed Word in view of his work to preach the gospel, heal the sick, and forgive sins: "For inasmuch as the Word of God was man ... in this respect did the Spirit of God rest upon Him, and anoint Him to preach the Gospel to the lowly."[23] The Word and the Spirit relate to God as his two hands, showing the Father's disposition to save all flesh through the Son's Spirit-anointed flesh. God is not afraid to get his hands dirty, as it were, in the real world. By stressing the materiality of salvation, Irenaeus also speaks against the Gnostics' idea of a "spiritual" salvation for an elite group achieved through special knowledge because it denies God's work through the flesh and the efficacy of the gospel for all flesh.[24] The Father above is not interested in spirits transcending or escaping bodies into a heavenly realm, but in the salvation of all flesh through his Son and Spirit in a new creation. The perfect Father's work of recapitulation aims not for a special group but for the salvation of the whole race of Adam. Finally, the Spirit's resting upon the Son at his anointing makes it possible for others to be saved by receiving the same Spirit through the Son: "Therefore did the Spirit of God descend upon Him, [the Spirit] of Him who had promised by the prophets that He would anoint Him, so that we, receiving from the abundance of His unction, might be saved."[25] Receiving the Spirit "as a gift from His Father," the Lord then does "confer it upon those who are partakers of Himself, sending the Holy Spirit upon all the earth."[26] We see

---

[20] Ibid., 3.18.3, in ANF 1:446.
[21] On the cosmic anointing of the Word in Justin Martyr and Irenaeus, see Orbe, *La unción del Verbo*, 67–72, 521–7; on the cosmic anointing in Irenaeus, see also McDonnell, *The Baptism of Jesus in the Jordan*, 57–60, 116–23.
[22] See Luis F. Ladaria, "El P. Antonio Orbe: La gnosis y la teología prenicena," *Revista española de teología* 67, no. 4 (2007): 422, 431–2.
[23] Irenaeus, *Against Heresies* 3.9.3, in ANF 1:423. Here Irenaeus cites Isa. 61:1-2 (cf. Lk. 4:18-19).
[24] See Ladaria, "La gnosis y la teología prenicena," 429.
[25] Ibid.
[26] *Against Heresies* 3.17.2, in ANF 1:445.

continuity between the Son and the adopted sons, since the Spirit anoints the Word not in his divinity but in his humanity, in order for humanity to receive anew the Spirit of holiness lost by Adam and thus be restored to the image of the Son, the prototypical and eschatological Adam, by sharing in the Son's resurrected and immortal flesh.[27] The Son of God, according to his divinity, did not need to be anointed with the Spirit, but "if the Word wants to save humans, he must be anointed as man."[28] The mystery of the anointing has a soteriological trajectory intended for our benefit.

The Word Deifies in the Spirit: Athanasius Responds to the Arians

The Arians too operated with a kind of Spirit Christology, supporting an adoptionist view of Jesus' identity. When applied to Arianism, a term given to the followers of a presbyter named Arius (AD 256–36), adoptionism refers to the idea that Christ is adopted by God as a son by grace, or as other "men who have received the Spirit by participation."[29] For the Arians, the Son is "from God," or begotten of the Father, but only in the same manner humans and all created beings have their beginning from God.[30] Being begotten means being created. Arius' commitment to the immutability or impassibility of God does not allow him to see how the Son, who undergoes a human history in which he is anointed and exalted by God, can in any way be divine by nature. Arians use biblical texts dealing with the anointing and exaltation of the Son (Ps. 45:7-8, Phil. 2:9-10) to show that he "received a reward … and would not have had it, unless He had needed it … having gained it from virtue and promotion."[31] Jesus' need and effort shows he is a creature. Committed to divine immutability, Arians interpreted Jesus' anointing as a change he undergoes in time and as part of a journey of obedience that earns him a prize from God—qualities implying ontological necessity on

---

[27] "Now the final result of the work of the Spirit is the salvation of the flesh. For what other visible fruit is there of the invisible Spirit, than the rendering of the flesh mature and capable of incorruption?" Ibid., 5.12.4, in ANF 1:538.
[28] Orbe, *La unción del Verbo*, 519 (translation mine).
[29] Athanasius, *First Discourse* 11.37-8, in NPNF² 4:328.
[30] Athanasius, *Defence of the Nicene Definition* 5.19, in NPNF² 4:162.
[31] Athanasius, *First Discourse* 11.37, in NPNF² 4:328.

his part and thus a nature unbecoming of God. Being a creature, the Word is "susceptible to improvement in the moral order" and thus "earned from God being anointed by the Spirit as a reward," in the same way that "later on he would earn definitive exaltation and his enthroning as 'god' as a prize for his passion and death."[32]

If the Gnostics read the anointing of Jesus through a dualistic lens that privileges the realm of spirit above (or instead of) the salvation of created flesh, the Arians read the same event through a hermeneutic that privileges divine immutability. Since God cannot get his hands dirty in the world, God as such cannot enter the world and save it. So God must do so through the Son as a creaturely intermediary, who on account of his good works is deified by the Spirit so that others can follow in his footsteps. As an adopted son by participation in the Spirit, Jesus opens the possibility for humans to be like him by sharing in God's Spirit. But Jesus does so only insofar as he becomes a paradigm for others to follow. Although Arians retain a strong sense of continuity between the man Jesus and other human beings, they do so at the expense of Jesus' unique identity as the divine Word, begotten of the substance of the Father before the creation of the world. According to the Arians, the relationship between the Father and the Son belongs only to the realm of the economy, not to the immanent realm of divine being. Technically speaking, God was eternally "alone" in his own self and only becomes a Father when he creates (begets) a Son in time.[33] Therefore, not only the Son but also the Spirit with whom he is anointed are ontologically subordinate to God. In Arianism, we see an adoptionist interpretation of the Spirit's role in the Son at his baptism, how the Spirit-anointed Son relates to God as his special but subordinate creature, and how the Spirit includes other humans to experience the anointing and exaltation of Christ should they follow his example of virtue and works.

Not unlike the Gnostics, Arians are driven ultimately by ontological concerns, meaning that their interest lies in what constitutes the *ontos*, "being" or "substance" of reality—especially, the ontology of God. Gnostics and Arians appeal to philosophical tenets that serve as principles of biblical interpretation. Gnostics see God as "spirit" and Arians as "immutable," and these commitments in turn guide their understanding of Jesus and his anointing in baptism. If the Arians attribute Jesus' being anointed and

---

[32] Orbe, *La unción del Verbo*, 612–13 (translation mine).
[33] "'God was not always a Father;' but 'once God was alone, and not yet a Father, but afterwards He became a Father.'" Athanasius, *First Discourse* 2.5, in NPNF² 4:308.

exalted as "god" to his moral progress, the Gnostics see the anointing of Jesus as a singular moment of progress in his illumination or awakening concerning his "spiritual" identity and mission.[34] Although Irenaeus and Athanasius are not unaware of ontological concerns in their theology, their ultimate interest lies in an incarnational soteriology or view of salvation. Much like Irenaeus' principle that God saves all flesh through the flesh, Athanasius argues that, although the Word as God is immutable in his own nature, the Word became flesh so that human flesh might be saved through him. Against the Arian presentation of Jesus as a creature who becomes deified, Athanasius responds that the Word "was not man, and then became God, but He was God, and then became man, and that to deify us."[35] Yet flesh cannot save flesh without God's involvement. So the divine Word, who is of the "same substance" (*homoousios*) of the Father (meaning, as the Nicene Creed would put it later, that the Son is "God of God"), takes matters into his own hands and assumes human flesh so that he might then anoint and exalt our flesh by his Spirit. The anointing of the Word with the Spirit in the flesh presupposes the Word's incarnation and makes possible the participation of human persons in his Spirit by the grace of adoption.

Anointed with the Spirit at the Incarnation to Supply Humans with His Spirit

To preserve the divine dignity of the Word in response to an Arian reading of his anointing, Athanasius first stresses that the Word as God is not the receiver but "the Giver of grace."[36] The Word does not partake of the Spirit like other created beings, as if he needed the Spirit: "All other things partake of the Spirit, but He, according to you, of what is He partaker? [O]f the Spirit? Nay, rather the Spirit Himself takes from the Son … and it is not reasonable to say that the latter is sanctified by the former."[37] Here we have another variety of Justin's burden (introduced in Chapter 1), that is, an attempt to defend the teaching that the Word as God does not need to be sanctified by the Spirit because he is already holy by nature with the Father and the Spirit. In the unity of the holy Trinity, the Son is begotten of the Father and the Spirit takes from the Son. The expressions "begotten" and "takes from"

---

[34] Orbe, *La unción del Verbo*, 613.
[35] Athanasius, *First Discourse* 11.39, in NPNF[2] 4:329.
[36] Ibid., 11.40–1, in NPNF[2] 4:329–30.
[37] Ibid., 5.15, in NPNF[2] 4:315.

are simply ways of saying that the Spirit is, as it were, of the same stock (divinity) as the Son, just as the Son is of the same stock as his Father. By drawing a distinction between the Word as God and human Spirit-bearers, Athanasius makes an ontological point. The Word is Son by nature, not a son by grace. Yet this is a penultimate assertion made for the sake of a more pressing point about salvation. Ontology serves soteriology. The mysteries of the Trinity and salvation come together. As the Son exists "in the Spirit as his own image" and the Father exists "in the Son" in their communion with one another, so also in the economy of salvation "there is one holiness which comes from the Father through the Son in the Holy Spirit" in their communion with us.[38] The Son's holiness not only makes him distinct from the saints in nature but is also communicated to the saints by grace via the Spirit.

The Word as God is not anointed or sanctified with the Spirit, but he is anointed as a human in order to sanctify all human flesh.[39] While remaining "in nature unalterable," the Word out of love takes on "alterable flesh" in order to condemn sin in the flesh so that sinners might be free to fulfill the law by the Spirit's indwelling.[40] Athanasius highlights the soteriological trajectory of the anointing by saying that when the Son is "anointed in a human respect, *we* it is who in him are baptized; since also when He is baptized, *we* it is who in Him are baptized" (italics mine),[41] or that "when He received the Spirit, *we* it was who by Him were made recipients of It" (italics mine).[42] The presence of the Spirit in the incarnate Son becomes a condition in the economy of salvation for humans to share in his bodily exaltation and receive the indwelling of the Spirit.

> The Saviour ... being God ... and being Himself He that supplies the Holy Ghost, nevertheless is here said to be anointed, that ... He might provide for us men, not only exaltation and resurrection, but the indwelling and intimacy of the Spirit.[43]

---

[38] Athanasius, *Letters to Serapion on the Holy Spirit* 1.20.4, in *Works on the Spirit: Athanasius the Great and Didymus the Blind*, trans. Mark DelCogliano, Andrew Radde-Gallwitz, and Lewis Ayres (Crestwood, NY: St. Vladimir's Seminary Press, 2001), 84–5.

[39] Athanasius observes that "it is not the Word, considered as the Word and Wisdom, who is anointed with the Spirit which He Himself gives, but the flesh assumed by Him which is anointed in Him and by Him; that the sanctification coming to the Lord as man, may come to all men from Him." *First Discourse* 12.47, in NPNF² 4:334.

[40] Ibid., 12.51, in NPNF² 4:336. Here Athanasius refers to Rom. 8:3-4, 9.

[41] Ibid., 12.48, in NPNF² 4:335.

[42] Ibid., 12.47, in NPNF² 4:333.

[43] Ibid., 12.46, in NPNF² 4:333.

Khaled Anatolios sees a Nicene form of "Spirit Christology" at work in Athanasius' teaching that "the Word, who in his divinity is the giver of the Spirit, becomes the receiver of the Spirit in the kenotic self-humbling of his humanity."[44] In a Nicene framework, such Spirit Christology could only be grasped within a Trinitarian logic in which the unity of the Word/Logos and God the Father was affirmed as the presupposition for the mystery of the Word's humility in his incarnation. In Athanasius' theology of sanctification, it is precisely because the Word is both the perfect giver as God and perfect receiver as man of the Spirit that human reception of the Spirit is not only possible but secure.[45]

When speaking of the Son's reception of the Spirit in the flesh for our sake, Athanasius does not always appear to distinguish between the sanctification and anointing of the Son's flesh. Together with other biblical terms like "mission" and "appointment," Athanasius sees "anointing" as one of many ways Scripture speaks more generally of the mystery of the incarnation, that is, "the union of God the Word with the Man from Mary."[46] Accordingly, Athanasius at times uses the term "anointing" (or chrism) to refer not only to the Father's anointing of the Son with the *Spirit* at the Jordan but also to the Son's *divinity* coming into union with his humanity at the incarnation: "For I the Word am the chrism, and that which has the chrism from Me is the Man; not then without Me could He be called Christ, but being with Me and I in Him."[47] The Word is already sanctified in his humanity with the Holy Spirit (or his own divinity) at the incarnation, and thus his anointing at the Jordan does not seem to add anything to his humanity per se, although it does make it possible for humans to receive his sanctification.[48]

Notwithstanding this peculiar feature of his theology, Athanasius still offers us an incipient Spirit Christology that reads anointing texts through an incarnational hermeneutic, according to which the Word is sanctified or anointed in the flesh in order to anoint the flesh with his Spirit. Unlike the Arians who thought of the Word as a creature begotten of the will of God, Athanasius speaks of the Word as being begotten of the nature of God, namely,

---

[44] Anatolios, *Retrieving Nicaea*, 124.
[45] Ibid., 125.
[46] Athanasius, *Fourth Discourse* 35, in NPNF² 4:447.
[47] Ibid., 46, in NPNF² 4:447.
[48] See Sánchez, *Receiver, Bearer, and Giver*, 25-7; Orbe reads in Athanasius' proposal a "first sanctification" of the Savior at the incarnation (personal sanctification) and a "second grace of sanctity" not for him but for us—a second grace that involves the "anointing of his body" at the Jordan. See Orbe, *La Unción del Verbo*, 612 (translation mine).

begotten as "an offspring proper to the Father's essence ... very God, existing one in essence with the very Father."[49] Athanasius also incorporates the Spirit into his confession of the unity of the Father and the Son. As the Son partakes of the Father's essence, so also the Spirit partakes of (or takes from) the Son's essence.[50] More than Irenaeus, Athanasius advances the discussion of the Son's being begotten of the Father. Yet like Irenaeus, Athanasius' ultimate interest lies in the Word's solidarity with the human race, which moves the divine Word to be anointed with the Holy Spirit in order to sanctify or deify persons. Athanasius guards the distinction between the Son and the Spirit. The Son alone becomes incarnate; the Spirit deifies the Son in the flesh and, in him, deifies others. Athanasius also focuses on the Son as the subject of his actions in the mystery of the incarnation, which includes all the events of his mission—including his anointing. As we noted before, this leads him at times to speak of the Word as the subject who anoints himself with his own Spirit (or his own divinity), rather than—as in the case of Irenaeus—of the Father as the one who anoints the Word with his Spirit.[51] Representing an Alexandrian way of speaking, Athanasius focuses on the Word as the subject of his own Spirit-oriented actions in the mystery of salvation. Irenaeus speaks more in terms of the Father as the subject of Spirit-oriented actions on the incarnate Word. We see in these emphases different possibilities for thinking through the relationship between the Son and the Spirit in articulating a Spirit Christology. Athanasius' reading of the baptism of Jesus offers building blocks for interpreting Spirit-events in the life of Jesus, distinguishing the incarnational and pneumatic dimensions of the Son's identity, reflecting on the ontological unity and distinction of the divine persons, and showing how the goal of the Son's life in the Spirit lies in imparting his Spirit to others.

Neither a "Christ" nor a "Son": Irenaeus and Athanasius on the Identity of the "Spirit"

In this second section, we look at some issues raised by early church fathers that are still relevant for contemporary constructions of Spirit Christology,

---

[49] Athanasius, *First Discourse* 3.9, in NPNF² 4:311.
[50] Ibid.
[51] Sánchez, *Receiver, Bearer, and Giver*, 26.

such as the Spirit's personal identity in the Trinity, the relative ambiguity in the early church's understanding of "Spirit," their interpretations of the anointing of Jesus, and the contrast between Syriac-Antiochene and Alexandrian approaches to the role of the Spirit in Christ. Let us begin with the Spirit's identity. In our discussion of early orthodox responses to heterodox views of the baptism of Jesus, we noted how Gnostics and Arians operate with versions of Spirit Christology that respectively denied the union of the Word and the flesh prior to his baptism (incarnation) and the begetting of the Word from the Father's essence (divinity). Each of these heterodox views assumed a certain view of the "Spirit" in the anointing of Jesus. For some Gnostics, the "Spirit" is the preexistent "Christ" or the Sophia (Wisdom) part of a dyad "Christ-Sophia," which temporarily uses the man Jesus as an instrument to beget spiritual children of the Father through *gnōsis*. Like the spiritual "Christ" who descends upon the man Jesus, the "Spirit" similarly emanates from the mind of the Father. By contrast, like the Son whose origin is from the will of the Father, the Arians see the "Spirit" with whom the Father anoints him as a creaturely instrument assisting the Son in his promotion to deified status. Whereas the Gnostics place the "Spirit" on the side of the divine mind or the spiritual world of the eons above, the Arians by contrast place the "Spirit" on the side of the creaturely realm.[52] Either way, whether "Spirit" denotes a being who emanates from a spiritual mind above (Gnostics) or one originating in time according to the divine will (Arians), this "Spirit" does not enter the flesh of the Son in order to save human flesh from sin and death.

Irenaeus and Athanasius assume and teach the divine status of the "Spirit" together with the Word. Citing Ps. 33:6, Irenaeus attributes the Father's work of creation to "His Word and Spirit."[53] The Gnostic denial that the Father above is also the creator of the world amounts to a form of "impiety" or "blasphemy" against Christ and the Holy Spirit, by whom God made all things.[54] Although Irenaeus focuses on the Spirit in the economy of creation and new creation, he does point out that "with Him [i.e., God the Father] were always present the Word and Wisdom, the Son and the Spirit,"[55]

---

[52] These contrasting views of "Spirit" are analogous to the distinction Orbe draws between Gnostics and Arians on the Word's generation from the Father. Ladaria notes that, according to Orbe, Gnostics and Arians can speak of a begetting of the Word from the Father's will, but they differ in that the former see their begetting as an emanation from a spiritual substance and the latter as a creation with a beginning in time. See Ladaria, "La gnosis y la teología prenicena," 422 n. 13.
[53] Irenaeus, *Against Heresies* 1.22.1, in ANF 1:347.
[54] Ibid., 2.19.9, in ANF 1:387 (cf. *Against Heresies* 4.3, in ANF 1:462).
[55] Ibid., 4.20.1, in ANF 1:487.

in the sense that they were with the Father "anterior to all creation."[56] Yet the main stress falls on the materiality of the Spirit, on how the Father's Word and Spirit "become united with the ancient substance of Adam" in order to make humanity alive again.[57] When Gnostics deny the salvation of the flesh, that the Spirit "dwells in bodies" to make them God's temple and members of Christ's body, they commit blasphemy.[58] The Spirit brings its works to their proper end in the resurrection of the body, that is, in "the salvation of the flesh ... rendering the flesh ... capable of incorruption."[59] Although Irenaeus does not offer a systematic defense of the Spirit's divine identity, he does place the Spirit (Wisdom) with the Father and the Son before creation and portrays it as a distinct personal reality in the life and work of the Trinity.[60] Irenaeus perceives that the identification some Gnostics make between the spiritual Christ and Spirit-Sophia descending upon Jesus at the Jordan not only denies the incarnation but also robs the Spirit of its own identity in the mystery of the Word's anointing for our sake.

Athanasius develops his theology of the Spirit's divinity to defend the unity of the Trinity. He does so against the Tropikoi (from Gk. *tropos*, likely meaning a heterodox interpretation), an Arian group that, unlike full-blown Arians, held that the Son was not a creature while also maintaining that the Spirit remained subordinate to the Father. The Tropikoi see the Holy Spirit as an angelic creature, different from the angels "only in degree."[61] Athanasius contends that this position results in the introduction of a "foreign" nature into the Trinity, which reduces the Trinity "to the level of creatures," or "a dyad plus a creature," dividing the unity of the Trinity into "two distinct natures, because the Spirit ... is different in substance" from the Father and the Son.[62] How then should we think rightly of the Spirit? Athanasius offers a succinct answer: "For if they were to think correctly about the Word, they would also think soundly about the Spirit, *who proceeds from the Father* [Jn 15:26] and, being proper to the Son, is given by him to the disciples and to

---

[56] Ibid., 4.20.3, in ANF 1:488.
[57] Ibid., 5.1.3, in ANF 1:527.
[58] Ibid., 5.6.2, in ANF 1:532.
[59] Ibid., 5.12.4, in ANF 1:538.
[60] Citing Manlio Simonetti, Ladaria observes that Irenaeus tends to use "Wisdom" in reference to the Spirit's work of creation and "Spirit" in reference to its work in the economy of salvation. Luis F. Ladaria, *El Dios vivo y verdadero: El misterio de la Trinidad* (Salamanca: Secretariado Trinitario, 1998), 146.
[61] Athanasius, *Letters to Serapion* 1.1.2, p. 53.
[62] Ibid., 1.2.3–4, p. 55.

all who believe in him."[63] In a nutshell, Athanasius neatly summarizes how to speak of the Spirit in relation to the Father, the Son, and human persons. To say that the Holy Spirit "proceeds from the Father" and is "proper to the Son" means that the Holy Spirit shares not only in the same divine works with them but also in the same divine substance with them in the unity of the Trinity. Like the expression "takes from," which we introduced earlier, Athanasius also uses terms like "proceeds from" and "proper to" in order to highlight, respectively, that the Holy Spirit is of the same stock (divinity) as the Father and the Son.

In affirming this unity of the Trinity and within such unity, Athanasius makes a distinction between the Son and the Holy Spirit. In response to the Tropikoi's question, "If the Spirit is not a creature but proceeds from God the Father, why isn't he also called a son?,"[64] Athanasius explains that the Scriptures reveal "an order and unity in the Holy Trinity"[65] according to which the Holy Spirit is distinct from the Son while also being inseparably united to him and the Father. Scripture presents the mystery of sonship and holiness in a Trinitarian way. Christ alone is "the true Son" of God, not the Spirit, "but when we are made sons in the Spirit, it is clear that we are called children of God in Christ."[66] The three are distinct and yet work together to make creatures sons (and daughters) by grace. Likewise, in their intradivine unity, "the Son is in the Spirit ... so too is the Father in the Son;" correspondingly, in their common work, "there is one holiness which comes from the Father through the Son in the Holy Spirit."[67] We see a Trinitarian order in unity among the three and in their sanctifying work toward us. Athanasius argues for the Spirit's divinity on the basis of his work of deification, or making us partakers of God by grace. By showing how the Holy Spirit makes human persons sharers in the divine life by dwelling in us, Scripture

> shows that the anointing and the seal which is in us [i.e., the Spirit] does not belong to the nature of things which have been brought into existence, but to the Son, who joins us to the Father through the Spirit that is in him. ... And if he divinizes, there can be no doubt that his nature is of God.[68]

---

[63] Ibid., 1.2.5, p. 55.
[64] Ibid., 1.15.1, p. 76.
[65] Ibid., 1.20.1, p. 84.
[66] Ibid., 1.20.1, pp. 82–3.
[67] Ibid., 1.20.4, pp. 84–5.
[68] Ibid., 1.24.1–3, p. 90.

Since the Holy Spirit "is proper to the one Word," who is of the same substance as God the Father, it is then appropriate to confess the Spirit to be "proper to and the same as the one God in substance" (*homoosious*).[69] In his defense of the Spirit's divinity, Athanasius shows that the Spirit is neither a creature nor a son, but the Spirit who is inseparably united to the Son and the Father in their common works on our behalf and inseparably united to the Son and the Father by nature. Athanasius' reflections on the identity of the Spirit in relation to the Father and the Son in the economy of salvation and in the divine life raise a key question for Spirit Christology today, namely, how the field can contribute to a theology of the Trinity—an issue we explore further in Chapter 4.

A Peculiar Problem: When "Spirit" Means Divinity and "Anointing" Means Incarnation

In the context of their whole Trinitarian theology, it is clear that Irenaeus and Athanasius think of the Holy Spirit in distinction from and in unity with the Son. Yet at times, we find a peculiar use of the term "Spirit" (Gk. *pneuma*, Lat. *spiritus*) in their writings. Although this usage can be found in some authors after the fourth century, scholars usually see it as a "pre-Nicene" view of "Spirit" (discussed in Chapter 1) because it precedes the ecumenical councils of Nicaea (AD 325) and Constantinople (AD 381), which lay the foundation for a more mature theology of the person of the Holy Spirit.[70]

The Pre-Nicene Interpretation of Spirit as Christ's Divine Substance

We can call the pre-Nicene interpretation a *substantial* use of the term "Spirit," that is, one that signifies not the person of the Holy Spirit but the divine *nature* (substance) of the Word (Logos). According to this sense, the

---

[69] Ibid., 1.27.3, p. 96.
[70] For example, see Aloys Grillmeier, S.J., *From the Apostolic Age to Chalcedon (451)*, vol. 1 of *Christ in Christian Tradition*, 2nd rev. ed. (Atlanta, GA: John Knox, 1975), 200.

term "Spirit" refers not to the Holy Spirit but to the Son. Italian patristic scholar Manlio Simonetti (1926–2017) identifies three such uses of the term "Spirit" among early church fathers. Among the orthodox, "Spirit" can refer to the "divine nature" of the preexistent Christ, his "personal name," or a more direct identification between Christ and "the Holy Spirit."[71] The author lists examples from theologians in the East and the West, including Irenaeus and Athanasius. For instance, in an allegory where the Word (Logos) is portrayed as the father of the human race, Irenaeus points out that the Word creates spiritual children by pouring out upon them "the life-giving seed— that is the Spirit of the remission of sins."[72] At first, the expression appears to refer to the Holy Spirit, but later on Irenaeus identifies "the seed of the Father of all," with "the Spirit of God, by whom all things were made" and who "was commingled and united with flesh."[73] Given its reference to the prologue of Jn 1, this text finally identifies the "Spirit" with the preexistent Logos in his role as creator.[74] Simonetti also demonstrates that, by adopting a peculiar interpretation of the distinction between "flesh" and "spirit" in Rom. 1:3-4, some church fathers, including Athanasius, at times associate "flesh" with Christ's humanity and "spirit" with his divinity.[75] In other words, the terms "flesh" and "spirit" are not understood in a historical or eschatological sense to mean two *stages*, respectively, the earthly life of Christ as a descendant of David "according to the flesh" and the resurrection life he comes into "according to the spirit" (or Spirit). Instead, the terms are used substantially or ontologically to refer to the two *natures* of Christ.

Either directly or indirectly, some early church fathers also identified the "Holy Spirit" with the preexistent Word (Logos), particularly in their interpretation of the Annunciation in Lk. 1:35: "The Holy Spirit will come upon you, and the power of the Most High will overshadow you; therefore the child to be born will be holy; he will be called Son of God." The text

---

[71] Simonetti, "Note di cristologia pneumatica," 201–32; cf. Grillmeier, *From the Apostolic Age to Chalcedon (451)*, 190–206.
[72] Irenaeus, *Against Heresies* 4.31.2, in ANF 1:505.
[73] Ibid.
[74] Simonetti asserts that the expression "the Word of the Father and the Spirit of God, having become united to the ancient substance of Adam" (*Against Heresies* 5.1.3) identifies the preexistent Word with the Spirit. See "Note di cristologia pneumatica," 214. However, in the context of the preceding and following statements, in which Irenaeus distinguishes between the Word's incarnation and the Spirit's imparting to humans (*Against Heresies* 5.1.1), and between the two "hands of God" in Adam's creation (*Against Heresies* 5.1.3), it is probably better to read Irenaeus' expression as an inclusive one that brings in one expression the Word's union to his flesh (incarnation) to bring about the Spirit's union to human persons (gift of the Spirit).
[75] Simonetti, "Note di cristologia pneumatica," 206. He cites Athanasius, *Letters to Serapion* 4.19.

places "the Holy Spirit" and "the power of the Most High" in a parallelism, a common way of saying the same thing in two different ways. In Luke's usage, "Spirit" and "power" function as closely related terms (cf. Lk. 4:14, 24:49; Acts 1:8, 10:38). However, in interpreting this text, Irenaeus first speaks of the Holy Spirit's descent upon Mary, and then by using the expression "the Son of the Most high God the Father of all" associates the second term with the Word "who effected the incarnation."[76] Irenaeus does not directly identify the Holy Spirit with the Word, but he does so indirectly by associating "the power of the Most High" not with the Holy Spirit but with "the Son Most High." Some fathers' association of "the power of the Most High" with Christ comes from the Pauline literature, where the apostle calls Christ "the power of God" (1 Cor. 1:24).[77] For instance, Athanasius sees "the power of the Most High" as a reference to the Word "who visited the holy virgin Mary," but also notes that "the Word in the Spirit formed the body and accommodated it to himself."[78] Even here Athanasius focuses not so much on the Holy Spirit's visitation of Mary to bring about the incarnation but on the Word's formation of a body from Mary and his assuming of such body unto his person. However, while speaking of the Word as the subject of the incarnation, Athanasius nonetheless adds that the Word does such work "in the Spirit"—a type of phrasing that brings the Holy Spirit back into the picture. None of the above examples ultimately take away from the orthodox fathers' broader incarnational and Trinitarian logic. But their occasional ambivalence in the use of the term "Spirit" raises an important question for a Spirit Christology today, namely, how do we distinguish the proper works of the Son and the Spirit in various events of Christ's life such as his conception and anointing?

The Interpretation of the Anointing as the Incarnation of Christ

Returning to the anointing of Jesus, we observed earlier how for Irenaeus this unction signifies the Holy Spirit who descends on the incarnate Word at his baptism so that he might do his mission and send the Spirit to us. In Athanasius' case, the anointing or chrism signifies, more broadly, either the

---

[76] Irenaeus, *Against Heresies* 5.1.3, in ANF 1:527.
[77] Simonetti, "Note de cristologia pneumatica," 219.
[78] Athanasius, *Letters to Serapion* 1.31.11, p. 102.

"Holy Spirit" or the "divinity" of the Word that sanctifies his human flesh at the incarnation so that humans too might be sanctified by the Word in the Spirit (or sanctified in the Word by the Spirit). When Athanasius states that the Word is "the chrism" and that which has the chrism from the Word is "the Man" (i.e., his humanity), the Alexandrian theologian represents a tradition that identifies the anointing with the incarnation and ascribes the event not to the Spirit but to the Logos (Word). We may call this move an *incarnational* interpretation of the anointing, as opposed to a more historical one referring specifically to the baptism of Jesus. After Athanasius, a classic example of this interpretation in the East comes from Gregory of Nazianzus, for whom the name "Christ" can signify "His Godhead … the Anointing of His manhood."[79] Similarly, John of Damascus (*c.* AD 675–749) states that Christ "in His own person anointed Himself; as God anointed His body with His own divinity, and as Man being anointed. For He is both God and Man. And the anointing is the divinity of His humanity."[80] In both of these examples, "anointing" refers more specifically to the divinity of the Son, which at the incarnation or personal union anoints his flesh or human nature. Earlier on, we pointed to examples of an interpretation of Lk. 1:35 in Irenaeus and Athanasius that associates "the power of the Most High" not with the Spirit but the Word.[81] Other prominent examples in the West include Tertullian and Augustine, who more directly interpret "the Holy Spirit" in Lk. 1:35 as the "Word." Tertullian argues that "the Spirit of God in this passage must be the same *as the Word.* … For both the Spirit is the substance of the Word, and the Word is the operation of the Spirit, and the Two are One (and the same)."[82] Augustine (AD 354–430) agrees that the Lord Jesus Christ "received it [i.e., the Spirit] as man, and therefore He is said to be full of grace, and of the Holy Spirit," but then goes on to argue that "Christ was *certainly not anointed* with the Holy Spirit, when He, as a dove descended upon Him *at His baptism*" (italics mine).[83] Rather, Christ was "anointed … when the Word of God was made flesh, *i.e.* when human nature … was joined to God the Word in the womb of the Virgin, so that with it it became one person. Therefore it is that we confess Him to have been born

---

[79] Gregory Nazianzen, *The Fourth Theological Oration* 21, in NPNF² 7:317.
[80] John of Damascus, *An Exact Exposition of the Orthodox Faith* 3.3, in NPNF² 9:47.
[81] "It is noteworthy that the all but unanimous exegetical tradition of Luke I,35 equated 'the holy spirit' and 'the power of the Most High' which were to come upon Mary, not with the third person of the Trinity, but with Christ Who, preexisting as spirit or Word, was to incarnate Himself in her womb." J. N. D. Kelly, *Early Christian Doctrines*, 5th rev. ed. (London: A.&C. Black, 1977), 144–5.
[82] Tertullian, *Against Praxeas* 26, in ANF 3:622.
[83] Augustine, *On the Holy Trinity* 15.26.46, in NPNF² 3:224.

of the Holy Spirit and of the Virgin Mary."[84] The anointing of Jesus does not occur at the time of his baptism, "for at that time He deigned to prefigure His body, i.e. His Church, in which especially the baptized receive the Holy Spirit."[85] For Augustine, Christ is not anointed with the Holy Spirit at his baptism, but the Word anoints himself when he joins his flesh to his person at the incarnation. It is also from that time that Christ personally has the Holy Spirit in his humanity. Yet Christ's baptism still has significance, not for Christ per se but for his body, the church. The baptism of Christ does not seem to add anything to his own identity, since Christ is already anointed in the flesh at the incarnation. But the event has an ecclesial significance or trajectory. It reveals to us a blessing flowing from the Word's condescension in his incarnation. Such blessing lies in the gift of the Holy Spirit to his body, the church, in her baptism.

Gregory of Nazianzus, John of Damascus, and Tertullian share a *substantial* interpretation of "Spirit," signifying the divine Word. Furthermore, Gregory, John, and Augustine share Athanasius' *incarnational* view of the anointing. All authors interpret the anointing as a metaphor for the divinity of the Word and move such anointing from his baptism to his birth, transposing the anointing at Jordan to the moment of the personal union. Finally, like Irenaeus and Athanasius, Augustine makes room for an *ecclesial* interpretation of the anointing, according to which the Spirit whom Christ received in his humanity can be communicated to the saints by the grace of adoption. Thus the church fathers retain the salvific purpose of the anointing, its participatory character. Having said that, something is lost in translation in the aforementioned efforts. A partial eclipse of the Holy Spirit in the events of Jesus' life and mission takes place, so that Spirit-events such as the birth and baptism of Jesus are read as Logos-oriented events.[86] Since the Logos already anoints his humanity with his Spirit (or his own divinity) from birth, the baptism at Jordan does not appear to be a constitutive event for the Logos in the flesh. Instead, the baptism functions as a "revelatory" moment for others of Christ's prior divinity or possession of the Spirit from birth, or as an "exemplary" event for others to know Christ as God, Messiah, or giver of the Spirit to the church.[87] As Cantalamessa puts it, the Holy Spirit

---

[84] Ibid.
[85] Ibid.
[86] For a discussion of early church Logos-oriented readings of birth and baptism texts, see Sánchez, *Receiver, Bearer, and Giver*, 34–46.
[87] Ibid., 30.

"intervenes in Jesus' baptism … more to attest to the divinity of Jesus than to anoint him as the Messiah."[88] As a result, the significance of the anointing lies only in what it means for us, which is right and salutary, but at the expense of reflecting further on what it means for Jesus. Jesus' baptism holds an "active significance" in that "Jesus anoints us," but it is difficult to see how the event has a "passive significance" for Jesus as one "anointed by the Father."[89]

Although the various peculiar interpretations of the anointing of Jesus thus far mentioned did not affect the substance of the orthodox theologians' commitment to faith in the Trinity and the incarnation, their views raise questions concerning the identity of the Spirit and its relationship to the Word and the events of his life and mission. What are the proper works of the Son and the Spirit in the mystery of Christ? How do these works relate to each other? Moreover, how should one speak of events in the life of the incarnate Son in which the Spirit is present and active? For instance, in events such as his birth, anointing, and resurrection, is the Son doing something, or is something being done to the Son? Or both? Related to this, are these events revealing something about the Son that already took place, or are they defining who the Son is in a new way? These are important questions in the field of Spirit Christology today.

Christological Tensions: Thinking through the Spirit's Role in Christ's Humanity

Taking account of our survey of early orthodox responses to heterodox views of the baptism of Jesus, we can now take stock of their contributions for the field of Spirit Christology today. In doing so, we acknowledge that Irenaeus' and Athanasius' contributions precede other important developments in the expression of the church's teachings on the Trinity and the incarnation, both in terms of ecumenical church councils and particular theologians. We will speak to one of those tensions in Christology later in this section. For now, we point out that Irenaeus' and Athanasius' responses to the heterodox illustrate a fundamental concern for distinguishing between the Word (Son)

---

[88] Cantalamessa, "The Incarnation and the Mystery of the Anointing: Christology and Pneumatology in the Early Centuries of the Church," in *TAT*, 188.
[89] Ibid., 188.

and the Holy Spirit, ascribing to the former the union at the incarnation and to the latter the work of uniting persons to the Word. They are aware that the economic relationship between the Word and the Spirit for our sake has its roots in a prior immanent relationship with the Father, observing that their threefold unity in their work to make humans holy reveals an eternal triunity in holiness among themselves. Against heterodox interpretations of the anointing of Jesus that privileged the great ontological divide between God and creatures, the orthodox press on linking the Word and the Spirit to the economy of salvation, noting that ultimately God is about taking on flesh to save the flesh. Irenaeus and Athanasius see the Spirit in the baptism of Jesus as a condition for his giving of the Spirit to others, noting the relative continuity between the presence of the Spirit in Jesus and in the saints, as well as the discontinuity between Jesus as giver of the Spirit and others as participants in his Spirit. While both theologians see the baptism of Jesus as a unique historical event in the economy of salvation, Irenaeus sees the Jordan as a genuinely new event in which the Word is made "Jesus Christ" by the Father's anointing with the Spirit for the sake of his mission and giving of the Holy Spirit to others. A bit more guarded, Athanasius tends to see the anointing at Jordan as a revelation for others of the Word's prior sanctification of his flesh with the Spirit (or divinity) at the incarnation, which also prefigures his sanctification of the saints with the same Spirit. In terms of the subject of the anointing, Irenaeus speaks of the Father's anointing of the Son with the Spirit (anointing), whereas Athanasius speaks of the Word's anointing of his own flesh with the Spirit (or his own divinity). In these reflections, we have partial yet substantive answers to Christological and Trinitarian issues frequently raised in Spirit Christology today.

Drawing attention to a peculiar *substantial* interpretation of the "Spirit" (meaning the divine nature or substance of Christ) as evident in an *incarnational* interpretation of the anointing (= incarnation, personal union) among some orthodox theologians, our study also highlighted the problem of reading events such as the birth and baptism of Jesus through a Logos-oriented lens to the detriment of the place of the Spirit in such events. Such a reading makes the divine Word (Logos) the anointing of his human flesh at the incarnation, in some cases eclipsing the role of the Holy Spirit in the sanctification of the Word's flesh at birth (incarnation) and his subsequent anointing for mission at the Jordan. Athanasius sees the sanctification of the Word's flesh as synonymous with his anointing from the time of the incarnation and as the work of the Word who sanctifies his own flesh at that time. The Son is sanctified in the flesh from the moment of the union in order to sanctify the flesh with the Spirit after his exaltation. The anointing at baptism reveals this salvific reality, but does not appear to bring it about. By contrast, we observed how Irenaeus distinguishes between the Word's union with his flesh at the union (incarnation) and the Father's anointing of the enfleshed Word with the Spirit at his baptism to make him Christ and communicate his anointing to others with the gift of the Spirit. The baptism appears not merely as a revelation of an already established reality, but as a defining event that affects the Word in the flesh so that the flesh (humanity) might receive his Spirit.

A Christological Tension in the Early Church's Threefold Meaning of the Anointing of Jesus

Given the various interpretations of the baptism of Jesus offered by heterodox and orthodox theologians, Cantalamessa offers three ways of interpreting the event in a way that sums up the dominant pattern and best thinking of the early church fathers on the matter by the fourth century. First, the baptism of Jesus must be seen as a *"Trinitarian* anointing," which involves a "personal" interpretation of the Spirit "as a 'person' and not only as a divine nature."[90] Second, the baptism of Jesus points to "a *historical* anointing," an event that "indicates the investiture of Jesus as the Messiah" for our salvation.[91] The anointing at Jordan, strictly speaking, points neither to an earlier incarnational anointing nor to an earlier cosmic anointing. Moreover, Cantalamessa contrasts Jesus' prior sanctification and personal possession of the Spirit from the incarnation to his subsequent anointing with the same Spirit at the Jordan: "But unlike the powers that Jesus possessed because of the fullness of the Holy Spirit in him due to the hypostatic union (which are not transferable to others), the effects that come from the anointing at baptism appear destined to be communicated to the church."[92] Early church theologians recognize that Jesus has the Spirit in himself from the time of the union, but his anointing at baptism in some sense makes it possible for others to partake of his Spirit by grace.

Third, and related to the last point, the baptism of Jesus must be seen as an *"ecclesial* anointing," that is to say, as the moment in which the Son is

---

[90] Ibid., 183.
[91] Ibid., 184.
[92] Ibid., 184–5.

anointed with the Spirit in a fresh way so that others might be anointed with the same Spirit.[93] Cantalamessa explains the uniqueness of the Jordan with a quote from Orbe's treatise on the anointing of the Word:

> In principle the incarnate Word was the Savior from the time of his conception. Only in the Jordan was the human nature of the Word, as such, sanctified with a Spirit destined to be given to human beings. ... The humanization of the Spirit begins in the baptism at the Jordan and not before. The Pneuma sent by the Father sanctified Jesus in one instant and with him, *secundum primitias* [according to the firstfruits], the church.[94]

By describing the anointing of Jesus at his baptism as a Trinitarian, historical, and ecclesial event, Cantalamessa lays out for us a framework to appreciate key contributions of early church fathers toward a Spirit Christology. Their nascent "Spirit Christology" lays the groundwork for thinking about the Trinitarian, Christological, soteriological, and ecclesial trajectories of the Spirit's presence and activity in, through, and with the incarnate Son.

The threefold meaning of the anointing also reveals a tension in the articulation of the identity of Christ from a pneumatic angle in the early church. Earlier on, we noted how Cantalamessa points out that the anointing of Jesus has both active and passive significance, that is to say, that Jesus does something to us through the event (active) and that something is done to Jesus in the event (passive). By doing so, the author highlights the hesitancy among some fathers to speak of the baptism in the passive sense. The reason lies partly in the heterodox use of the event to deny Jesus his incarnation and divinity. The author also finds reason for such hesitancy in the church's anti-Arian move toward the "ontologization of Christology," which tends to privilege "what exists from the beginning, the *archē* of things, their metaphysical constitution and not their historical becoming."[95] The question about the active or passive interpretation of the anointing of Jesus is a more fundamental question about the proper way to think about the Son-Spirit relation in describing the events of Jesus' life and mission. The early church leaves us with something of a tension in its conception of this relation. On the one hand, we see the boldness of the orthodox theologians in establishing Christ's possession of the Spirit from the beginning of his life. On the other hand, we see the timidity of some to speak of Christ's becoming

---

[93] Ibid., 185.
[94] Ibid. Here Cantalamessa cites Orbe, *La unción del Verbo*, 633.
[95] Cantalamessa, "The Incarnation and the Mystery of the Anointing," 186.

anointed by the Spirit later at his baptism. How then should we think of the Spirit's activity throughout Jesus' life? For instance, does the Spirit reveal to others at Jesus' baptism and resurrection the glory he already has as the Son of God? Or does the Spirit also anoint the Son for mission and raise him from the dead, bringing about something new in the history of the Son through its involvement in these events? Is the Spirit's sanctification of the Son in his humanity something that happens all at once, or does the Son also grow in some sense in such sanctification through his ongoing obedience to the Father against the attacks of Satan and for the sake of our salvation? Chapter 5 shows how a number of theologians deal with these issues today.

A Christological Tension in Syriac-Antiochene and Alexandrian Spirit Christologies

The Christological tension inherent in describing the Son-Spirit relation can be seen further in the distinct emphases of Syrian-Antiochene and Alexandrian traditions in the East. In a brief study of the indwelling of the Spirit in Christ, French Orthodox theologian Boris Bobrinskoy notes that, in contrast to the Syriac and Antiochene traditions represented by Basil of Caesarea and John Chrysostom (AD 349–407), Gregory of Nazianzus represents an Alexandrian tradition, which makes him "more reluctant than St. Basil to investigate the mystery of Christ's humanity and the mode of the Spirit's presence within that humanity."[96] The question of the "mode" of presence and activity of the Holy Spirit in the human life and work of the Son remains a significant one in the contemporary field of Spirit Christology, and Bobrinskoy shows how the Cappadocian fathers—Basil, Gregory of Nazianzus, and Gregory of Nyssa—approach the same issue from different theological traditions.

To highlight the inseparable unity of the Holy Spirit and the Son in all events of his life and mission, Bobrinskoy calls attention to a classic text from Basil's treatise on the Holy Spirit:

> When we speak of the economy of salvation accomplished for man by our great God and Savior Jesus Christ, who will deny their having been

---

[96] Boris Bobrinskoy, "The Indwelling of the Spirit in Christ: 'Pneumatic Christology' in the Cappadocian Fathers," *St. Vladimir's Theological Quarterly* 28, no. 1 (1984): 64.

accomplished through the grace of the Spirit? ... First of all, the Lord, he was made an unction and was inseparably united to the flesh of the Lord. ... After this every operation was accomplished with the co-operation of the Spirit. He was present when the Lord was tempted by the devil ... He was inseparably united with him while he worked miracles ... And he did not leave him when he had risen from the dead.[97]

Basil speaks without hesitation about the Spirit's role in Christ and his work. Christ's work of salvation is "accomplished through the grace of the Spirit." The Spirit is "present" with him but also "inseparably united to the flesh of the Lord," so that Christ's "every operation was accomplished with the co-operation of the Holy Spirit." By contrast, Bobrinskoy notes how Gregory of Nazianzus, in one of his Pentecost sermons, "is even reluctant to speak of the operation of the Spirit *in* Jesus: (The Spirit dwelt in Christ) not as energizing, but as accompanying him who is his equal (XLI.11)."[98] Gregory tends to downplay the "active operation of the Spirit in Jesus."[99] If Bobrinskoy is correct about the Alexandrian influence on Gregory, then it makes sense to understand Gregory's hesitancy in the context of Athanasius' response to the Arians. We noted, for example, how Gregory, like Athanasius, spoke of the anointing or chrism of the Word as a reference not to what happened to the Word at his baptism but to what the Word did at his incarnation.

In contrast to his friend Theodore of Mopsuestia, who tended to speak of the Spirit as if Christ were "the simple receptacle of the Spirit" rather than "the living and unique *locus* [place] of the full presence of the Spirit who belongs to him alone," John Chrysostom represents a balanced Antiochene position that affirms "the divinity of Christ without in any way diminishing the action of the Spirit within him."[100] Chrysostom "affirmed unequivocally that Jesus was spiritual because the Spirit had 'fashioned'

---

[97] Ibid., 60. The citation is from *De Spiritu Sancto* XVI.39. For another translation, see Basil, *On the Holy Spirit* 16.39, in NPNF² 8:25.
[98] Bobrinskoy, "The Indwelling of the Spirit in Christ," 61.
[99] Ibid., 62. Here Bobrinskoy cites Gregory's identification of the name "Christ" with his "divinity" and his use of anointing as a metaphor for the incarnation:

> He is "Christ" because of his divinity. For this is the anointing of his humanity; it does not, as is the case with all other anointed ones ... sanctify by its action (*energeia*), but by the full presence (*parousia*) of the Anointing One (the Spirit). The result is that he who (as anointed Christ) anoints (humanity) is called "man," and makes that which is anointed "god" (*Or.* XXX.21).

For another translation, see Gregory Nazianzen, *The Fourth Theological Oration* 21, in NPNF² 7:317.
[100] Bobrinskoy, "The Indwelling of the Spirit in Christ," 61.

him, and that the Spirit acted in and through his humanity, in which he dwelt as in a sanctuary."[101] The diversity of schools of thought in the early church concerning the dynamics of the Spirit's role in the mystery of Christ offers guidance for speaking robustly about the indwelling and ongoing activity of the Spirit in the incarnate Son while also upholding his identity as the incarnate Word and giver of the Spirit. Basil's powerful description of the Holy Spirit as "inseparably united to the flesh of the Lord" reveals the underlying theological concern—also shared by Irenaeus and Athanasius—for grounding the sanctification (deification) of human flesh in the mystery of the Holy Spirit's indwelling presence and activity in and through Christ's flesh.

To understand the Eastern Alexandrian tradition represented by Athanasius and then Cyril of Alexandria, we must review and inquire further into the similar concerns that drive their responses to the Arian (Athanasius and Cyril) and Nestorian (Cyril) controversies in the fourth and fifth centuries. Arius and Nestorius are like night and day in that the former denies the divinity of the Word and the latter, precisely against Arius, affirms it in the strongest possible way. Yet interestingly enough, they both operate with a commitment to divine impassibility as an ultimate ontological principle in their theological approach—a move that gets them in trouble. In Arius' case, Jesus cannot be God because Jesus is a passible creature. In Nestorius' case, the Logos cannot suffer because he is God, so only the humanity of Christ does. In response to Arius' subordination of the Word (Logos) in relation to the impassible God, the Alexandrian tradition highlights the ontological *unity* of the Father and the Son. In response to Nestorius' separation of the divine (impassible) Word (Logos) from his humanity (or Christ as man), it posits in the strongest terms the personal *unity* of the Son. Neither Athanasius nor Cyril denies the divine impassibility of the Word, but this ontological premise serves a penultimate function in service to soteriology. If the Word is a human creature who becomes deified (Arius), how can he deify the flesh? Therefore, Athanasius teaches that the Word, who is God, becomes human for our sake so that he might deify humanity.[102] Similarly, if only the humanity of Christ died, but not the Word (Nestorius), then, how can the Word give life to the flesh? Therefore, Cyril observes that not only the human nature of Christ but the person of the Word died in the flesh so that He might give life to the flesh

---

[101] Ibid., 65 (cf. 61).
[102] Cf. Athanasius, *First Discourse* 11.39, in NPNF² 4:329.

(humanity).[103] In articulating an apologetic response informed by their soteriological concerns, Athanasius and Cyril share a tendency to speak of the divine Word as the personal subject of his own actions in the economy of salvation, the fullness of the Logos' (and his own Spirit's) presence in his humanity from the time of the incarnation (union), what the events in the economy of salvation mean not for the Word but for us, and the cosmic or universal significance of the Word's incarnation for humanity as a whole.[104] Earlier in this chapter, we explained how the aforementioned Alexandrian theological accents play out in Athanasius' interpretation of the anointing of the Word at the Jordan. In short, the Word anoints his humanity with his own "Spirit" (which can mean either his "divinity" or the "Holy Spirit"). The Father does not come into the picture as the person who sends the Holy Spirit upon his incarnate Son (as in Irenaeus). Moreover, this anointing does not take place as a new moment at the Jordan, but already happens at the incarnation when the human nature of the Word is in full possession of the Spirit—the Jordan being only a revelation for others of a prior reality. Therefore, the Word anoints his humanity not for himself (even in his human nature) but for our sake, so that humanity might receive the anointing of his own Spirit in Christian baptism. The significance of the anointing lies not in what it means for the Son's humanity throughout the various events of his life and mission, but in what it means more universally for our salvation. Due to these factors, it is understandable that the Alexandrian tradition gives less attention to the historical particularity and

---

[103] Consider Cyril's last two anathemas against Nestorius, in which the Alexandrian highlights how the Nestorian position on the union of Christ leads to a disjointed account of salvation. Anathema 11:

> Whosoever shall not recognize that the Word of God suffered in the flesh, that he was crucified in the flesh, and that likewise in that same flesh he tasted death and that he is become the first-begotten of the dead, for, as he is God, he is the life and it is he that giveth life: let him be anathema.

Anathema 12:

> Whosoever shall not confess that the flesh of the Lord giveth life and that it pertains to the Word of God the Father as his very own, but shall pretend that it belongs to another person who is united to him [i.e., the Word] only according to honour, and who has served as a dwelling for the divinity; and shall not rather confess, as we say, that that flesh giveth life because it is that of the Word who giveth life to all: let him be anathema.

Cyril of Alexandria, *The XII Anathematisms of St. Cyril against Nestorius*, in NPNF² 14:217.

[104] Sánchez, *Receiver, Bearer, and Giver of God's Spirit*, 41–3.

ongoing activity of the humanity of the Word, or to the ongoing presence and work of the Holy Spirit throughout his human life and mission.

To account for the pneumatic dimension of Christ's human history, which is partially eclipsed by the Alexandrian tradition, we can look more closely to the Eastern Antiochene tradition's way of dealing with the Spirit's activity in Jesus. Given that Cyril of Alexandria condemns Nestorius, who comes from the Antiochene approach advanced by Theodore, it makes sense to look briefly at Theodore's pneumatic Christology. To review, in Bobrinskoy's estimation, Theodore tends to think of Jesus Christ more as a "receptacle of the Spirit"—as an Alexandrian theologian might say—than as the "unique *locus* [place] of the full presence of the Spirit who belongs to him," while Chrysostom affirms Christ's divinity "without in any way diminishing the action of the Spirit within him."[105] Be that as it may, there is no doubt that Theodore has a strong sense of the pneumatic trajectory of Jesus' life.[106] He speaks of the grace or power of the Spirit dwelling in Christ, in a way that his human temple (or the assumed man) is fit for union or "conjunction" with the Logos,[107] is anointed at the union to live a "perfect life,"[108] and is capable of being shared by other humans through baptism into Christ's death and resurrection.[109] Yet the way in which Theodore frames this pneumatic trajectory presents some challenges. For instance, his distinction between the divine Logos and the assumed man—a classic way of framing his Antiochene

---

[105] Bobrinskoy, "The Indwelling of the Spirit in Christ," 61.

[106] See Sánchez, "The Holy Spirit and the Son's Glorification," 87–8.

[107] "Christ-in-the-flesh, while he was not yet in his nature so that he was united with God the Word, necessarily needed the mediation of the gift of the Spirit. … And this conjunction was accomplished through the gift of the Spirit." Theodore of Mopsuestia, *Commentary on the Gospel of John*, trans. Marco Conti (Downers Grove, IL: IVP Academic, 2010), 137; similarly, referring to Jn 1:33, Theodore writes that Christ was "first born in the Spirit, and through the Spirit was united to the Only-Begotten so that he acquired the true dignity of sonship and communicates to us the gift of the Spirit by which we are also regenerated and received among his children according to the power of each one" (23).

[108] "And after receiving every perfect grace, which he received thanks to his anointing, he lived a perfect life of great integrity in a way that is it not possible for human nature." Theodore, *John*, 137. For Theodore, Christ is anointed with the Spirit in the body not at his baptism but from the time of its union or conjunction with God the Word (71).

[109] Therefore, the assumed man also received a share in that which is the principle of all goodness on behalf of all humanity because we will participate in all the things that happened to him—in the resurrection, in the ascension into heaven and in the kingdom and glory. … It follows, then, that we will also receive the grace of the Spirit so that we may be regenerated by its power by symbolically fulfilling through baptism the event of the death and resurrection of Christ. … "All the grace of the Spirit," he says, "is with me because I am joined together with God the Word, and I received true sonship. From the grace that is in me and with me a small portion will come upon you so that you may also be called sons of God, even though you are quite far removed from the honor that I have as the Son." (Theodore, *John*, 137)

approach—can be seen as leading logically to a Christology that speaks of the assumed man almost as a distinct person in a way that does not account fully for the Logos as the only personal subject of his human actions.[110] If the pneumatic trajectory of Christ's human life receives significant attention, the view of the union as a conjunction of natures instead of a hypostatic union seems less satisfying—at least from an Alexandrian perspective.

Perhaps more significant, Theodore's argument that the Holy Spirit dwells in the assumed man Christ as "grace" or "power" but not according to its "nature" leaves him open to the criticism that Christ only has the Spirit as a power external to his person but not as an equal or more naturally as "his own Spirit"—a problem that Cyril observes in Nestorius.[111] Theodore's distinction between grace and nature in pneumatology comes through in biblical interpretation.[112] Daniel Keating has observed that Theodore's reading of the "not yet" in Jn 7:39 (a text we discussed in Chapter 2) is driven by an *ontological* concern for distinguishing properly between "the person and the divine nature" of the Spirit, which is immutable, and "the gift of his grace which is imparted to the saints" after Christ's ascension.[113] Citing John O'Keefe, Keating argues that Theodore's distinction between nature and grace aligns with his interest in protecting God's impassibility from the

---

[110] Thus the Second Council of Constantinople (AD 553) condemns Theodore for the teaching that "the Word of God is one person, but that another person is Christ, vexed by the sufferings of the soul and the desires of the flesh." *The Second Council of Constantinople: The Capitula of the Council*, in NPNF² 14:315.

[111] The distinction between the Spirit as "power" and "nature" is behind Cyril's anathema against Nestorius:

> If any man shall say that the one Lord Jesus Christ was glorified by the Holy Ghost, so that he used through him a power not his own and from him received power against unclean spirits and power to work miracles before men and shall not rather confess that it was his own Spirit through which he worked these divine signs; let him be anathema. (Cyril of Alexandria, *The XII Anathematisms of St. Cyril against Nestorius*, in NPNF² 14:214-15)

Moreover, since Theodore sees the grace of the Spirit as the mediating gift that brings about the conjunction of the Logos and the assumed man, he is also susceptible to the criticism that the grace of the Spirit is what makes the assumed man worthy of sonship. This criticism is behind the Second Council of Constantinople's condemnation of Theodore for teaching that Christ "as a mere man was baptized ... and obtained by this baptism the grace of the Holy Spirit, and became worthy of Sonship." *The Second Council of Constantinople: The Capitula of the Council*, in NPNF² 14:315.

[112] On the contrast between Theodore's and Cyril's exegesis on Jn 7:39, see Sánchez, "The Holy Spirit and the Son's Glorification," 81–2.

[113] Daniel A. Keating, "'For as Yet the Spirit Had Not Been Given': John 7:39 in Theodore of Mopsuestia, Augustine, and Cyril of Alexandria," in F. Young, M. Edwards, and P. Parvis, eds., *Studia Patristica* 39 (Leuven: Peeters, 2006), 234.

mutability of creation.[114] Keating points out that Cyril's reading of Jn 7:39 as a promise of our sharing in the Holy Spirit's own *person/nature* through the Son has in view a critique of Theodore's teaching that we share only in the Spirit's indwelling *grace*. Behind the nature-grace distinction lies an important Christological question, namely, whether the incarnate Logos has the Spirit as "his own" or by *nature* because he is God in the flesh (Cyril's position), or whether the Logos, precisely because he is impassible, has the Spirit only as a *human* temple and thus by *grace* like the rest of us (Theodore's position).[115]

Cyril's interpretation of the same text gives us further insight into the pneumatic dimension of Alexandrian Christology. Echoing Athanasius' theology of human participation in the divine life (deification), Cyril teaches that the uniqueness of the Spirit's gift after Christ's glorification lies in the divine Spirit's full dwelling in human persons to restore in them the divine image lost by their forefather Adam in Eden. Through a Christological reading of Gen. 2:7 in light of Jn 20:22, Cyril interprets God's life-giving breath in Adam as the Holy Spirit who dwells in him and keeps him in the divine image until Adam sins and the Spirit flees from him and the rest of corrupted humanity.[116] In God's economy of salvation, the Spirit who departed

---

[114]Ibid., 237.

[115]As an example of Theodore's ontological concern, consider the following:

> In saying: "When the Paraclete is come, whom I will send unto you," He refers to the grace of the Spirit which He was about to bestow on them. He was not going to send unto them the Divine nature of the Spirit which was everywhere, but He said this of the gift of the grace which was poured upon them.(Theodore of Mopsuestia, *Commentary on the Nicene Creed*, trans. Alphonse Mingana, ch. 10, http://www.tertullian.org/fathers/theodore_of_mopsuestia_nicene_02_text.htm#C10)

> Although eighth- and ninth-century Spanish theologians Elipandus of Toledo and Felix of Urgel, who linked Christ's grace of sonship to his baptism, were susceptible to the criticism leveled against Antiochene theologians in the East, Cavadini explains that they operate within a non-adoptionist Western christological paradigm, according to which *"by assuming* flesh or a body, etc., the *Word*, the 'Only-begotten' with regard to nature, becomes [for us] the 'First-born in adoption and grace.'" See John C. Cavadini, *The Last Christology of the West: Adoptionism in Spain and Gaul, 785–820* (Philadelphia: University of Pennsylvania Press, 1993), 33.

[116]After his resurrection from the dead, he breathed on his disciples and said, "Receive the Holy Spirit". ... In the beginning, as the Spirit bearer Moses said to us, the creator of all took dust from the ground, fashioned a man and "breathed into his face the breath of life." And what is the breath of life but plainly the Spirit of Christ. ... Since the Spirit, who can form and keep us in the divine imprint, flew away from humanity, the Savior graces us once again with this Spirit, bringing us back to that original dignity and refashioning us into his image. (Cyril of Alexandria, *Commentary on John*, trans. David R. Maxwell, vol. 1 (Downers Grove, IL: IVP Academic, 2013), 5.695–6, pp. 310–11)

from the first Adam returns to the human race in a definitive way through the second Adam's breathing of the firstfruits of the Spirit on his disciples after his death and resurrection, so that they might be renewed after the incorruptible image of their risen Lord.[117] Cyril echoes Irenaeus' theology of recapitulation, according to which the Logos does over again the failed history of Adam by assuming the nature of Adam and receiving the Spirit, so that humans might receive the Spirit once again. For Cyril, there is a genuine economic *newness* to the gift of the Spirit in the new covenant. The Spirit had not yet dwelled fully in the saints in the sense that the Spirit still had to form Christ's disciples after the bodily image of their glorified Lord. The thrust of Cyril's account of the Spirit is soteriological. Yet his insistence that the Spirit communicates himself fully to the saints so that the saints could share by adoption in the divine life aligns with—and indeed, depends on—the notion that the divine Spirit (and not only its power or gifts) dwells fully in the flesh of the Word as "his own Spirit." It is because the Word is one with the Spirit by nature that the Spirit also dwells in his flesh in all fullness and is with him in all his works. Even though Cyril does not dwell on the historical dynamics of the Spirit's presence and activity in the various events in the Word's humanity, he opens a way forward to reflect on the implications of the full communication of the Spirit to the flesh of the Son and through him to us in a way that the integrity of the hypostatic union is maintained. The contemporary field of Spirit Christology attempts to deal with the tension evident in Alexandrian and Antiochene Christologies between achieving a full incarnational Christology that is grounded in the Logos' assumption of a human nature filled with his own Spirit, while doing justice to the historical particularity and becoming of the Logos in his Spirit-empowered human life and mission.

Significantly, Bobrinskoy suggests a way to incorporate the insights of Syriac-Antiochene and Alexandrian Christologies into a broader Trinitarian account of salvation. He proposes that the baptism of Jesus reveals a New Testament pattern and "movement" of divine activity, a "schema Father-Spirit-Christ" according to which "the Father is the origin, the Spirit is the mediator who descends and rests on the Son, who permits His incarnation and sends Him."[118] This pattern highlights the Son's identity as one who

---

[117]Pairing Jn 20:22 with Gen. 2:7, Cyril argues that "Christ restores his own Spirit in his disciples as the first fruits of a nature renewed to incorruption and glory in the divine image." Cyril of Alexandria, *Commentary on John*, 12.135, p. 369; see also Keating, "'For as Yet the Spirit Had Not Been Given,'" 236–7.

[118]Bobrinskoy, *The Mystery of the Trinity*, 65–6.

receives and bears the Spirit, the Christ "in whom resides the fullness of grace, of wisdom, of power, of authority and holiness, that is, the fullness of the Spirit."[119] Anchored especially in the Syriac tradition, this pneumatological dimension of Christology, which focuses on Christ "as the term in whom the fullness of the Divinity rests, the Spirit of grace and holiness," complements the more traditional sequence Father-Christ-Spirit.[120] Although Bobrinskoy does not specifically say so, the traditional sequence aligns more closely with an Alexandrian Christology, which assumes the priority of the personal union (incarnation) over the presence of the Spirit in the flesh of the Son.[121] Grounded especially in the mystery of Pentecost, Bobrinskoy argues that the Father-Christ-Spirit schema "best complements the first, and, linked to the first, best accounts for the proper mission of the Holy Spirit."[122] The incarnate Son who receives and bears the fullness of the Spirit from the Father for his mission becomes the glorified Lord who sends and gives the Holy Spirit for its mission in the world. In light of the biblical and patristic witness to a reciprocity of the missions of the Son and the Holy Spirit in God's salvation, in which both the Son is acted on by the Spirit and the Spirit is sent by the Son, we see how a Spirit Christology invites us to think about the identity of Jesus the Christ in a broader Trinitarian perspective—an important task in Spirit Christology that comes up especially in the next chapter. In the mystery of God, the Son is never alone. The Holy Spirit is always with him, not foreign to him. The Holy Spirit is the Son's own Spirit. In short, the Spirit of God rests on the Son and the Son of God gives the Spirit. In this reciprocity of the divine persons, the mystery of God is made accessible to us as a mystery of salvation in which the Holy Spirit plays a prominent role as both the person who enters the Son's flesh for his work of salvation (Father-Spirit-Christ) and is sent by the Son to save the flesh (Father-Christ-Spirit).

Questions

(1) Compare and contrast the Gnostic and Irenaeus' interpretations of Jesus' baptism. Do the same for the Arian and Athanasius' interpretations. In

---

[119]Ibid., 66.
[120]Ibid., 66–7.
[121]On the theological basis and function of the Father-Christ-Spirit pattern in Athanasius and Cyril of Alexandria, see Sánchez, *Receiver, Bearer, and Giver*, 26–7, 41–3, 55–6.
[122]Bobrinskoy, *The Mystery of the Trinity*, 68.

your analysis, illustrate how these theologians differ in their views of Jesus and the Spirit, and how God deals with the world.

(2) Cantalamessa identifies three views of the anointing of Jesus in the early church: historical, incarnational, and ecclesial. Describe each of these positions and give examples of theologians who hold each of them. In your description, reflect on what each position wants to highlight about Jesus' identity, including his relationship with the Spirit.

(3) How does Bobrinskoy characterize the distinction between Antiochene and Alexandrian ways of describing the Spirit's relationship with Christ? Reflect on the advantages and disadvantages of each approach.

4

The Spirit in the Trinity: Spirit and Logos Christologies in Trinitarian Key

In the preface, we listed three main questions the field of Spirit Christology raises for theologians today. The first one asks how the Spirit's role in Jesus contributes to our understanding of the incarnation and God's salvation through him (Christology and soteriology). Next comes the study of the Trinitarian implications of Jesus' life in the Spirit. What are the proper works or missions of the Son and the Spirit in God's plan of salvation, and which biblical and theological models best depict the relations among the persons of the Trinity? Finally, a Spirit Christology asks how the Son's life in the Spirit relates to human persons, particularly how to think of the discontinuity and continuity between the presence and activity of the Spirit in the Son and in the adopted children of God. The next three chapters focus more directly on how systematic theologians from various traditions and from around the world have developed answers to these questions. In this chapter, we look at the work of Jürgen Moltmann (Protestant, German) and David Coffey (Catholic, Australian) to see how their Spirit Christologies contribute to Trinitarian theology.

Moltmann frames his Spirit Christology in the context of a Trinitarian ontology of the cross, which is then applied to deal with questions about the personhood of the Holy Spirit and its relationship to the Father and the Son. In critical dialogue with historical developments in Catholic theologies of the incarnation and grace, Coffey's proposal offers arguably the most comprehensive account of the Trinity in the field of Spirit Christology to date. In drawing out the Trinitarian implications of their proposals, Moltmann and Coffey interact significantly with two prominent issues. The first one is the Eastern Orthodox churches' preference for speaking about the Holy Spirit's relation to the Son in a way that does not take away from the priority of the person of the Father in the life of the Trinity. For reasons we will explain later, the East confesses the Holy Spirit's procession from the Father (as stated in the original Niceno-Constantinopolitan Creed), in distinction from the Western churches which speak of the Holy Spirit's procession from the Father "and the Son" (*filioque*, in Latin). Theologians in the East feel that bringing the Son into the Spirit's procession takes away from the Father's unique person. Moltmann and Coffey attempt to answer this ecumenical problem between the East and the West by allowing for the teaching—with support in the East—that the Holy Spirit proceeds from the Father and receives from the Son. They explain the meaning of this proposal in their own ways. The second issue Moltmann and Coffey are especially sensitive to in their proposals is the critique heard among a number of contemporary theologians that the Spirit's procession from the Father and the Son makes the Holy Spirit seem like a purely "passive" person in relation to the other two. In their own ways, both theologians attend to this concern and offer ways in which the person of the Spirit might be seen properly in its "active" being in relation to the Father and the Son. In the economy of salvation and in the intradivine life, Moltmann speaks of the third person as the glorifying Spirit and Coffey of the Spirit as interpersonal love.

The Kenotic Spirit: Jürgen Moltmann on Christology and Trinitarian Theology in the Key of a Pneumatology of the Cross

Lyle Dabney, a former doctoral student of Jürgen Moltmann, has proposed a pneumatology of the cross as a critical response to Luther's theology of the cross. Referring to thesis twenty-one of Luther's Heidelberg Disputation (1518), Dabney claims that "with regard to the Spirit he [i.e., Luther] fails to 'call the thing what it is' because he fails to root his understanding of the

Spirit in the cross."¹ Dabney correctly interprets Luther's theses as a critique of the human attempt to know God through reason and nature as opposed to "through suffering and the cross" (thesis twenty). However, he argues that the reformer reduces the Spirit's role to the human person: "For while he [i.e. Luther] defines the Spirit formally in terms of the Trinity, he defines the Spirit materially, rather, in terms of the human."² By orienting the Spirit's work "not to the cross ... but rather to community and forgiveness and resurrection," Luther's treatment of the third article of the Creed in his Large Catechism (1529) illustrates the problem of the "medieval subordination of Pneumatology to Christology."³ As a result, all major Reformers focus on the Spirit's work "in the event of human proclaiming and believing the Gospel" but overlook grounding the Spirit's identity "in the incarnation of the Son, in his mission, in his suffering and death and resurrection."⁴ The Spirit's identity is explored in terms of his work of crucifying and raising sinners, but not in terms of the Spirit's presence and activity in the suffering Christ and the implications of this insight for the doctrine of God.

Dabney perceives a shift toward a theology of God based on the cross in Karl Barth's "declaration that 'The crucified Jesus is the image of the invisible God' [KD II/2, p. 132]; a claim that, if taken to heart, flies in the face of the entire theological tradition which had attributed the sufferings of Christ on the cross to his human nature alone in order to protect the notion of divine *apatheia*."⁵ "Apatheia" is the Greek word for "impassibility" or lack of suffering. Applied to the theology of God, *apatheia* is the idea that, in distinction from suffering creation, God the creator cannot suffer. If God suffered, then, divinity would succumb to the creaturely order of things and no longer be divinity. Dabney alludes to the classic way theologians sought to deal with this problem in light of the incarnation, namely, by clarifying that the divine Word suffered in the flesh, but not in his divinity. Dabney, however, wishes to say more, and he believes Barth opened the way for conceiving of the "God of the cross" as a "suffering, not an apathetic God."⁶ After Barth, Dabney sees in Moltmann's *Crucified God* a decisive move "to

---

¹D. Lyle Dabney, "*Pneumatologia Crucis*: Reclaiming *Theologia Crucis* for a Theology of the Spirit Today," *SJT* 53, no. 4 (2000): 514. For his dissertation, see D. Lyle Dabney, *Die Kenosis des Geistes: Kontinuität zwischen Schöpfung und Erlösung im Werk des Heiligen Geistes* (Neukirchen-Vluyn: Neukirchener Verlag, 1997).
²Dabney, "*Pneumatologia Crucis*," 515.
³Ibid.
⁴Ibid., 515–16.
⁵Ibid., 518–19.
⁶Ibid., 519.

the explicitly trinitarian question of the suffering of the threefold God on the cross" and thus to "a fundamental advance in the doctrine of God."[7] Luther saw in the cross the revelation of the Father's heart or gracious disposition to love his suffering creatures, but could not see the cross as the revelation of the Father's own suffering in relation to the Son's suffering and death. Moltmann advances the discussion with the "realization that the cross defined not just the disposition but the very being of God in the world."[8] The new development in the theology of the cross lies in the shift from soteriology to ontology, from seeing the cross in terms of *anthropo*logy to seeing it as *theo*logy proper, from its effect on humans to its effect on the Trinity.

The Kenotic Spirit's Active Role in Christ's Life, Death, and Resurrection

Reflecting on Jesus' cry of dereliction, Moltmann observes that "for the Father this cry represents the experience of the loss of the Son and for the Son it signifies an experience of abandonment by the Father. But what of the third person of the Spirit?"[9] Based on Mark's portrayal of Jesus, who "as the *Christ*, the one defined by the Spirit ... freely takes up the suffering of the cross," Dabney outlines his proposal for a pneumatology that sees the "*Spiritus Crucis*" not only at work after Christ's death but also as "the motive force in the mission of Jesus from Galilee to Golgotha" and "the Spirit of Life that leads Jesus to his death."[10] Dabney's thesis is that whereas the cross means an experience of "*absence*" for the Father and the Son in that the former feels the "loss" of his Son and the latter feels the "abandonment" of the Father, "what the Spirit experiences is a function not of *absence*, but of *presence*. For the Spirit of the Cross is *the presence of God with the Son in the eschatological absence of the Father*."[11] In the *Crucified God*, Moltmann only speaks of the kenosis of the Father and the Son revealed on the cross, with the Holy Spirit coming only afterward as "the one who 'brings the dead to life'"; therefore, Moltmann ends up portraying the third person as "a

---

[7] Ibid., 520.
[8] Ibid., 519.
[9] Ibid., 523.
[10] Ibid., 523. For a fuller account of his *pneumatologia crucis*, Dabney directs us to *Die Kenosis des Geistes*.
[11] Dabney, "*Pneumatologia Crucis*," 524.

crossless Spirit, indeed one who stands finally in contradiction to the God of the cross."[12] Dabney enriches Moltmann's kenotic Trinitarianism with a Spirit-oriented trajectory.

Dabney portrays the Spirit as one who bridges the "chasm" between the Father and the Son on the cross: "Thus, whereas the cry of Jesus reveals the yawning chasm of loss and desolation that opens to separate Father and Son, no such chasm exists between the Crucified One and the *Spiritus Crucis*, the One who suffered death on the cross and the *Spiritus Vivificans*."[13] The author adds that "it is precisely the kenotic work of the Spirit of life to plunge himself into death, hell and the grave, to 'empty himself' into the abyss of death and raise the one who, by virtue of that self-same Spirit, gave himself to death on the cross to gain new life for all creation."[14] The Spirit's kenosis in the crucified Christ's experience of "death, hell, and the grave" opens the door for assurance that the same Spirit will accompany God's suffering people in their experience of forsakenness, conforming them to Christ's cry of dereliction in anticipation of the resurrection.

Dabney shows that Moltmann progressively included in his works a vision of the Spirit's unique personhood in the perichoretic Trinity (*The Trinity and the Kingdom*), its role as the giver of life in all creation (*God in Creation*), and its determining presence in Jesus' messianic mission, death, and resurrection (*The Way of Jesus Christ*).[15] Significantly, Moltmann situates his treatment of the Spirit's role in Jesus' death within a "Spirit Christology," according to which Jesus "is present in the power of the Spirit, not merely in his last moment on the cross but in all his moments from birth onwards."[16] By descending on and dwelling in Jesus for his mission, the Spirit of God takes on the role of the "Shekinah" or God's abiding presence with Israel in her sufferings.[17] Like Dabney, Moltmann speaks of "a 'condescending' of the Spirit ... a *kenosis of the Holy Spirit*, which emptied itself and descended from the eternity of God, taking up his dwelling in this vulnerable and mortal human being Jesus."[18] The kenosis of the Spirit reveals something of its unique identity. First, the Spirit "binds itself to Jesus' destiny" and, therefore,

---

[12] D. Lyle Dabney, "The Advent of the Spirit: The Turn to Pneumatology in the Theology of Jürgen Moltmann," *Asbury Theological Journal* 48, no. 1 (1993): 98.
[13] Dabney, "*Pneumatologia Crucis*," 524.
[14] Ibid.
[15] Dabney, "The Advent of the Spirit," 100–1.
[16] Moltmann, *The Way of Jesus Christ*, 76; Jesus' "whole being is the warp and weft of the Spirit" (86).
[17] Ibid., 90. See also Jürgen Moltmann, *The Spirit of Life: A Universal Affirmation*, trans. Margaret Kohl (Minneapolis, MN: Fortress, 1992), 47–51, 54–5.
[18] Moltmann, *The Way of Jesus Christ*, 93; cf. Moltmann, *The Spirit of Life*, 61–2.

"participates in his weakness, suffering, and death on the cross."[19] Second, by descending on Jesus, the Spirit shows its disposition "to communicate itself through Jesus to other men and women."[20] Jesus receives the Spirit to give the Spirit. At his baptism, Jesus does not receive the Spirit for his mission "as a private person, but *pars toto*, representatively, as one among many, and as one for many."[21] Alluding to Augustine's image of the Spirit as the "bond of love between the Father and the Son," Moltmann refers to the Spirit as "the bond in the division" experienced by the Father's and the Son's mutual surrender on the cross.[22] The Spirit's suffering with Christ on the cross flows from the Spirit's own cruciform personhood. He proposes that "the sufferings of the Spirit" or "the self-emptying of the Spirit" make possible for Christ to suffer death through the "power" of the eternal Spirit (cf. Heb. 9:14), so that by his death he might defeat death with the result that now "indestructible life is opened up to all the dying."[23]

Moltmann calls his pneumatology a "theology of the cross."[24] Since the Shekinah Spirit is Jesus' "*companion* in suffering," Moltmann calls for a "*pneumatologia crucis*" that "stresses the operation of the Spirit in Jesus' passion and death."[25] Reflecting on Jesus' self-offering on the cross in Heb. 9:14, he clarifies that the Spirit is not only "the power that makes him [i.e., Jesus] ready to surrender his life" to the Father but also the power that "itself sustains this surrender."[26] The Spirit is not merely an immediately empowering force on Jesus during his life, but an abiding sustaining presence in him. As Jesus' companion unto death, the Spirit's work in him can be seen from the side of death or from the side of the new creation. From the side of death, Moltmann suggests that "in the strength of the indwelling and sym-pathetic divine Spirit, Jesus endures the God-forsakenness vicariously, on behalf of the God-forsaken world; and by doing so he brings the world God's intimate nearness."[27] From the side of the new creation, the Spirit is the sustaining power of Jesus' death because it is "the power of indestructible life" (see Heb. 7:16), so that "then we are already looking beyond this death

---

[19] Moltmann, *The Way of Jesus Christ*, 93.
[20] Ibid., 94.
[21] Ibid.
[22] Ibid., 174; cf. Eberhard Jüngel, *God as the Mystery of the World*, trans. Darrell L. Guder (Edinburgh: T&T Clark, 1983), 346, 368–76.
[23] Moltmann, *The Way of Jesus Christ*, 174.
[24] Moltmann, *The Spirit of Life*, 70.
[25] Ibid., 62.
[26] Ibid., 63.
[27] Ibid., 65.

to Jesus' rebirth from this same divine, quickening power of the Spirit."[28] In the Spirit, Jesus dies and is raised from the dead. In the Spirit, Jesus dies lovingly for us to bring us to God's embrace; in the Spirit, his resurrection has the power to sustain our lives beyond death so that we might share in God's own life.[29]

The Glorifying Spirit's Active Personhood in the Trinity

Moltmann's argument for a kenosis of the Spirit has implications for Trinitarian theology. The pneumatology of the cross, in Moltmann's critique of divine *apatheia*, points to an *"inward self-humiliation"* in the life of God.[30] Not only the incarnation but creation also assumes *"God's self-humiliation,"* since out of his own being's self-communicating love "the Creator has to concede to his creation space in which it can exist."[31] Through this divine self-limitation, this outward space God creates out of himself, he suffers with, from, and for the world.[32] In distinction from process theology, however, Moltmann's panentheism points out that God suffers not out of a deficiency of his being but out of a superabundance of love for creation.[33] The cross does not merely reveal the death of God but a "death *in* God," which is God's active suffering in his being with creation.[34] Moltmann's and Dabney's pneumatologies of the cross accent the kenotic Spirit's identity as a unifying or bonding presence amidst the chasm of the Son's experience of the Father's abandonment. By interceding for God's creatures in sighs of lament and protest for the current state of an unjust and decaying world, the Spirit also sustains them during their experiences of God's absence amidst

---

[28] Ibid.
[29] For a brief account of his holistic pneumatology, see Jürgen Moltmann, *The Source of Life: The Holy Spirit and the Theology of Life* (Minneapolis, MN: Fortress, 1997), 10–25.
[30] Jürgen Moltmann, *The Trinity and the Kingdom: The Doctrine of God*, trans. Margaret Kohl (Minneapolis, MN: Fortress, 1993), 119.
[31] Ibid., 60.
[32] Ibid., 61.
[33] "One cannot speak of the openness of God's love to the world and to time in the same way as the creature which is open to the world and to time out of a lack of being. Rather one must speak of the openness of God's love on the ground of divine abundance and superabundance of being." See Jürgen Moltmann, "The Trinitarian History of God," *Theology* 78 (1975): 638; cf. Moltmann, *The Trinity and the Kingdom*, 23; and Jürgen Moltmann, *Crucified God: The Cross of Christ as the Foundation and Criticism of Christian Theology*, trans. Margaret Kohl (Minneapolis, MN: Fortress, 1993), 230.
[34] Moltmann, *Crucified God*, 207, 227.

their sufferings. Out of the experience of God's absence, the Spirit who raised Christ from the dead also empowers God's suffering creatures to lament in the hope of resurrection and new creation.[35]

Moltmann observes a certain one-sidedness in the way Trinitarian relations are traditionally portrayed in the language of origin and sending, both in terms of how the persons relate to one another (immanent Trinity) and to the world (economic Trinity). The flow of the Trinitarian life moves from its origin in the Father who sends the Son and the Holy Spirit into the world, and this pattern or order reveals an intra-Trinitarian origin.[36] This classic model of the Trinity is "necessary" in the church's reflection because it clarifies that the messianic history of Jesus—including his being sent by the Father, his being anointed with the Spirit sent by the Father upon him, and his sending of the Spirit who proceeds from the Father to others—is none other than "the history of God."[37] Moreover, this descending Trinitarian pattern shows that the history of God is an "*open mystery* ... the *love of God* which proceeds out of itself ... The Trinity of the sending and seeking love which is open from the beginning."[38] Consistent with Moltmann's ontology, this openness shows God's willingness to suffer and experience history not out of some deficiency of being but out of his love for creation.

What is still missing is a complementary way of locating the history of God revealed in Jesus in its broader eschatological context, so that we see the Trinitarian relations not only in terms of "the eternal history of Christ *out of* God" but also as "the eschatological goal of the history of Christ *in* God."[39] In the "*Trinity in sending*" model described above "all activity goes out from the Father, the Son is both active and passive, but the Holy Spirit is only passive."[40] The Spirit is passively sent by the Father through the Son, but what does the Father actively receive from the Spirit through the Son? In short, glorification or transfiguration.[41] If the history of God is seen from its eschatological future and goal, a complementary "Trinity in glorification" model emerges according to which the Holy Spirit has an active role in glorifying the Father through his Son's obedience unto death and the Son

---

[35] See Moltmann, *The Spirit of Life*, 73–7.
[36] Moltmann, "The Trinitarian History of God," 636.
[37] Ibid., 637.
[38] Ibid.
[39] Ibid., 639.
[40] Ibid.
[41] See Moltmann, *The Trinity and the Kingdom*, 122–8.

through the Father's raising him from the dead.[42] The glorifying Spirit also brings about the unification of humanity with the Son and the Father through the renewal of the fellowship of creation for the worship of God, which in turns brings about the final unification of the Son with the Father at the end of history.[43] As "the unifying God," the Holy Spirit fulfills the history of God's openness to creation in order to bring creation into God.[44] Moltmann prefers to speak of the "unification" of God in the future or as the end of salvation history, rather than of the "unity" of God in eternity. In the classic Trinity in sending model, the "unity" of God is presupposed as an established reality even apart from the history of God; but the model of the Trinity in glorification clarifies that such unity can only be arrived at in light of the "unification" of the Trinity that has yet to happen in the future and is anticipated partly in Christ's resurrection.[45] The history of God, which includes the suffering of the Son on the cross and the glorifying work of the Spirit, does not only reveal the economic Trinity but "determines the inner life of the triune God from eternity to eternity."[46] This shift from unity to unification in describing Trinitarian relations is consistent with Moltmann's eschatological ontology, according to which the end of history does not merely reveal what has always been the case from the beginning but actually defines reality anew. Moltmann's Trinity in glorification corresponds to his "doxological Trinity," which transcends the distinction between the economic and the immanent Trinity: "When everything is 'in God' and 'God is all in all', then the economic Trinity is raised into and transcended in the immanent Trinity. What remains is the eternal praise of the triune God in his glory."[47]

Moltmann sees the Spirit's passive role in the sending model of the Trinity on its own as problematic for a Trinitarian theology because it seems to reduce the Spirit to the power of God and Christ. The active role given

---

[42] Moltmann, "The Trinitarian History of God," 640.
[43] Ibid., 641.
[44] Ibid., 642.
[45] Moltmann asserts that "the unity of God is the ultimate, the eschatological goal and it contains within itself the total unification of the world with God and in God. Therefore in the eschatological view the unity of God is combined with the salvation of the world, just as his glory is combined with his glorification through everything that lives." Ibid.
[46] "Just as the cross of the Son puts an impress on the inner life of the triune God, so the history of the Spirit moulds the inner life of the triune God through the joy of liberated creation when it is united with God." Ibid., 161.
[47] Ibid.

to the Holy Spirit as the glorying and unifying God in the Trinity highlights its unique and distinct subjectivity and personhood. As Moltmann puts it,

> The Spirit is not an energy proceeding from the Father or from the Son; it is a subject from whose activity the Son and the Father receive their glory and their union, as well as their glorification through the whole creation, and their world as their eternal home … the Holy Spirit as the centre of the act, which is to say as "person."[48]

This concern for ascribing the Spirit a more active personhood is at the forefront of Moltmann's Trinitarian response to the *filioque* controversy. His proposal must be located in the broader framework of the contemporary interest among Western theologians to overcome the Eastern (Greek) critique of the Western (Latin) church for unilaterally including the *filioque* clause in the Nicene Creed—a clause not found in the original Greek version of the Creed. Filioque is the Latin word for "and the Son" and, when included in the third article of the Creed, confesses that the Holy Spirit "proceeds from the Father *and the Son*" (*filioque*). Besides the unilateral move by the West to add to the Creed without consulting the East, the basic critique of the *filioque* is that the clause does not acknowledge the priority of the person of the Father in the procession of the Holy Spirit (cf. Jn 15:26). Moltmann is sympathetic to this critique, agreeing that the Holy Spirit in a sense proceeds "solely" from the Father.[49] Yet this does not yet explain how the Holy Spirit relates to the Son. To remedy this, the author distinguishes between the person or *hypostasis* of the Holy Spirit and its perichoretic *form*. Perichoresis means that the persons of the Trinity exist in a reciprocal communion with one another. While the Holy Spirit proceeds from the Father in terms of his personal or hypostatic "existence" (a statement that aligns with Moltmann's "Trinity in sending" pattern), the author notes that in terms of the perichoretic intercommunion of the three persons the Holy Spirit's procession from the Father cannot be expressed without some reference to the Son (since, after all, the Father is never without his Son). Thus Moltmann suggests that the *filioque* be expanded with the expression "the Spirit proceeds from the Father in the eternal presence of the Son" or "*proceeds from the Father of the Son*" (emphasis in the original).[50]

Even though these expressions say more about the Son-Holy Spirit relation in the *filioque*, they are still drawn in the framework of what

---

[48] Ibid., 126.
[49] Ibid., 183.
[50] Ibid., 184–5.

Moltmann later on calls a "monarchical concept of the Trinity" (akin to his term "Trinity in sending"). In this model, the Spirit's personal existence is from the Father and the Son (immanent Trinity) and corresponds to the Spirit's mission from the Father and the Son in history (economic Trinity). The author notes that this Trinitarian order (Father-Son-Spirit) applies especially to "the sending of the Spirit through Christ on the foundation of the resurrection;" but if applied in a one-sided way through the *filioque*, the Holy Spirit is "put in third place in the Trinity, and subordinated to the Son."[51] The Spirit appears as a passive person in the Trinitarian life. Yet if we think in terms of a Spirit Christology, drawing attention to "Christ's own history in the Spirit," a complementary Father-Spirit-Son Trinitarian pattern emerges in which "Christ comes from the Father in the Spirit."[52] In order to account for more reciprocal ways of thinking about the Trinitarian relations, Moltmann develops the notion of a more perichoretic view of the Son-Spirit relation. Adopting Epiphanius' famous expression, "the Holy Spirit proceeds from the Father and receives from the Son," Moltmann suggests that the Holy Spirit receives from the Son "his relational, perichoretic form."[53] In continuity with his "Trinity in glorification" model discussed earlier, in which the Holy Spirit plays an active role in glorifying the Father and the Son, Moltmann defines "the *form* of the Holy Spirit" as "his face as it is manifested in his turning to the Father and to the Son, and in the turning of the Father and the Son to him ... the Holy Spirit in the inner-trinitarian manifestation of glory."[54] The resulting interpretation of the creed in a way that moves beyond the *filioque* should read as follows: "*The Holy Spirit, who proceeds from the Father of the Son, and who receives his form from the Father and the Son*" (emphasis in the original).[55] The author later refers to this Spirit-Son-Father pattern as the "eucharistic concept of the Trinity" and commends it as the best way to highlight the Spirit's active personhood in relation to the other two persons: "Here all activities proceed from the indwelling Spirit, all mediation takes place through the Son, and the Father is purely the recipient of the thanksgiving and songs of praise of his creatures."[56] Ultimately, Moltmann sees the perichoresis of the three

---

[51] Moltmann, *The Spirit of Life*, 293.
[52] Ibid.
[53] Moltmann, *The Trinity and the Kingdom*, 186; Epiphanius (367–403) uses this expression drawn from Jn 16:14-15 in his *Ancoratus* of 374 to show the Spirit's dependence on the Son. But he does not explain how to interpret the expression. See Congar, *I Believe in the Holy Spirit*, vol. 3, 27.
[54] Moltmann, *The Trinity and the Kingdom*, 187.
[55] Ibid.
[56] Moltmann, *The Spirit of Life*, 298.

persons of the Trinity as the ultimate ontological principle for talking about God, and thus as moving beyond all linear models of the Trinity (including the monarchical and eucharistic Trinity models). In the communion of the persons, all the relations are simultaneous and reciprocal, and this perichoretic reality becomes "the most important theological objection to the Filioque."[57] It is this perichoretic unity of the divine persons that best manifests the type of communion human persons are called to image and "experience in love, in friendship, in the community of Christ's people which is filled by the Spirit, and in the just society."[58]

Moltmann's pneumatology of the cross, grounded in a Spirit Christology, illustrates how the Spirit is not merely sent by the Son after his mission but serves an active role in the Son's mission. The Spirit empowers Jesus throughout his life, sustains him in death with his presence, and vivifies him in the resurrection. Moving beyond reducing the Spirit as proceeding from the Father and the Son (*filioque*), the Spirit also plays an active role in the Trinity as the glorifying Spirit in whom the Father and the Son face the Spirit and vice versa in a simultaneous or perichoretic manifestation of glory. The Spirit also accompanies those who share in the Spirit of life amidst their sufferings, cries out in them its discontent with an unjust world, and fills them with the hope of God's justice and a sharing in Christ's glory in an eternal Trinitarian doxology. By linking the Spirit to Christology, Trinitarian theology, and anthropology, Moltmann offers a proposal for addressing the types of questions raised by a Spirit Christology today.

The Spirit as Interpersonal Love: David Coffey on the Contribution of Spirit Christology to the Theology of the Trinity

Australian Catholic theologian David Coffey has offered a mature Trinitarian synthesis of Logos and Spirit Christologies. In *Deus Trinitas*, Coffey pairs the former with a "descending, Johannine Christology," corresponding to the traditional "procession" model of the Trinity in which the Holy Spirit

---

[57] Ibid.
[58] Ibid., 309; cf. Moltmann, *The Source of Life*, 89–102.

proceeds from the Father and the Son; and the latter with an "ascending, Synoptic Christology," aligning with a more comprehensive "return" model of the Trinity in which "Jesus, having been sent forth from the Father, *returns* to him through his life and death in the power of the Holy Spirit" (italics mine).[59] Methodologically, before proposing models that describe the eternal relations among the persons of the Trinity (immanent Trinity), the author tracks two major "biblical" models of the Trinity in the New Testament, namely, the mission and the bestowal (later called return) models. A description of these models and their implications for understanding the Spirit's role in the Trinity, the life of Christ, and our lives follow.

The Return Model of the Trinity

The "mission model," which follows the pattern "Father–Son–Holy Spirit," highlights "the outward movement of the Son and the Holy Spirit from the Father."[60] Coffey finds "the clearest and most explicit" example of this pattern in Jn 15:26, where Jesus promises he will send the Paraclete from the Father to his disciples.[61] Inspired in Augustine's view of the Holy Spirit as the mutual love of the Father and the Son (also known as the "mutual love theory"), Coffey initially called the second biblical pattern—characterized by the order "Father, Holy Spirit, Son"—the "bestowal model" because it describes "the bestowal of the Holy Spirit by the Father and the Son on each other."[62] Later on, the bestowal model is incorporated or expanded into a more comprehensive "return model," which follows the order "Father Holy Spirit–Son–Holy Spirit–Father," and in doing so adds "the return of the Son in the Holy Spirit to the Father."[63] This return scheme acknowledges that the New Testament does bear witness not only to the Father's sending of the Son and the Holy Spirit to save the world but also to "the return of Christ, and of us with him, to the Father, in the power of the Holy Spirit."[64]

Biblical texts that speak of the Father's bestowal of the Holy Spirit on his son Jesus, such as at his baptism at the Jordan (Mk 1:9-11), and especially

---

[59] Coffey, *Deus Trinitas*, 4–5. The "procession" model is the immanent side of the biblical "mission" model in which the Holy Spirit is sent by the Father and the Son (cf. 21). Moreover, the biblical "return" model of the Trinity has its corresponding immanent model "in which the Holy Spirit is seen as the objectivization of the mutual love of the Father and the Son" (4).
[60] Ibid., 43.
[61] Ibid., 34.
[62] Ibid., 44.
[63] Ibid.
[64] Ibid., 35.

from the very beginning of his existence (Mt. 1:18-25; Lk. 1:26-38; cf. Jn 3:34), lead to reflection on the "sinlessness" of Jesus as God's beloved son.[65] In keeping with Jesus' role as the Servant of Yahweh (see Isa. 42:1 in the baptism narrative), the bestowal of the Holy Spirit on him results in his "unswerving fidelity and obedience to the Father throughout life and especially in his death."[66] Coffey finds in these texts the biblical foundation for Augustine's more speculative mutual love theory. By identifying the Spirit with God's "love" in an interpersonal sense, Coffey can describe the Father-Son relation in terms of the Spirit in whom they exist for (love) one another. He sums up his proposal as follows: "The Spirit is the love of the Father for Jesus, poured out on him in a radical and unique way and experienced as such on the part of Jesus. The Spirit, through the answering love it evoked from him, enabled him to live his whole life in dedicated obedience to the Father's will."[67] Because the Son's love for the Father in the Spirit is expressed in his human life, Coffey speaks somewhat innovatively of the Spirit as "humanized" in the Son, and thus sees a sort of "incarnation" of the Holy Spirit (as love) in the life of Jesus.[68] In doing so, Coffey depicts the Spirit's presence in Jesus in a way that is similar but not equal to the divine Son's presence in his own humanity (incarnation). As he puts it, "in a way analogous to the Incarnation of divine being in human being in the person of Jesus, there is an incarnation of divine love in human love in the love of Jesus, this latter incarnation being the Holy Spirit."[69] While a Logos Christology focuses on the incarnation of divine *being* in the person of the Son, a Spirit Christology emphasizes the "incarnation" or "humanization" of divine *love* (Spirit) in the divine Son as expressed in his human love for the Father and for us.

Not only does Coffey speak of the Spirit interpersonally as the Father's love for Jesus and as Jesus' reciprocal love for the Father but also as the love of Jesus poured out for other humans as a result of his obedient self-giving to the Father unto death. The latter sense can be gleaned from Jn 19:30 (read in conjunction with Jn 7:38-39 and 19:34-35), where John uses the Greek expression *paredoken* (meaning "delivered up" or "handed over") to mean not only that Jesus physically died but also that he gave the Holy Spirit to the church.[70] The Holy Spirit appears as the fruit of the cross, as

---

[65] Ibid., 37.
[66] Ibid.
[67] Ibid.
[68] Ibid., 39.
[69] Ibid.
[70] Ibid., 39–40.

it were, the overflow or outpouring of Jesus' self-giving to the Father unto death.[71] Similar to Vanhoye's and others' interpretation of Heb. 9:14, Coffey sees the reference to "Christ, who through eternal Spirit offered himself without blemish to God" as further proof that Jesus' act of self-offering in death, "which gathered up and reexpressed the obedience and love that characterized his whole life, was performed in the power of the Holy Spirit conferred on him by God."[72] Coffey sums up his biblical reflection on the Spirit as the mutual love of the Father and the Son as follows:

> The Father bestows the Holy Spirit on Jesus as his love for him. ... Jesus further appropriates this unique Gift of the Spirit ... in the course of his life through his unfailing obedience and answering love of the Father, and in his death definitively returns to the Father in love by returning the Holy Spirit to him (though without thereby losing it himself). From this truly biblical theology the Holy Spirit emerges as the mutual love of the Father and the Son, even though, as Augustine pointed out, nowhere does Scripture actually call the Spirit love.[73]

The Spirit Proceeds from and Is the Mutual Love between the Father and the Son

From a biblical (functional) theology of the movement of the Spirit from the Father to Jesus and from Jesus to the Father, Coffey arrives at an immanent (ontological) theology of the Holy Spirit as the interpersonal love in whom the Father and the Son exist. Two benefits of this return model of the immanent Trinity lie in their capacity for generating a more ecumenical view of immanent Trinitarian relations and a clearer picture of what makes the person of the Holy Spirit unique in the Trinitarian life. In terms of the immanent Trinity, Coffey shows how his return model of

---

[71] The pneumatic reading of Jn 19:30, 34 (in light of Jn 7:37-39 and other texts) is commonly adopted in contemporary Catholic theology. For exegetical reflections, see Felix Porsch, *El Espíritu Santo, defensor de los creyentes: la actividad del Espíritu según el evangelio de san Juan*, trans. Severiano Talavero Tovar (Salamanca: Secretariado Trinitario, 1983), 31-4, 102-7; and Antonio García-Moreno, "El Espíritu Santo, fruto de la Cruz," in Pedro Rodríguez, José R. Villar, Ramiro Pellitero, José Luis Gutiérrez, and José Enériz, eds., *El Espíritu Santo y la Iglesia* (Pamplona: Universidad de Navarra, 1999), 71-7; for systematic reflections, see O'Donnell, "In Him and Over Him," 35-7; and Joseph H. P. Wong, "The Holy Spirit in the Life of Jesus and of the Christian," *Greg* 73, no. 1 (1992): 69-72.
[72] Coffey, *Deus Trinitas*, 40.
[73] Ibid., 41 (cf. 48).

the Trinity can assist in thinking through the *filioque* controversy. Let us recall that the Eastern (Greek) church's main critique of the Western (Latin) addition of the clause "and the Son" (*filioque*) to the Nicene Creed is both its unilateral inclusion in an ecumenical creed and its lack of appreciation for the priority of the Father in the procession of the Holy Spirit (cf. Jn 15:26). While sympathetic to the Eastern critique, Catholic theologian Yves Congar has argued that the *filioque* belongs fundamentally to the structure of Western Trinitarian theology, according to which the distinction of the persons is derived from the unity of God. Because the Holy Spirit proceeds from the Father "and the Son," a clear distinction in the one God emerges between the generation of the Son and the procession of the Holy Spirit from the Father.[74] By drawing such distinction, the Holy Spirit appears as a distinct person. The Latin framework also highlights in the strongest possible way the consubstantial unity of the Father and the Son, which deals satisfactorily with the historical problem of Arianism—a historical reason for the addition of the *filioque* in the Western version of the Creed.[75] In basic agreement with this consensus, Coffey sees the *filioque* as the Western formulation of the traditional "procession" model of the Trinity and its "dogmatic intent" as yielding "the hypostatic distinction of the Holy Spirit."[76]

Yet he also sees the need for a complementary biblical and patristic expression of the Trinity that, while affirming the Son's role in the Holy Spirit's procession from the Father can also acknowledge the Father's monarchy. Such an expression would approximate the intent of Augustine's historic assertion that, although the Holy Spirit proceeds from the Father and the Son, the Holy Spirit proceeds "principally" (*principaliter*) from the Father.[77] In the Trinitarian order, there is always a priority of the Father in relation to the Son. To attend to the Eastern concern, Coffey commends the use of St. Gregory of Nyssa's expression "the Holy Spirit proceeds from the Father and receives from the Son," which in his estimation fits well with his more comprehensive "return" model of the Trinity.[78] When interpreted in the

---

[74] Congar, *I Believe in the Holy Spirit*, vol. 3, 373.
[75] Ibid., 213.
[76] Coffey, *Deus Trinitas*, 47.
[77] Ibid., 53. For Augustine's expression, see *On the Holy Trinity* 15.26.47, in NPNF² 3:225.
[78] Gregory uses the expression "the Spirit comes from the Father through the Son" (known as the *per filium*, meaning "through the Son"). Congar notes that these expressions speak to "a certain dependence on the part of the Spirit, in his being, with regard to the Son" or point out that "the Son played a part in the intra-divine existence, although that part was not of a causal nature [as in the case of the Father]." Congar, *I Believe in the Holy Spirit*, vol. 3, 32.

framework of Augustine's mutual love theory, Nyssa's expression can show that the Holy Spirit logically proceeds from the Father *first* as his love for the Son.[79] Yet in Coffey's return model, the Holy Spirit is also the Son's reciprocal love for the Father. This latter point further clarifies what the Holy Spirit *receives* from the Son in the immanent Trinity, namely, "the character of being the Son's love for the Father."[80] Bringing both processional and return models together in a Western account of the immanent Trinity, Coffey, following Thomas Aquinas, suggests that the Holy Spirit both "proceeds from" the Father and the Son and "occurs between them, in so far as he is their mutual love."[81] With these contributions, Coffey shows the ecumenical productivity of his "procession" and "return" models of the Trinity for dealing with the *filioque* controversy. Moreover, the Holy Spirit cannot be seen merely as passive in relation to the Father and the Son because, in its interpersonal being, the person of the Spirit is the mutual love in whom they exist for one another.

The Spirit's Sanctifying Role in the Incarnation and Grace

There is yet another benefit of Coffey's proposal. At the level of the economic Trinity (the divine persons in relation to human persons), the return model yields a richer (Trinitarian) way of describing what it means for God to communicate his own life (self-communication) to humanity in both the incarnation and in the mystery of grace. To understand the author's contribution in this area, we need to grasp his desire to overcome a certain way of conceiving the relationship between God and the world in Catholic scholastic theology. In describing God's relation to creation, scholastic theologians emphasized the unity of the triune God and his unified works in the world, according to the axiom "the works of the Trinity toward the world are indivisible" (Lat. *opera ad extra indivisa sunt*). To allow for distinctions among the divine persons, they used the doctrine of *appropriation* as a

---

[79] Coffey, *Deus Trinitas*, 63.
[80] Ibid.
[81] Coffey, "Did You Receive the Holy Spirit When You Believed?," 62; Coffey notes that the Holy Spirit "proceeds *as* the mutual love of the Father and the Son … while the first [procession model] is concerned with the bare *fact* of the procession of the Holy Spirit, the second [return model] is concerned with the *manner* of the procession" (64). For Coffey's full proposal on the *filioque*, see ibid., 42–74.

strategy. Accordingly, certain works can be especially appropriated to one divine person (say, creation to the Father), even though all persons act as the one God in the world. However, if pushed to the extreme, this move can lead to odd conclusions. Can one, for instance, speak of the incarnation as a work that can be equally appropriated to any of the divine persons, or is this work unique to the person of the Son, since in biblical narrative only the second person of the Trinity becomes incarnate? Karl Rahner observed this problem in the neo-scholastic theology of the Trinity and argued that the incarnation cannot be merely "appropriated" to the Son but must be an act "proper" to his person.[82] Could something similar be said of the Holy Spirit's indwelling of the graced person? This move too was difficult to achieve since, in scholastic theology, the indwelling of the graced person was ascribed to the three divine persons acting in indivisible unity toward the human creature. Rahner moves beyond the neo-scholastic theology on this point, arguing that the one God communicates his own self to the human creature in grace according to what is proper to each person of the Trinity in its own peculiarity.[83] Here Rahner makes room for later theologians to inquire into what is peculiar to the person of the Holy Spirit in its sanctifying indwelling of the human person.

A former colleague of Coffey at Marquette University, Del Colle argues that through the use of "anointing" and "spiration" language neo-scholastic thinkers such as Scheeben and Mersch started to make room for ways to articulate the uniqueness of the Holy Spirit's proper work (*proprium*) in relation to humanity.[84] By drawing attention to the Holy Spirit's role in the sanctification of the Son's humanity (incarnation) and especially human persons by adoption (grace), Del Colle shows how a Spirit Christology can yield a robust theology of the third person that links the theology of the Trinity to the mystery of salvation. The author commends Coffey's contribution toward recovering a proper work for the Spirit in Western theology.[85] The problem with Western theology, and its limited use of the order Father–Son–Spirit in the "procession" model of the Trinity, lies in seeing the Spirit's sanctifying mission merely as "appropriated" to it (since the Father and the Son also sanctify) and as occurring only after the Son's mission comes to completion in his death and resurrection.[86] What is

---

[82] Rahner, *The Trinity*, 23.
[83] Ibid., 34–5.
[84] Colle, *Christ and the Spirit*, 78–9.
[85] For Coffey's full proposal, see "*Did You Receive the Holy Spirit When You Believed?*," 10–42.
[86] Coffey, *Deus Trinitas*, 41–2.

missing from this picture is the recognition of the Holy Spirit's "proper" sanctifying mission and the simultaneity of its mission with that of the Son from the first moment of his human existence. To remedy this, Coffey argues that the Holy Spirit's proper mission is to create and sanctify a human nature in a way that makes possible its "unity with the Son" (incarnation) and also brings graced persons into "*union* with the Son" (grace).[87] Here Coffey's Spirit Christology follows the pattern "Father–Holy Spirit–Son–Holy Spirit–Father" of the return model. Applied to our sanctification, the model shows that Spirit makes us holy by causing us "to be caught up in Christ's response of love to the Father, so that we participate in their mutual love, which of course is the Holy Spirit in action."[88] Coffey notes, however, that unlike the Son's incarnation in which a human nature is united to his divine person, the Spirit's indwelling in human persons does not make them divine persons (or incarnations of the Spirit supplanting the third person).

Considering Coffey's overall proposal, one notes how his comprehensive return model has the capacity to address important issues raised by Spirit Christology today. He shows how Jesus and the Spirit relate to one another in a biblical narrative of the Trinity, how this narrative offers a basis for thinking about the Holy Spirit as the interpersonal love of the Father and the Son in the immanent Trinity in a way that does not do away with but complements a Logos Christology's processional model. He also illustrates how the proper mission of the Holy Spirit in the economic Trinity lies in its unique sanctifying role to bring a human nature to unity with the Son in the incarnation and human persons to union with the Son in grace.

---

[87] Ibid., 42; Coffey argues that "in the one act, of the Father, in the Holy Spirit, the sacred humanity is created, sanctified substantially, and joined in hypostatic union to the divine Son" (108). Coffey agrees that there is a sense in which the Son's incarnation logically precedes its sanctification by the Spirit, if the term sanctification is understood to mean a derived holiness like that of the saints. However, in the case of the Son, his sanctification is not derived but proper to his person. Using the distinction between "accidental" and "substantial" sanctification, Coffey asserts that because the Holy Spirit is oriented toward Christ (an orientation he calls "entelechy"), the latter's incarnation can be seen as the Spirit's act. Such assertion sees the Son's sanctification to be proper to his own person (substantial) and not merely a habitual sanctification as in the case of other saints (accidental). See Coffey, *"Did You Receive the Holy Spirit When You Believed?,"* 105–10 (cf. 40); Ladaria, however, notes that "accidental" sanctification, when applied to Christ, simply means that the Son's humanity does not change substantially as a result of the Spirit's creation and sanctification of this humanity. It is a humanity already assumed and constituted by the Logos who alone unites it to his person, even if the Spirit also creates this humanity, sanctifies it, and is ever active in it throughout the Son' life. I resonate with Ladaria's warning about inverting the order Father-Son-Spirit by assigning the union to the Spirit instead of the Logos, even if union and sanctification are simultaneous. See Ladaria, *La Trinidad*, 189, 197–9.
[88] Coffey, *"Did You Receive the Holy Spirit When You Believed?,"* 103.

A Concluding Reflection

Moltmann locates the Spirit's kenosis in the divine life in order to highlight God's suffering love for creation. This move requires a relational ontology of divine love embracing creation rather than an ontology of being that distinguishes between God and creation or between the economic and immanent Trinity. Moltmann's proposal also requires a perichoretic ontology in which the divine equality among the persons admits no order or *taxis* among them. What if Moltmann's legitimate concern for a perichoretic ontology of the Trinity is included within a Trinitarian ontology that still allows for the distinction between God and creation, as well as proper distinctions among equally divine persons? Why not have the best of both worlds?

To avoid the risk of compromising God's transcendence and freedom in relation to creation, or collapsing the economic into the immanent Trinity, Moltmann's Trinitarian theology could include Coffey's relational or perichoretic conception of the Spirit as the personal love in whom the Father and the Son exist for one another. Indeed, Coffey's return model of the Trinity aligns to some extent with Moltmann's eucharistic and doxological models.[89] But unlike Moltmann's doxological model, the return model does not do away with the order of Trinitarian relations in which the Spirit proceeds from the Father and the Son (*filioque*) or from the Father through the Son (*per filium*).[90] Maintaining some form of the processional model, which both the West and East agree to on biblical and theological grounds, would be congenial to Moltmann's admission that there is room for a Trinity in the sending (or monarchical) model, even if—as he rightly notes—it is not the only way to speak about the Trinity.[91] Without dismissing the *filioque*, we may call Coffey's return model an *in spiritu* model of the Trinity, according to which the Father begets the Son and the Son is begotten of the Father in the Spirit, who is their mutual love.[92]

---

[89] Del Colle, "A Response to Jürgen Moltmann and David Coffey," in Bradford E. Hinze and D. Lyle Dabney, eds., *Advents of the Spirit: An Introduction to the Current Study of Pneumatology* (Milwaukee, WI: Marquette University Press, 2001), 341.
[90] For Coffey's full integration of the processional and mutual love models, see *Deus Trinitas*, 33–65; for a similar proposal, see Ladaria, *La Trinidad*, 219–36.
[91] Colle, "A Response," 341.
[92] "I hold that in the immanent Trinity the Son returns to the Father 'in' the Spirit, but that is possible only because the Son is co-principle with the Spirit." David Coffey, "Spirit Christology and the

The processional model yields a descending Trinity that is distinct from and free for loving creation, and the mutual love model shows how the impassible Spirit enters our own broken lives—a form of kenosis, as it were—to bring us into the loving embrace of the Father and the Son. Correspondingly, our sharing in God's life occurs by the Spirit's gratuitous descent from above into our lives, which the processional model grounds. The mutual love model clarifies in a Trinitarian way how the Spirit of Christ brings about such sharing in God's life by grace.

Questions

(1) At the end of Chapter 3, Bobrinskoy proposes a "Father-Spirit-Christ" Trinitarian pattern that complements the traditional "Father-Christ-Spirit" order or *taxis*. How does his proposal align with Moltmann's and Coffey's models of the Trinity? What concerns drive these two authors' proposals?

(2) What does Moltmann's kenotic Spirit tell us about God's character, the Spirit's identity, the Spirit's activity in Jesus, Trinitarian theology, and the Spirit's work in our lives? Answer the same question, replacing "kenotic Spirit" with the term "glorifying Spirit." How do the kenotic and glorifying aspects of the Spirit relate to each other?

(3) What does Coffey's "return model" of the Trinity tell us about who the Spirit is, how the Spirit relates to the Father and the Son, and what the Spirit does in Jesus and in us?

(4) Define the term *filioque* and explain the controversy behind the use of this term. Show how Moltmann and Coffey use their Spirit Christologies to deal with the *filioque* issue.

Trinity," in *Advents of the Spirit*, 335. For my proposal in this direction, see Sánchez, *Receiver, Bearer, and Giver*, 132–47.

5

Who Do You Say That I Am? The Complementarity of Spirit and Logos Christologies

In the previous chapter, we looked at two major figures, a Protestant (Moltmann) and a Catholic (Coffey), who have incorporated the insights of a Spirit Christology into their broader systematic and Trinitarian programs. In this chapter, we look at how three theologians integrate Spirit and Logos Christologies in the context of their respective Christological traditions. They are Leopoldo Sánchez (Lutheran, United States, originally Chile-Panama), Myk Habets (Reformed, New Zealand), and Skip Jenkins (Pentecostal, United States). Similar to Coffey's and Del Colle's Spirit Christologies, they retrieve, expand, and adapt partially eclipsed elements of their traditions.

Studies in Spirit Christology today bring attention to often forgotten teachings in Christian traditions concerning the Holy Spirit's role in Christology and Trinitarian theology. Theologians in the field see as part of their task the retrieval of these biblical, patristic, Reformation, and post-Reformation insights in the formulation of Christology, trying to understand how they shed light on and, in light of recent research or current questions, be developed or expanded upon. The last section of this chapter looks at how three theologians working from their traditions retrieve ways in which their own theological heritage contributes to a robust Spirit Christology that stands in continuity with Scripture and the Trinitarian theology and

Christology of Nicaea and Chalcedon. We will present these representative theologians in the chronological order of the main historical voices they seek to retrieve in their Spirit Christologies. Although argued ecumenically in conversation with theological traditions not their own, Sánchez, Habets, and Jenkins take seriously the historical contexts and theological frameworks aligning most closely with their own Lutheran, Reformed, and Pentecostal traditions. Each theologian has not only interacted with contemporary works in their proposals but also reimagined underutilized or underdeveloped Christological and pneumatological elements from their own traditions.

Coming from the Lutheran tradition, I develop the Logos Christology of the German theologian Martin Chemnitz (1522–1586) in a pneumatic trajectory by proposing a pneumatic category or *genus* of the Spirit (*genus pneumatikon*) that highlights the humanity of the Son's reception of the Holy Spirit and its gifts for his work of salvation. Reformed theologian Myk Habets finds especially in the incipient Spirit Christology of English Puritan theologian John Owen (1616–1683) a fresh way to posit the direct influence of the Holy Spirit on the assumed humanity of the Son and in all his works. Finally, Pentecostal theologian Skip Jenkins sees in the Christology and pneumatology of Scottish "proto-Pentecostal" pastor Edward Irving (1792–1834) a way of articulating the Holy Spirit's role in making holy and empowering the fallen humanity the Son assumed in order to save, sanctify, and empower other humans by the same Spirit. Although all these contemporary theologians draw out the Trinitarian implications of their proposals, particularly in conversation with theologians such as Luis Ladaria, Thomas Weinandy, and David Coffey, this chapter focuses on their retrievals of classic voices from their traditions in the development of a "mutual complementarity" approach to Spirit Christology.[1]

---

[1] All theologians offer responses to the *filioque* controversy. Jenkins's proposal aligns with and expands on Coffey's, Myk Habets's is closest to Weinandy's. Although somewhat critical of Weinandy's reasons for supplementing the *filioque*, I appreciate his insight into the Holy Spirit's place in the Son's generation from the Father. However, my own proposal as a whole draws significantly from Ladaria's and Coffey's appreciation for the integration of both procession and mutual love models of the Trinity in the West. All theologians listed here are sensitive to the need for a perichoretic view of Trinitarian relations that does not do away with the order or *taxis* of Trinitarian processions. See Jenkins, *A Spirit Christology*, 241–91, 297–319; Habets, *The Anointed Son*, 220–7; and Sánchez, *Receiver, Bearer, and Giver*, 110–47.

Logos and Spirit Christologies: A Diversity of Approaches toward Complementarity

Reflecting on the relationship between Logos and Spirit Christologies, Dutch Reformed theologian Cornelis van der Kooi has distinguished between three different approaches to the question of "how we have to qualify the presence of God in Christ."[2] Van der Kooi calls the first approach the "substitute" model. Its adherents see Spirit Christology "as a substitute for Logos Christology" because they argue mainly that the latter "threatens the humanity of Jesus."[3] In the first chapter, we discussed Roger Haight's proposal as an example of this approach.[4] We called it a "post-Nicene" Spirit Christology, not in a chronological sense but in a theological sense, in order to highlight its aim to revise significantly the Christological and Trinitarian teachings inspired by the Council of Nicaea (AD 325), such as those of Constantinople (AD 381) and Chalcedon (AD 451). Van der Kooi observes that at times favoring the "substitute" model was driven by "the presupposition that a 'higher' Logos Christology was in fact a later development in the history of the church."[5] However, it is now common to acknowledge that the New Testament already has the highest Christology possible, one that identifies Jesus with Yahweh.[6] In spite of its criticism of Logos Christology, the author appreciates the model's approach to see Jesus "first and foremost as a human being, one of us," and its awareness that Jesus "as redeemer was also the one who has to be followed."[7]

---

[2] Cornelis van der Kooi, "On the Identity of Jesus Christ: Spirit Christology and Logos Christology in Converse," in *TAT*, 193; cf. Cornelis van der Kooi, *This Incredible Benevolent Force: The Holy Spirit in Reformed Theology and Spirituality* (Grand Rapids, MI: Eerdmans, 2018), 38–45.
[3] Van der Kooi, "On the Identity of Jesus Christ," 198–9.
[4] As examples of the substitute model, van der Kooi discusses Haight and Hendrikus Berkhof. See *This Incredible Benevolent Force*, 47–51.
[5] Van der Kooi, "On the Identity of Jesus Christ," 199.
[6] See Carlos Raúl Sosa Siliezar, *La Condición Divina de Jesús: Cristología y Creación en el Evangelio de Juan* (Salamanca: Ediciones Sígueme, 2016); Larry W. Hurtado, *Lord Jesus Christ: Devotion to Jesus in Earliest Christianity* (Grand Rapids, MI: Eerdmans, 2003); and Richard Bauckham, *God Crucified: Monotheism and Christology in the New Testament* (Grand Rapids, MI: Eerdmans, 1998).
[7] Van der Kooi, "On the Identity of Jesus Christ," 199.

Next, van der Kooi speaks of the "alternative" model, according to which "Spirit Christology and Logos Christology … are two parallel avenues for expressing what was so unique about Jesus."⁸ He sees Dutch Catholic theologian Piet Schoonenberg as the main example of an approach that asserts both Christologies "are each independently able to say everything that ought to be said in a Christology."⁹ Schoonenberg's Spirit Christology seeks to overcome the potential danger of "docetism" in a Logos Christology's description of the incarnation as enhypostatic—meaning that the "human nature" of the Logos is not its own hypostasis (anhypostatic) but has its existence in the hypostasis or person of the Logos (enhypostatic)—which can give the impression that Jesus is not a "human being" or "fully human."¹⁰ Docetism (from the Greek dokéō, which means "to seem") is the idea that Christ is essentially divine and only "seems" to be human. To make Christology intelligible to the modern mind, which understands the human person to be "a center of freedom and self-consciousness," Schoonenberg proposes to speak of an "inverted enhypostasis" of the "divine nature" of the Logos "in the human nature of Jesus."¹¹ In this way, Schoonenberg seeks to see the Logos not as "the central personalizing element in Jesus Christ, but the other way around, his humanity as the personalizing element."¹²

By saying that "the divine Logos is enhypostatic in the human nature of Jesus," Schoonenberg wants to highlight how the Logos enters "a process of becoming, of change under the human condition" in which "the Spirit as the power of God … is the decisive factor in the life and acts of Jesus."¹³ In response to critics, Schoonenberg eventually speaks of a *"reciprocal enhypostasis,"* which claims that "the mystery of Jesus Christ consists only in the fact that God, in revealing himself, was present in the highest degree in the human person Jesus … because that fact … *includes* that the human person of Jesus is present in, sustained by, enhypostatic in God's Logos."¹⁴ This is Schoonenberg's way of holding two assertions dialectically or in paradoxical tension with one another, namely, that God the Logos only exists as the human person Jesus (inverted enhypostasis of the Logos in

---

⁸ Ibid., 200; cf. van der Kooi, *This Incredible Benevolent Force*, 51–5, 64–5.
⁹ Van der Kooi, "On the Identity of Jesus Christ," 200. For Schoonenberg's thought, see "Spirit Christology and Logos Christology," and *El Espíritu, la Palabra y el Hijo* (Spanish translation of the original *De Geest, het Woord en de Zoon*).
¹⁰ Van der Kooi, "On the Identity of Jesus Christ," 201.
¹¹ Ibid., 200–1.
¹² Ibid., 200.
¹³ Van der Kooi, *This Incredible Benevolent Force*, 53.
¹⁴ Schoonenberg, "Spirit Christology and Logos Christology," 365.

Jesus) and that this is only the case because the human person Jesus only exists in the divine Logos (akin to the classical teaching on the enhypostasis of Jesus or, more precisely, the human nature of Jesus, in the person of the Logos). Significantly, Schoonenberg goes on to say that a Spirit Christology can achieve the same result as a Logos Christology, offering an account of God's presence in Jesus on its own—the only exception being that one cannot speak of Jesus as having his existence in the person of the Holy Spirit. He writes:

> Because the Spirit is equally divine as the Logos, the Spirit too is not only present in Jesus, but also embraces, contains and sustains his human reality, although we do not say that it is enhypostatic in the Spirit. ... [Jesus] *is* divine by the Spirit's presence pervading him ... in both christologies Jesus can be seen as fully divine and fully human.[15]

Schoonenberg speaks of both the Logos and the Spirit (also known as Wisdom) as becoming personalized in the human being Jesus. Logos and Spirit are only extensions of the one God until, in the history of Jesus Christ, they *"become persons"*—the Logos at the incarnation, and the Holy Spirit at Jesus' glorification (resurrection/ascension).[16] Van der Kooi has doubts about the plausibility of Schoonenberg's language of a historical becoming of the one God into Trinitarian persons in the human history of Jesus, including its accompanying proposal that a Spirit Christology on its own can carry the whole weight of a Logos Christology.[17]

Like the "substitute" option, the "alternative" one shows a concern for recovering Christ's full humanity through a Spirit Christology over against what is perceived to be a docetic risk in Logos Christology. But neither one of these options integrates both Christologies. This leads us to what van der Kooi calls the "mutual complementarity" approach, which "holds Spirit Christology to be a substantial complement to the Logos tradition ... on the

---

[15] Ibid., 365; cf. Schoonenberg, *El Espíritu, la Palabra y el Hijo*, 151–3.
[16] Schoonenberg, "Spirit Christology and Logos Christology," 368.
[17] By entering a process of becoming, of change, and human conditions, the figure of the Logos becomes personalized. So the humanity of Christ is the supporting and bearing factor that effects an ongoing process of the Logos becoming a person. In this process the Spirit as the power of God ... as Wisdom ... is the decisive factor in the life and acts of Jesus. ... The question can be raised as to what exactly the Logos or Wisdom is in this interpretation. Is it a *sphere of divinity*, a *force field* that only becomes personalized in the human self-consciousness of Jesus? Do we then still meet God in person in Jesus Christ?
 Van der Kooi, "On the Identity of Jesus Christ," 202 (cf. 206); see also Sánchez, *Receiver, Bearer, and Giver*, 58–62.

Trinity and Christology from the fourth and fifth centuries."[18] In the first chapter, we called this approach Nicene (Chalcedonian) Spirit Christology because of the role Nicaea and the subsequent councils it inspired played in the church's formulation of its Trinitarian, Christological, and pneumatological foundations. Methodologically, "mutual complementarity" proceeds by reintroducing those "pneumatological elements in the biblical witness that were forgotten or suppressed in the course of the development of doctrine … [in order] to deepen and enrich Logos Christology."[19]

We can only speak of the Logos in terms of the New Testament witness to the life and mission of the man Jesus of Nazareth, who is the Son of God and lives by the power of the Holy Spirit. The challenge for systematic theology is to bring together these filial (sonship) and pneumatic (Spirit) aspects of Jesus' identity.[20] The descending (Logos/Son) Christology of the Gospel of John and Paul's epistles must be retained because it prevents us from reducing Jesus to a man inhabited by the Spirit and "articulates the unique anchoring of his Sonship in God."[21] Logos Christology assists a Spirit Christology by clarifying that the man Jesus who bears the Spirit of God is none other than the Son of God in the flesh. The ascending Christology of the synoptic gospels, which van der Kooi associates with a Spirit Christology, also enriches a Logos Christology because it "enlightens and clarifies the inner dynamics by which the Sonship of Jesus is realized" in the history of salvation for our benefit.[22] A Spirit Christology allows us to think of the Logos in terms of his concrete humanity, so that "not only does the humanity of Jesus find its center in the Word, but also … the Word fully subsists in and through the humanity of Jesus … in such a way that the order of humanity is not removed."[23] There is a sense in which, because God took upon himself our humanity, the infinite is capable of the finite (*infinitum capax finiti*), in a way that created human nature remains distinct from the divine nature.[24] Van der Kooi is not only interested in preserving Jesus' humanity over against a potential risk of docetism in Logos Christology. More importantly, his concern lies in seeing the Logos come to us precisely as a human being, Jesus of Nazareth, who by the Spirit's power learns obedience as a Son to

---

[18] Van der Kooi, "On the Identity of Jesus Christ," 203; cf. Gregory J. Liston, "A 'Chalcedonian' Spirit Christology," *Irish Theological Quarterly* 81, no. 1 (2016): 74–93.
[19] Van der Kooi, "On the Identity of Jesus Christ," 203.
[20] Van der Kooi, *This Incredibly Benevolent Force*, 61.
[21] Ibid., 66.
[22] Ibid.
[23] Ibid., 69.
[24] Ibid.

his Father, so that upon completion of his mission he might make others children of the Father by the gift of his Spirit. Jesus is distinct from us and also like us, since he is true God and true man. But he is also unique and similar to us in terms of the presence of the life-giving Spirit in him. As the author puts it, "Jesus is fully human but definitely not an ordinary human being" because unlike us, he has already been raised from the dead, and "where he is, we are *not yet*. Here the work of the Spirit is needed. If there is to be a bridge between Christ and us in this world of estrangement, it has to be built by the Spirit."[25] Spirit Christology facilitates an account of human participation in the divine life, in Jesus' gift of the Spirit of God to us.

The Spirit Makes the Son's Human Nature Suitable for His Work of Salvation: Sánchez's Pneumatic Retrieval of Martin Chemnitz

Affectionally called "the second Martin," Martin Chemnitz is an influential theologian and pastor of the second-generation disciples of Martin Luther. He is one of the main authors of the Formula of Concord (1577), a document that intended to unify German Lutherans divided over doctrinal matters after Luther's death. Chemnitz's work, *The Two Natures in Christ* (1570), represents a classic treatment of post-Reformation Lutheran Christology that claims continuity with the creeds and councils of the church. It is a Logos-oriented incarnational Christology from above, meaning that, methodologically, the author's presentation moves from the divine to the human natures of Christ, and then from the person to the work of Christ. To develop a Lutheran incarnational Spirit Christology, it is important to understand how classic Lutheran Christology works before we see how its grammar might be congenial to a Spirit-oriented trajectory.

Lutheran Christology draws significantly from the Alexandrian tradition. As we observed in Chapter 3, Athanasius and Cyril, who represent this tradition, share a tendency to speak of: (1) the Word as the personal subject of his theandric (joint divine and human) actions in salvation, (2) the fullness of the Logos' (and his own Spirit's) presence in his human nature

---

[25] Ibid., 70.

from the time of the incarnation (personal union), (3) what the events in the economy mean not for the Word but for us, and (4) the cosmic or universal significance of the Word's incarnation for humanity as a whole. Due to these theological accents, the Alexandrian tradition gives less attention to the historical particularity and active role of the Word's humanity, or to the progressive activity of the Holy Spirit in such humanity.

The classic Lutheran Christology represented by Chemnitz inherits and embodies the basic elements of the Alexandrian tradition. Like Athanasius and Cyril, Chemnitz interprets the anointing of the Son not as his anointing by the Father with the Spirit at the Jordan but as the Logos' anointing of his own humanity with his divine nature at the hypostatic "union" or as the indwelling or "unction" of the Holy Spirit in the Logos' human nature from the moment of the union.[26] By moving the Spirit-anointing of Christ from the Jordan to the incarnation, and by using the term "spirit" in both substantial (the Logos' divinity) and personal (the Holy Spirit) senses to signify such anointing, Chemnitz inherits the partial eclipse of pneumatology in Christology seen among some early church fathers. Furthermore, because Christ already has the fullness of deity and the Holy Spirit in the flesh from the moment of the incarnation, Chemnitz tends to think of events in Christ's life taking place after the incarnation as revelatory for others of his glory rather than as defining for his own humanity. For example, after considering a number of Western scholastic positions on Christ's growth in wisdom, Chemnitz interprets Christ's "advance in wisdom" in Lk. 2:52 to mean that "He did not advance in Himself but in the view of others to whom He more

---

[26] Chemnitz asserts that

Christ was anointed according to His human nature "above all His fellows" (Ps. 45:7), not only with infused gifts of the Spirit, nor only with the indwelling of the Spirit through grace … but also because the divine nature of the Logos with its total substantial fullness dwells personally in His assumed nature. … Therefore, it is not called a union but an unction of the Spirit, for the union of the divine and the human in Christ takes place through the overshadowing of the Holy Spirit. (Luke 1:35).

Martin Chemnitz, *The Two Natures in Christ*, trans. J. A. O. Preus (St. Louis, Missouri: Concordia, 1971), 328 (cf. 248); Chemnitz cites approvingly John of Damascus on the substantial view of "spirit" and the incarnational view of the anointing: "For He anointed Himself. As God He anointed His body with His own deity. As man He was anointed, for the deity is the unction of the humanity" (379). Chemnitz also cites Athanasius: "The assumed flesh was anointed with and sanctified by the Logos" (347). Cyril adopts Athanasius' synonymous use of sanctification and anointing to refer to the Spirit's presence in Christ from the moment of the union (cf. 468); for Cyril's position, see José Miguel Odero, "La unción de Cristo según S. Cirilo Alejandrino," in *Credo*, vol. 1, 203–8.

and more manifested His gifts."[27] By this assertion, he likely means that the Logos' divine nature or attribute cannot advance. But the question remains as to whether the human nature can advance in wisdom. Here Chemnitz assumes a distinction often employed in a Logos Christology between Christ's *possession* of wisdom from the moment of the union and his *use* of the same during his life. The use shows forth something Christ already has so that others might behold it, but it is less clear how the use shows an advance in Christ's human nature per se. As Chemnitz puts it, Luke's intention in the passage is to highlight that "the divine wisdom which dwelt personally in complete fullness in the assumed humanity, when it willed and insofar as it wished, manifested itself more and more through the flesh."[28] These examples show how an interpretation of the anointing and Christ's advance in wisdom within the framework of a Logos Christology raises questions about the historical particularity and unique significance of these Spirit-events in the Logos' human life and work. Before addressing these issues, we need to understand Chemnitz's Christology.

Three Kinds of Statements on the Incarnation: Understanding Chemnitz's Logos Christology

Lutheran Christology communicates a strong sense of the *unity* of the person of Christ. It speaks of the incarnation (personal union) as a communication of divine and human properties (Lat. *communicatio idiomatum*) in the one person of Christ. To illustrate further the various ways in which such communication of properties takes place, Chemnitz works with three *genera* (from Lat. *genus*) or "kinds" of statements about the incarnation.[29] Divine properties include attributes such as omnipotence, omnipresence, and omniscience; attributes proper to the human nature include birth, growing in age, and suffering and dying. Let us briefly look at the three genera. The *genus idiomaticum* (Lat. *idioma*, meaning "property") ascribes divine and human properties to the *person* of Christ. It is the kind of *genus* that allows us to make statements such as "the Word died on the cross" (according to the human nature) or "Jesus is my Lord and God" (according to the divine

---

[27] Chemnitz, *The Two Natures in Christ*, 250.
[28] Ibid., 251.
[29] On the three *genera*, see Chemnitz, *The Two Natures in Christ*, 157–79, 215–31, 241–6.

nature). The next two *genera* are more pertinent to our study. The *genus apotelesmaticum* (Lat. *apotelesma*, meaning "work") allows us to say that the properties of Christ's divine and human natures cooperate with one another according to what is proper to each nature. When we say, for instance, that Jesus' blood purifies us from all sin (1 Jn 1:7), this work of purification takes place through the death of Jesus (human property), who has the power to cleanse us from sin (divine property).[30] Chemnitz sees this *genus* as an expression of the church's teaching in the Third Council of Constantinople (AD 680-1) that the one person of Christ has both divine and human wills working in communion with one another in all his works.[31] Chemnitz follows the Council in observing that "these natural wills and activities in Christ are not in conflict or contrary to one another, but the one works with the other … and the human is subject to and subordinate to the divine."[32] In keeping with the Alexandrian emphasis on the divine Logos as the one subject of his theandric works, and given the distinction between God and creation, the activity of the assumed human nature is seen as subordinate to the divine nature of the Logos.

In regard to the human nature, the *genus apotelesmaticum* deals only with its *natural* attributes (e.g., being born, dying) in contrast to other supernatural gifts and divine qualities *received* by the human nature from outside of it. To

---

[30] Chemnitz explains

> that the human race cannot be freed from the bondage of sin and death in any other way than that the Son of God Himself by His divine power, through death, in the same body which He made His own in the incarnation should destroy the power of death. For the wrath of God cannot be appeased by human satisfaction or human powers, nor can death be destroyed and life restored. For this is a work of divine power. Yet these things do not occur outside the flesh, for the blood of the Son of God cleanses us from sin (1 John 1:7). … The person of the Redeemer accomplishes the work of redemption according to each nature, so that the work of redemption is the work of the person, not only in the humanity but also in the deity, yet with the property of each nature preserved in this classification. (Ibid., 221)

[31] The Council fathers

> declare that in him [Christ] are two natural wills and two natural operations indivisibly, inconvertibly, inseparably, inconfusedly. … And these two natural wills are not contrary the one to the other (God forbid!) as the impious heretics assert, but his human will follows and that not as resisting and reluctant, but rather as subject to his divine and omnipotent will. (*The Third Council of Constantinople: The Definition of Faith*, in NPNF²14:345)

The teaching is directed against the Monothelite view that Christ only had one will and operation in his two natures, so that the human nature endowed with a rational soul is left without its own will and operation. On the Monothelite controversy, see Chemnitz, *The Two Natures in Christ*, 233-40.

[32] Chemnitz, *The Two Natures in Christ*, 238.

deal with those received attributes, Chemnitz points to the need for a third and final *genus*.[33] The *genus maiestaticum* (Lat. *maiestas*, meaning "majesty") teaches that the Logos communicates divine attributes to his assumed human nature. As an example, Chemnitz points out that Christ's "flesh has been made life-giving (John 5:26 and 6:27)."[34] Chemnitz cites Athanasius and Cyril in support of the interpretation of these texts under the *genus maiestaticum*, showing again the affinity of Lutheran and Alexandrian Christologies.[35] Because of the personal union, the Word's power to give life (a divine property) is communicated to and received by his human flesh so that it can cooperate in all works of Christ leading to the salvation of the flesh (humanity). Chemnitz is aware of the critique that the third *genus* can be understood as a "commingling, conversion, or equating" of the natures, but argues that such an interpretation would conflict with "the analogy of faith regarding the differences between the natures and the essential attributes" of each.[36] There must be a communication or perichoresis (interpenetration) of attributes without confusion of natures that makes it possible for the assumed human nature to "effectually cooperate in all the works of Christ."[37] In keeping with the distinction between God and creation, such perichoresis is not reciprocal, meaning that the divine nature of Christ does not receive attributes from the human nature.[38] Chemnitz develops a hermeneutical rule on the humanity of Christ under the third *genus*, arguing that "when we

---

[33] Chemnitz notes that it is not enough for a complete Christology

> if we only teach under the first *genus* that the attributes of the natures are attributed or communicated to the person, and under the second classification that each nature in Christ performs in communion with the other that which is proper to it. For in addition to these two *genera* we must also point out that the human nature in Christ, besides retaining its properties intact, has received innumerable supernatural … gifts as a result of its hypostatic union with the deity … we must posit still a third category or *genus*. (Ibid., 245)

[34] Ibid., 244.
[35] Ibid., 260, 349, 367–70; Cyril of Alexandria's position, adopted at the Council of Ephesus (AD 431), reads:

> Whosoever shall not confess that the flesh of the Lord giveth life and that it pertains to the Word of God the Father as his very own, but shall pretend that it belongs to another person who is united to him [i.e., the Word] only according to honour, and who has served as a dwelling for the divinity; and shall not rather confess, as we say, that that flesh giveth life because it is that of the Word who giveth life to all: let him be anathema. (Cyril of Alexandria, *The XII Anathematisms of St. Cyril against Nestorius*, in NPNF² 14:217)

[36] Chemnitz, *The Two Natures in Christ*, 268.
[37] Ibid., 285.
[38] Ibid., 246.

have Scriptural testimony attributing to Christ's human nature something which is above, beyond, or even contrary to [human] nature, we should not be caught on the horns of this dilemma, that either we must deny the reality of His human nature or interpret the passages of Scripture which sound otherwise in such a way that we believe nothing about Christ's human nature which is above or contrary to nature."[39] Chemnitz asks us to hold two realities about Christ's human nature in paradox or tension without seeking a complete resolution. Human logic follows scriptural logic.[40] He repeatedly illustrates the majestic *genus* through the analogy of the heated sword: "Just as the quality of shining and giving heat is communicated to heated iron," so also do the attributes of the divine nature of the Word (shining and giving heat) are given to the assumed humanity (heated iron) through and because of the personal union.[41] Yet in this perichoresis the heat and the heated iron remain distinct.

The Genus Pneumatikon: Bringing the Holy Spirit Back into Lutheran Christology

Having looked at the main features of Chemnitz's incarnational Logos Christology, our next question is whether this Christology offers some building blocks for reflecting on the Holy Spirit's role in the Son's humanity. This question is, of course, not one that Chemnitz asks. However, throughout his treatment, he offers some frames of reference that are productive for thinking through the complementarity of Logos and Spirit Christologies. Because Chemnitz is not seeking such a complementarity as an aim in his treatise, there are times when his statements on the Logos and the Spirit are not integrated and need further articulation. Part of my own work on Chemnitz constitutes an attempt at developing and extending his thoughts in dialogue with the contemporary field of Spirit Christology. Key to my proposal is the addition of a fourth *genus* to Lutheran Christology, namely, a *genus pneumatikon* or *genus habitualis*, which can speak more fully to the active presence of the person and gifts of the Holy Spirit in the Logos' assumed humanity.[42] My contention is that the requirements of a Spirit

---

[39] Ibid., 482.
[40] Ibid., 485.
[41] Ibid., 268 (cf. 262–3).
[42] On my progression of thought on the fourth *genus*, see *Sculptor Spirit*, 37–41; "Sculpting Christ in Us: Public Faces of the Spirit in God's World," in *TAT*, 302–5; *Receiver, Bearer, and Giver*, 167–80;

Christology as a complement to an incarnational Christology can be met by incorporating this *genus* of the Spirit and its habitual gifts into the type of Logos Christology represented by Chemnitz. Those requirements include an account of the place of the Holy Spirit in Christ's human nature and life, the distinction and mutuality between the missions of the Son and the Spirit in Trinitarian theology, and the participation of human persons by grace in Christ's own Spirit. These requirements align with the Christological, Trinitarian, and soteriological benefits of an incarnational Spirit Christology.

The first step in my proposal lies in locating the *genus pneumatikon* within the matrix of Chemnitz's *genera*. The *genus* of the Spirit deals neither with *natural* attributes of Christ's human nature such as being born and dying (as in the *genus apotelesmaticum*) nor with *divine* attributes communicated by the Logos to his assumed human nature (because of the personal union) such as the power to give life (as in the *genus maiestaticum*).[43] Instead, the *genus pneumatikon* fits best in the middle of the other two *genera*, in a category Chemnitz refers to as supernatural created gifts—significantly, a category he adopts not from the Eastern Alexandrian tradition but from the Western scholastics. Scholastic Christology makes a distinction between the "grace of union" (Lat. *gratia unionis*), which refers to the Word's assumption of a human nature (aligning with a Logos Christology), and "habitual grace" (Lat. *gratia habitualis*), which refers to the special holiness of the Logos' humanity.[44] Corresponding to habitual grace, Chemnitz speaks of "supernatural gifts" (Lat. *hyperphysica*), which are "infused into the human nature of Christ in such a way that they inhere in it, as they say in the [scholastic] schools, formally, habitually, and subjectively."[45] Chemnitz also names them "created and finite gifts" (Lat. *gratuita dona & finita*) as a way to distinguish these gifts in Christ's human nature from those "essential, uncreated, and infinite

---

"The Holy Spirit in Christ: Pneumatological Christology As a Ground for a Christ-Centered Pneumatology," in Scott R. Murray, Aaron M. Moldenhaeur, Carl D. Roth, Richard A. Lammert, Martin R. Noland, Charles L. Cortright, and Michael J. Albrecht, eds., *Propter Christum: Christ at the Center* (St. Louis, MO: Luther Academy, 2013), 343–56; and "Pneumatology: Key to Understanding the Trinity," in John A. Maxfield, ed., *Who Is God?: In the Light of the Lutheran Confessions*. Papers presented at the 2009 Congress on the Lutheran Confessions (St. Louis, MO: Luther Academy, 2012), 137–9.

[43] Beyond the *genus apotelesmaticum*, Chemnitz explains that Christ's human nature cooperates with the divine nature "not only with its natural powers and activities ... but also with those supernatural gifts which it has received from the hypostatic union and possesses because they have been communicated to it." Chemnitz, *The Two Natures in Christ*, 246.

[44] See Thomas Aquinas, *ST* 3a, q. 6, a. 6.

[45] Chemnitz, *The Two Natures in Christ*, 248. For this section, I consulted the 1653 edition of *De Duabus Naturis in Christo*.

attributes of the Deity" (Lat. *essentialia increata & infinita Divinitatis Idiomata*) that the Logos communicates to his human nature.[46] In a broader Trinitarian framework, the distinction between uncreated and created gifts is congenial to a corresponding distinction between the mission of the Logos/Son who communicates essential attributes to his own human nature (*genus maiestaticum*) and the mission of the Holy Spirit who communicates habitual gifts to the same (*genus habitualis*). This would require that these habitual gifts be ascribed to the person of the Holy Spirit.

Therefore, the second step of my proposal is to attribute the supernatural created gifts to the person of the Holy Spirit. While Chemnitz attributes the communication of essential attributes to the assumed human nature to the person of the Logos (because of the personal union), he assigns the communication of habitual created gifts more generally to "the effects of the Deity" (Lat. *effectus Deitatis*) in Christ's human nature.[47] However, at times, Chemnitz indirectly assigns these gifts to the Holy Spirit. Which raises the question: To whom should the created gifts be ascribed? The effects or works of the Deity, or the Holy Spirit? I argue that, instead of ascribing these created gifts to the works all persons of the Trinity share in common, such gifts should be ascribed to the Holy Spirit. In that way, we can account for biblical texts that deal more specifically with the Holy Spirit's activity in the life of Christ. Second, a further clarifying distinction needs to be made between such created gifts of the Spirit in Christ's human nature and the person of the uncreated Spirit itself.[48] The former requires the latter. Thus the *genus* of the Spirit posits that the Holy Spirit itself is communicated to the Logos' human nature through indwelling or anointing (the term *genus pneumatikon* best gets at this idea), and consequently, that the gifts of the Holy Spirit are also received by the assumed human nature (the term *genus habitualis* best communicates this idea). Chemnitz himself implicitly invites a pneumatological reading of the supernatural created gifts. As an example, he reflects on Jesus' growth in strength and wisdom "in the Spirit" (Lk. 2:40, 52),[49] which means that "He learned to reprove the evil and choose the

---

[46] Chemnitz, *The Two Natures in Christ*, 247.
[47] Ibid.
[48] We have to be careful not to equate the category of habitual grace with the Spirit, but rather to see the person of the Spirit as the source of created or habitual gifts. On this point, I share McGarry's (citing Hughes) critique of theologies that risk reducing the person of the Spirit to "a depersonalized category of grace." See Joseph McGarry, "Formed by the Spirit: A Third Article Theology of Christian Spirituality," in *TAT*, 284–5.
[49] Chemnitz, *The Two Natures in Christ*, 249.

good."⁵⁰ When the Logos "willed to assume our infirmities, apart from sin, for our sakes, in order that He might be the victim for us" according to his human nature, he did so in a way that "these infused gifts [of strength and wisdom] ... might gradually and little by little increase and advance before God and men."⁵¹ Chemnitz locates the Spirit in Christ's humanity already at his conception and attributes his assumed human nature's purification and sanctification from sin (sinlessness) to the Spirit's intervention.⁵² Yet Chemnitz also seems to make room for the Spirit's ongoing leading of Christ throughout his life, in a way that is not only meant to reveal the divine wisdom he already has to others but allows for progressive human growth in his use of wisdom. On this point, he cites approvingly Luther's reading of Lk. 2:40: "Thus, although the Spirit was in Him from the beginning of His conception, yet His stature and reasoning ability increased in Him in the same manner as in other men. Thus the Spirit came upon Him more and more, and hence moved Him more and more."⁵³ We can state that the Son is filled with the Spirit from conception, and moved or urged by the Spirit throughout his mission.

The third step of my proposal lies in integrating Logos and Spirit Christological aspects in an account of salvation. We already noted that the *genus maiestaticum* corresponds to the mission of the Son, who alone assumes the human nature unto his person (incarnation), and the *genus pneumatikon* corresponds to the mission of the Holy Spirit, who indwells the assumed humanity. But how do they relate to one another? Here we recall the *genus apotelesmaticum*, which deals with the works the divine Logos does in cooperation with the *natural* attributes of his human nature for our sake. We now add the *supernatural* created gifts that, by the Spirit's presence and activity, are also operative in, with, and through the Logos' human nature. In the Son's kenosis or humiliation, he is thus conceived, sanctified, strengthened, advanced in wisdom, and moved to be obedient unto death by the strengthening of the Spirit. And the Son does this willingly for us and for our salvation. In the one person of Christ, his human will works under and with his divine will in our salvation—"under" because the human is always under the divine, and "with" because the humanity of the Son is his own living instrument or agent. Highlighting the instrumental role of the Logos'

---

⁵⁰ Ibid., 489.
⁵¹ Ibid., 490.
⁵² Ibid., 52, 56–7.
⁵³ Ibid., 384 (cf. 251).

humanity, Chemnitz asserts that the assumed humanity receives supernatural created gifts "in order that it can be the fully and properly prepared instrument with and through which the deity of the Logos exercises and carries out its activities."[54] Here the assumed humanity is passively conceived. Yet immediately afterward Chemnitz goes on to argue, echoing the church's condemnation of the Apollinarian heresy, that this assumed humanity "is not a soulless instrument … nor something inactive or without energy … but is an animated organ, living, intelligent, rational, which cooperates as a living and intelligent instrument, when the deity wills to accomplish divine activities through it."[55] Citing Cyril for support, Chemnitz sees Christ's assumed humanity more actively as "a cooperating agent in the performance of His miracles."[56] Chemnitz refers to a scholastic debate dealing with the question of whether the Logos operates directly through his human nature after the personal union or by means of his supernatural created gifts.[57] In our appropriation of Chemnitz, we might ask the question this way: Does the Logos act directly through his humanity after the personal union, or does he act through his Spirit-indwelt humanity in accomplishing his works? For Chemnitz, the answer is yes! Both the Logos and the Spirit are at work in the assumed humanity, the former through the communication of essential attributes and the latter through the communication of habitual gifts. There is no moment in which only the Logos or only the Holy Spirit works in, with, and through the assumed human nature. Rather, both persons act in communion with one another in the mystery of the incarnation. This is true even if the Logos, in his kenosis, does not always will to manifest his divine majesty through his flesh. The aim of Chemnitz's discussion is ultimately soteriological. The divine Logos undergoes a human journey for our sake. I want to clarify that, in that journey, the Holy Spirit has an important role to play. In the context of Chemnitz's Logos Christology, the clearer addition of the pneumatological component leads us to assert that "the divine Logos has chosen to do his work of salvation in, with, and through his humanity in which the Holy Spirit dwells and is active. That is how the Logos chooses to be God for us. From a Trinitarian angle, the Son and the Holy Spirit appear as inseparable companions in the Father's saving work."[58]

---

[54] Ibid., 252.
[55] Ibid., 253.
[56] Ibid.
[57] Ibid., 252.
[58] Sánchez, *Receiver, Bearer, and Giver*, 176. I have argued that a Spirit Christology complements and integrates insights from three major atonement theories. A Logos-oriented reading of these

One of the benefits of a Spirit Christology lies in its ability to show the continuity between the Spirit's presence in Christ and his saints. A Logos Christology best shows the discontinuity between the Son and the adopted sons (and daughters) of God. The Logos alone is God made flesh. We are not. But we share in his Spirit by grace. Our fourth and final step lies in showing how our pneumatological reading of Chemnitz's category of supernatural created gifts aligns with the gift of human sharing in the anointing of Christ. As we noted earlier, however, Chemnitz follows a patristic tradition that ascribes the anointing of Christ above others to the Logos' sanctification of his own assumed humanity at the personal union. Because his assumed human nature "is personally united with the Logos," such humanity—though consubstantial with ours—still "differs from the other saints not only by reason of His gifts, which by comparison excel the others in number and degree, but also by reason of the union He differs totally from the saints."[59] In these remarks, Chemnitz is arguing that as the incarnate Logos, Christ's humanity differs totally from ours. Not insofar as it is a human nature but insofar as essential attributes are communicated to it so that in cooperation with the divine nature of the Logos it might accomplish the work of salvation. If we consider that the Logos alone saves the flesh by assuming the flesh—an act that is only ascribed to the incarnate Word—then, it is clear that no other human being is capable to accomplish such salvation. The saints do not share in the Logos' capacity to save from sin, death, and the devil. However, when it comes to supernatural created gifts that inhere in human nature, Chemnitz teaches that such gifts are communicated both to the saints because the Holy Spirit dwells in them and to Christ because of the personal union.[60] When it comes to these gifts, Christ also differs from the saints in that his human nature—even

---

theories tends to pit the Latin (Anselm), exemplary (Abelard), and classic (Aulén) accounts against each other, depending on how much weight is given in each to the divine (objective) or human (subjective) aspect of God's salvation in Christ. A Spirit Christology shows how the Spirit is involved in all dimensions of the Son's identity and mission as vicar (Latin), victor (classic), and example (exemplary), and thus acknowledges the strengths of all approaches:

> These strengths are respectively and comparatively the central place of Christ's human obedience unto death in atonement (Anselm), the affirmation that reconciliation is always and exclusively the eschatological work of God against his enemies (Aulén on the classic approach), and the non-exclusive stress on the church's subjective appropriation of atonement in self-sacrificial Christ-like works of love (Abelard). (76)

[59] Ibid., 263.
[60] Chemnitz, *The Two Natures in Christ*, 247.

though consubstantial with ours in all things, except sin—has them in greater number and degree.[61] In explaining the difference between Christ and the saints, Chemnitz appeals not only to his identity as the Logos made flesh but also to the fullness of the Holy Spirit in his humanity: "Although gifts are conferred upon the other saints as God distributes to each the measure of faith (Rom. 12:6), yet to Christ alone is the Spirit not given by measure (John 3:34)."[62] Christ receives these gifts in his human nature for his work of salvation, which includes giving the Holy Spirit and its gifts to us. Following Irenaeus, Athanasius, and Cyril of Alexandria, Chemnitz places Christ's receiving and giving of the Spirit in the broader narrative of Adam's loss of the Spirit in the Fall due to sin and the Spirit's return to fallen humanity through the incarnation and anointing of Christ. Speaking on the significance of the Spirit-anointing of Christ's human nature for us, Chemnitz highlights Christ's generosity of "Spirit" in that he shares what he has fully with others.

> For our comfort we should consider why Scripture speaks this way, namely, that Adam through the Fall lost the Holy Spirit, and the flesh, because of its depravity, was not able to contain the Holy Spirit. But in the person of Christ human nature was again anointed with the Spirit, not in small measure but in such a way that He exercises all of His divine powers in Christ's human nature. In this way the Spirit with His gifts is poured out upon all flesh (Acts 2:4 ff.). … Christ as the Firstborn has received gifts from his Father according to His assumed nature for the benefit of men (Ps. 68:18). He is worthy to receive them (Rev. 5:12), while we are most unworthy. But having received these gifts, He does not keep them to Himself alone, but because we are His brothers according to the assumed nature (Heb. 2:11 ff.) and the flesh of His flesh (Eph. 5:30), He gives, communicates, and distributes them to His brothers according to His assumed nature, as the Head to its members.[63]

Reading Chemnitz's Logos Christology through the lens of a Spirit Christology brings greater clarity to his own work in light of contemporary concerns. It shows the ecumenical possibilities of an incarnational Spirit Christology that brings together strengths from the East and the West.

---

[61] Ibid., 248.
[62] Ibid., 250.
[63] Ibid., 328–9.

The Spirit Acts Directly on the Son's Human Nature: Habets's Retrieval of John Owen's Incipient Spirit Christology

To dispel the myth that a Spirit Christology has to be necessarily adoptionistic and to justify its orthodox grounding in the post-Reformation Reformed tradition, Habets commends Owen's early and groundbreaking contribution to Spirit Christology in his work *Pneumatologia* (1674).[64] In chapter three of the second book, Owen covers the "Work of the Holy Spirit with Respect unto the Head of the New Creation—the Human Nature of Christ."[65] Habets observes that Owen's aim in this section is to "defend Christ's uniqueness as the God-man without limiting his humanity in any way (incipient docetism)" and to "present Christ ... as the archetype of Christian existence, continually empowered, comforted, and sanctified by the Holy Spirit."[66] In his preface to the readers, Owen argues that, in defending the Spirit's divinity, he wishes to "declare and defend the faith of the catholic church against the Socinians"—a group that argued against the teachings of the Trinity and Christ's divine nature.[67] Owen sees his treatment on the Spirit's work in Christ's human nature as a sober, nonspeculative approach to the topic, which has "attended unto the doctrine of Scripture, our only infallible rule and guide, but also expressly considered what was taught and believed in the ancient church in this matter, from which I know that I have not departed."[68] Habets notes that Owen actually contributes to the tradition in a new way, moving the discussion on the Spirit in Christ further than his predecessors. Habets explains Owen's "distinctive insight":

> He argued that the eternal Son of God assumed human nature into personal union with himself, but—and this was the distinctive insight of his

---

[64] See Habets, "Spirit Christology: The Future of Christology?," in *TAT*, 217–32; cf. *The Anointed Son*, 208–12.

[65] Habets references John Owen, *Pneumatologia*, vol. 3, bk 2, chap. 3, in *The Works of John Owen*, 23 vols. on CD-ROM (Rio, Wisconsin: Ages Digital Library, 2000), 199–209. My references to *Pneumatologia* are from John Owen, *The Holy Spirit* (Grand Rapids, MI: Sovereign Grace, 1971), 159–88.

[66] Habets, "Spirit Christology: The Future of Christology?," 218.

[67] Owen, *The Holy Spirit*, 7.

[68] Ibid.

Christology—he held that all direct divine activity on that assumed human nature was that of the Holy Spirit. Prior to this time it was generally held that the Logos, the Son, determined the human life of Jesus directly, rather than indirectly, through the Holy Spirit.[69]

The Spirit's Direct Activity in Christ's Human Nature: Defending the Spirit's Divinity against the Socinians

Owen's position on the Holy Spirit's direct or immediate activity on Christ's human nature can be placed against the background of a certain Socinian argument against the divinity of the Spirit attributed to John Crellius (1590–1633). According to Crellius, and in continuity with standard Socinian teaching, there is only one God, the Father. Christ is neither divine in nature nor God incarnate (there is no "hypostatical union"), but merely an exemplary man who could be considered to be divine in the sense that "he was assisted by divine power."[70] This divine power comes from the Father, who is the one God, not from the Holy Spirit. Crellius does not believe that the Holy Spirit is a divine "Person" and, consequently, holds that there is no "help" or assistance it can "yield unto the most high God."[71] Crellius reasons as follows: Now, if the Son were considered to be divine and if his human nature were "personally joined to the second Person of the Deity," as the majority of Trinitarian theologians ("our Adversaries") posit, why would other Trinitarian theologians (such as Owen!) attribute instead Christ's "sanctification" to the Holy Spirit rather "than to the divine Nature or Person of Christ"?[72] Otherwise stated, if the divine Son, by virtue of the personal union, has communicated his supernatural gifts and divine properties to his human nature, why would he need the Holy Spirit to act upon his human nature? Owen adds that the Socinians also claimed that if the Spirit were to assist the human nature of the Son, then, this would imply that "an *immediate* work of the Holy Ghost should be interposed, in the same person,

---

[69] Habets, "Spirit Christology: The Future of Christology?," 218–19.
[70] John Crellius, *Touching One God the Father. Wherein many things also concerning the Nature of the Son of God, and the* Holy Spirit *Are Discoursed of*, bk. 1, section 2, chap. 32 (London: Kosmoburg, 1665; Ann Arbor: Text Creation Partnership, 2011), 161–4.
[71] Ibid., 164.
[72] Ibid.

between the one nature and the other."⁷³ It would appear as if, logically speaking, the Spirit is operating between the divine Logos and his human nature—a position that, if taken to its logical conclusion, would seem to undercut the integrity of the personal union. It is key to note that Crellius's aim in his reasoning is not to argue for either position but simply to use both positions to highlight the supposed logical inconsistency of the Trinitarian orthodoxy as a whole. The point of the Socinian argument is not to defend some classical orthodox view of Christ's divinity or the divine Logos' works through his own assumed human nature (whether directly or indirectly), but ultimately to deny the divine nature of the Holy Spirit. When placed in this context, Owen's argument for the Holy Spirit's immediate activity on the Son's human nature could be seen as an attempt to show that the Holy Spirit is no less than God but a divine agent in its own right. This is no doubt the greater purpose of *Pneumatologia*, and the section on the Spirit's acts in the Logos' human nature is simply one way into Owen's greater apologetic concern against anti-Trinitarian theologians.

How then could one answer the Socinian criticism about the logical inconsistency of two seemingly contradictory Trinitarian positions? How can one say that both the Logos and the Holy Spirit act upon Christ's human nature, especially if the Logos presumably communicates all his supernatural gifts and divine properties to his assumed human nature by virtue of the personal union? Or to put it crudely, if Jesus is really God, why does he need the Spirit? This question is similar to the one Trypho asked Justin (see Chapter 1), that is, "how He [Christ] can be demonstrated to have been pre-existent, who is filled with the powers of the Holy Ghost … as if He were in lack of them?" How does Owen deal with "Justin's burden" in his own time, and in response to the slightly more sophisticated Socinian version of the question? Owen proposes something of an integration of two schools of thought, acknowledging the hypostatic union as the Logos' proper work while emphasizing the pneumatic trajectory of his life and work. The Son's only "immediate" and "necessary" work or act upon his human nature is, strictly speaking, "the *assumption* of it into subsistence with himself," or "the inseparable subsistence of the *assumed nature* in the person of the Son."⁷⁴ The union is not attributed to the Spirit, but to the Logos. All other acts of God toward the Logos' humanity are said to be "voluntary" and can be especially ascribed or appropriated to the Holy Spirit as "the *immediate*,

---

⁷³Owen, *The Holy Spirit*, 160.
⁷⁴Ibid.

peculiar, efficient cause of all external divine operations" (emphasis in the original).[75] Summing up the distinct works of the Son and the Spirit with respect to the Son's human nature, Owen argues that, although all persons of the Trinity act indivisibly in all their works, the Holy Spirit can nevertheless be said to be especially "the immediate operator of all divine acts of the Son himself, even on his own human nature. Whatever the Son of God wrought in, by, or upon the human nature, he did it by the Holy Ghost, who is his Spirit, as he is the Spirit of the Father.[76] The Spirit acts immediately on the Son's humanity, but the Son is still the subject working through "his Spirit" in his humanity.

The Logos Works through the Spirit: On the Reformed Dynamics of Owen's Spirit Christology

Owen lays out the Spirit's works on Christ's human nature, namely, his conception, total sanctification (from conception), and growth in grace and wisdom; his anointing at baptism with gifts for his messianic (especially, prophetic) office, and his empowerment for miracles, exorcisms, and self-offering on the cross; his body's preservation from decay, the union of his body and soul in resurrection, and, finally, his body's glorification at the Father's right hand so that those who believe in him might also share in his glorification.[77] Commenting on the particularities and significance of Owen's outline, Habets notes its alignment with "Nicene and Chalcedonian orthodoxy," but also with "a staple Reformed emphasis on a *communio idiomatum* and the *extra Calvinisticum*."[78] The expression *communio idiomatum* means that, because the Logos assumed a human nature (personal union), there is a "communion of attributes" (divine and human) in the one person of Jesus Christ. What the expression *extra Calvinisticum* adds to the Reformed understanding is that, when speaking about such communion of attributes, the divine nature of Jesus Christ remains "outside" (*extra*) his human nature. Stated positively, the divine

---

[75] Ibid., 161.
[76] Ibid., 162.
[77] Habets, "Spirit Christology: The Future of Christology?," 220–2. For Owen's discussion, see *The Holy Spirit*, 162–83.
[78] Habets, "Spirit Christology: The Future of Christology?," 218–20.

Logos is fully united to his human nature, but never fully contained within or by his human nature. An overriding concern in this formulation is not only to distinguish clearly between the divine and human natures in Christ but also to highlight the genuine humanity of Christ. Habets sees in Owen's incipient Spirit Christology an answer to both concerns. The main way to do so is through the distinction between the personal union as the divine Logos' only direct or immediate operation on his human nature, and the rest of the Logos' life and mission as the Holy Spirit's immediate operation on his human nature. In terms of safeguarding Christ's true humanity, Habets draws attention to Owen's argument that Christ is, on the one hand, totally sanctified by the Spirit from conception "in order that his human nature could not fall prey to the human condition—the propensity to sin," but, on the other hand, "the actual exercise" of his sanctification is gradual as he grows in grace and truth.[79] This distinction between Christ's possession and exercise of the Spirit's sanctification speaks both to Christ's being distinct from us because he is the God-man filled with his Spirit, as well as his being like us because he is a human subject capable of growing in sanctification by the Spirit.[80] Owen fears that ascribing to the Logos' divine nature immediate acts on his human nature will lead to Apollinarianism— namely, the teaching that the divine Logos replaces Christ's human soul— and instead asserts that "being a perfect man, his rational soul was in him the immediate principle of all his moral operations, even as ours are in us. ... In their increase, enlargement, and exercise [in reference to his moral operations], there was required a progression in grace also; and this he had continually by the Holy Ghost."[81] Drawing from this text, Habets concludes, following Spence, that Owen advocates for "the view that Jesus Christ is *autokineton*—a self-determining spiritual principle, fully self-conscious and, as a creature, open and responsive to God, not determined

---

[79] Ibid., 220–1. Owen explains that

> the soul of Christ, from the first moment of its infusion [of all grace by the Spirit's work of sanctification], was a subject capable of a fulness of grace, as unto its habitual residence and in-being, though the actual exercise of it was suspended for a while, until the organs of the body were fitted for it. This [total sanctification], therefore, it received by this first unction of the Spirit. Hence, from his conception, he was "holy," as well as "harmless" and "undefiled," Heb. vii. 26; a "holy thing," Luke i.35; radically filled with a perfection of grace and wisdom, inasmuch as the Father "gave him not the Spirit by measure," John iii.34 (*The Holy Spirit*, 169)

[80] See Habets, "Spirit Christology: The Future of Christology?," 222–3.
[81] Owen, *The Holy Spirit*, 169.

by the Logos immediately. Owen's argument is that if this were not so then Christ would not be truly human."[82] Christ's human nature is not only truly human and consubstantial with ours but also sanctified, guided, empowered, sustained, and glorified by the Holy Spirit and its gifts. A final effect of Owen's incipient Spirit Christology is its invitation to ponder how believers share in the same Spirit who glorified Christ's human body. Spence sees this anthropological implication of Owen's Christology as one of his main contributions. As Spence puts it, if "the integrity of Christ's human nature … can only be maintained if the divine Word is recognized as operating on it not directly, or immediately, but rather indirectly by the Spirit," then, it is impossible to posit "that our experience of the Spirit does not violate the integrity of our humanity."[83] Otherwise stated, it is not by our human sharing in the Logos directly but in his Spirit that we bear the image of Christ in a truly human way.

A productive exchange takes place between Habets and Reformed theologian Oliver Crisp's critique of Owen's position.[84] Crisp's fundamental problem with Owen's Spirit Christology lies in that, by drawing a Spirit-mediated wedge between the divine Son and his human nature, it threatens the integrity of the personal union. Otherwise stated, the strong distinction of natures in the person of the Son illustrated by the introduction of the Holy Spirit as the divine agent who acts immediately on the Son's human nature fails to make room for the Son's own personal and direct actions on his assumed human nature. After the assumption of a human nature proper, the Son steps back and lets the Holy Spirit take over, so to speak, so that the Son no longer appears to be the personal subject of his own actions in an ongoing way. Crisp suggests that there is an underdeveloped reflection on the personal union in Owen's Reformed version of Spirit Christology.[85]

---

[82] Habets, "Spirit Christology: The Future of Christology?," 221; for a treatment of Owen's thesis, see Alan Spence, "Christ's Humanity and Ours: John Owen," in Christoph Schwöbel, and Colin E. Gunton, eds., *Persons, Divine and Human: King's College Essays in Theological Anthropology* (Edinburgh: T&T Clark, 1991), 74–97; cf. Kyle David Claunch, "The Son and the Spirit: The Promise of Spirit Christology in Traditional Trinitarian and Christological Perspective" (PhD diss., The Southern Baptist Theological Seminary, 2017).

[83] Spence, "Christ's Humanity and Ours," 96.

[84] The following summary is from Habets's engagement of Oliver D. Crisp, *Revisioning Christology: Theology in the Reformed Tradition* (Farnham: Ashgate, 2011). See Habets, "Spirit Christology: The Future of Christology?," 223–9.

[85] Reformed theologian McCormack has argued that the early Reformed Christology of John Calvin (1509–1564) is open to the charge of Nestorianism because, while it is strong on the unimpaired distinction of the two natures "*after* the union," it is still unable "to reflect more deeply on the hypostatic union itself." Bruce L. McCormack, *For Us and Our Salvation: Incarnation and*

Interestingly, there is a sense in which Crisp's critique brings up the same apparent logical inconsistency between two orthodox positions noted by the Socinians in their critique of orthodox theologians like Owen, which raises the question as to whether Owen has succeeded in fully integrating Chalcedonian Logos Christology with a Spirit Christology. Crisp's critique suggests that Owen's pneumatological emphasis does not yet adequately deal with a Logos Christology's concern for preserving the unity of the person and the communion of attributes not only at the personal union but throughout his entire life and mission. Significantly, this Reformed critique can be seen as congenial to a classic Lutheran Christology's concern for emphasizing the unity of Christ's person, and the Logos' direct involvement as the personal subject of his acts in, with, and through his assumed human nature. Habets's own response to Crisp is threefold. First, Owen's position does something a Logos Christology on its own does not immediately do, namely, take seriously the biblical witness to "Jesus' life lived in dependence on the Spirit—his conception, baptism, vocation, passion, exaltation."[86] Second, Owen's Christology still aligns with the councils because he assumes that the Son is, at least in the definition of the personal union, "the active willing subject" in the mystery of the incarnation.[87] For instance, in a broader Trinitarian perspective, Habets argues that Owen is open to the Son's ongoing involvement in his human life and mission, even if he does so by his Spirit. As Owen notes, "Whatever *the Son of God* wrought in, by, or upon the human nature, *he* did it by the Holy Ghost, who is *his* Spirit, as he is the Spirit of the Father" (italics mine). Third, and related to the point above, Owen's proposal can be construed in a Trinitarian way to show that he is interested in formulating a "dual agency at work, that of the Son and the Spirit, and both in personal ways" in the life of Christ.[88] To bring together Logos and Spirit Christologies, Habets suggests that "the Word is the subject who wills and acts, but does so within the conditions of human nature, and that necessitates he works by or through the Holy Spirit."[89]

In the background of Owen's argument and Habets's retrieval of it, there is an underlying critique of the risks of docetic or Apollinarian tendencies

---

Atonement in the Reformed Tradition, Studies in Reformed Theology and History, vol. 1, no. 2 (Princeton, NJ: Princeton Theological Seminary, 1993), 9.
[86] Habets, "Spirit Christology: The Future of Christology?," 225.
[87] Ibid., 226.
[88] Ibid., 227.
[89] Ibid., 228. "The eternal Son is the active subject of the incarnation, but he works on the human nature indirectly, through the Holy Spirit, as a real human person, Jesus bar [son of] Joseph, Jesus the Messiah" (229).

in Christology, which at times are said to align—at least in Habets's appreciation—with a Lutheran Christology of the *communicatio idiomatum* (i.e., communication of attributes).⁹⁰ Crisp's critique of Owen highlights typical Christological concerns not only some Reformed theologians but also Lutheran ones can share, namely, preserving not only the distinction of natures and attributes in the person of Christ but also the integrity of the personal union and the Logos' ongoing and direct activity in and through his own human nature. Although classic Lutheran Christology speaks of a *genus maeistaticum*, according to which the Logos, due to the personal union, communicates his divine majesty and power through his assumed humanity, Lutherans do not understand this communication as a "transfusion of the properties of one nature into the other" (Owen) nor as a transfer of attributes "across those natures" (Habets), if by these statements the conclusion is drawn that a confusion or mixing of natures or attributes, or a denial of Christ's human nature, takes place.⁹¹ Perhaps it is more productive to simply acknowledge a tension in Chalcedonian Christology, which warns against taking the unity of the person in the direction of a confusion of natures (a risk perceived by the Reformed in the Lutheran position), or the distinction of natures in the direction of a division of the person (Crisp's critique of Owen, but also a risk perceived by the Lutherans in the Reformed position).⁹² On the one hand, the pneumatic dimension of

---

⁹⁰ Ibid., 223, n. 45; 226, n. 59.

⁹¹ Owen, *The Holy Spirit*, 161; Habets, "Spirit Christology: The Future of Christology?," 226, n. 59; McCormack rightly notes that Lutherans are aware of the charge of Eutychianism leveled against them. See *For Us and for Our Salvation*, 4–5; The Formula of Concord's classic Lutheran position states:

> Such a communication or imparting did not take place through an essential or natural outpouring of the characteristics of the divine nature into the human, in such a way that the humanity of Christ has them of itself and apart from the divine essence, nor in such a way that the human nature in Christ had completely set aside its natural, essential characteristics and had either been transformed into the deity or had become in and of itself equal to the deity by means of these imparted characteristics, nor in such a way that from now on the same natural, essential characteristics and actions of both natures are of the same kind or even identical. ... For in no way shall the transformation, mixing, or equating of the natures in Christ or of their essential characteristics be held or allowed.

Formula of Concord, Solid Declaration [hereafter FC, SD], Art. 8, par. 62, in Robert Kolb and Timothy J. Wengert, eds., *The Book of Concord: The Confessions of the Evangelical Lutheran Church* (Minneapolis, MN: Fortress, 2000), 627.

⁹² McCormack sees the classic Lutheran position as a "direct" communion of natures (*communion naturarum*). He distinguishes this position from the mature Reformed position, according to which a real yet "indirect" communion takes place, "not of the natures between themselves but a communion of the natures through the Person of the union." This distinction aligns with a difference between an unmediated communion between the person of the Logos and the human nature (Lutheran) and a mediated communion between the natures through the person of the

Chemnitz's discussion of Christ's human reception of supernatural created gifts for his mission can be strengthened with Owen's explicitly biblical account of the Spirit's direct role in the assumed humanity. On the other hand, Chemnitz's insistence on the direct yet distinct activities of the Son and the Spirit in Christ's assumed humanity can deal with Crisp's critique of Owen on risking the integrity of the personal union through an exclusive mediation of the Spirit between the natures, and build on Habets's interest in maintaining the Logos' ongoing involvement in his Spirit-led life and work.

We find among theologians in the field of Spirit Christology a desire to be true to their respective traditions while working ecumenically on the integration of Logos and Spirit Christologies into a rich Christological, Trinitarian, and soteriological matrix. Despite their distinct theological traditions, and the different ways they nuance their positions, it is significant that both Sánchez and Habets, following Chemnitz and Owen respectively, ultimately agree that the divine Logos, who assumed a human nature unto his person, can be said to act in and by the Holy Spirit with respect to his human nature in a way that the divine persons cooperate with one another in God's work of salvation.

The Holy Spirit Sanctifies the Fallen Flesh of the Son: Skip Jenkins's Pentecostal Retrieval of Edward Irving

Given their focus on the divine Logos as the subject of his human actions and the universal significance of his humanity for salvation, Colin Gunton notes

---

Logos (mature Reformed). Yet McCormack acknowledges that the Reformed mediated position can make the person of the Logos seem like a third reality if pushed too far, harming the integrity of the union. In spite of this, the author still sees the unmediated union as important to steer away from the risk of a docetic Christology, in which God saves us "in" man as opposed to "as" man. See McCormack, *For Us and for Our Salvation*, 5, cf. 13–15 (cf. Habets, "Spirit Christology: The Future of Christology?," 226–7). A classic Lutheran response to the Reformed argument about the risk of mixing the natures is twofold. First, only Christ knows "of what this assumed human nature is capable above and beyond its natural characteristics without being destroyed." See FC, SD, Art. 8, par. 53, in *The Book of Concord*, 625. Second, Scripture itself speaks of the assumed human nature as receiving divine attributes without becoming divine, such as when "the blood of Christ cleanses us from all sin" (1 Jn 1:7) or "the flesh of Christ is a food that gives life" (Jn 6:48–58). See FC, SD, Art. 8, pars. 58–9, in *The Book of Concord*, 626.

that theologians like Athanasius and, to a lesser degree, Cyril of Alexandria display "a relative lack of interest" in the "historical particularity" of Jesus' humanity and tend to "reduce the humanity to a rather passive role."[93] To meet the challenge of contemporary Christology, which he characterizes as the need to articulate "an incarnation Christology which will yet do full justice to the historical particularity of Jesus and the detailed lineaments of his story," Gunton calls for a new look at "the place of pneumatology in christology."[94] He commends the retrieval of Edward Irving's teaching about the radical condescension or kenosis of Christ, namely, "that at the incarnation the Son did not assume the perfect, unfallen, flesh of Adam, but our fallen human nature."[95] Gunton sees Irving's teaching as "a version of the classic patristic teaching that what Christ does not assume, he does not heal."[96] The thrust of Irving's assertion does not concern the divine person of the Son, who is without sin "in his freely-willed acts of personal choice," but rather what he undergoes in his human nature for the salvation of fallen humankind.[97] How does the Spirit come into this picture? Jesus' sinlessness is attributed to the Spirit's sanctifying presence and action throughout his life. Such sinlessness is not seen statically as something he already possesses, but more historically as "Jesus' obedience to the Father through the Spirit … as the free response to an other" by the Spirit.[98] The Spirit did not only form the body of Jesus from conception but also anointed his soul so that, as Irving puts it in his reading of the temptation account, Jesus "did ever resist and reject the suggestions of evil."[99] By highlighting Christ's real human choices in his kenosis, Irving's Christology also shows Christ to be our example of obedience to the Father by the leading of his Spirit. As Gunton

---

[93] Colin Gunton, "Two Dogmas Revisited: Edward Irving's Christology," *SJT* 41 (1988): 359–60.
[94] Ibid., 361.
[95] Ibid., 365. Gunton cites Irving:

> For he condescended to dwell in concert and communion with flesh; to look up through fleshly eyes; by fleshly senses to converse with the great wickedness of the earth; and, through the faculties or the human soul, to commune with every impious, ungodly and blasphemous chamber of the fallen intellect and feeling of men. … For the Divine and Almighty Creator to empty Himself of Himself, to take the limitation of a creature, and bind Himself under the appointed law of action and suffering thereof, is very wonderful.

> The citation is from G. Carlyle, ed., *The Collected Writings of Edward Irving in Five Volumes*, vol. 5 (London: Alexander Strachan, 1865).

[96] Gunton, "Two Dogmas Revisited," 366.
[97] See ibid., 369 (citing Bishop Kallistos of Diocletia's interpretation of Irving).
[98] Gunton, "Two Dogmas Revisited," 369.
[99] Cited in ibid., 370.

puts it, Christ's "relation to the Spirit is the means whereby Jesus is enabled to be both truly human and, so to speak, prototypically human."[100]

The Spirit's Role in the Son's Human Obedience and Triumph Over Sin: Jenkins's Dialogue with Irving, Dunn, and Barth

Skip Jenkins argues that the incipient Spirit Christology of "proto-Pentecostal" theologian Irving is a promising framework for articulating an incarnational Spirit Christology that fuses into an intelligible vision the Pentecostal teachings on holiness (associated with sin dealt with by justification and sanctification) and power for witness (associated with Spirit baptism).[101] Jenkins sees Irving's teaching on "the eternal Son's assumption of *fallen* flesh as pivotal for such a fusion."[102] Jenkins mines Irving's Christological insight by studying his sermons and other works. According to Irving, the Word must assume the fallen nature of Adam, and not simply the human nature of Adam before the Fall or a human nature changed at conception, so that by his obedience he can conquer all weakness in his own body and rescue human creatures from their fallen state.[103] As God, the Son is already inherently holy, immortal, and incorruptible, but as a human being, the Son must receive these powers through the Holy Spirit. Although the man Jesus is holy from conception, his holiness is not inherent to his human nature but derived or received from God. Jesus is not holy because of the union of the Son with human nature (hypostatic union) but because of the Holy Spirit's union with (or more precisely, inhabitation or indwelling of) his human soul.[104] In his acts of obedience to the Father, Christ's human will acts in harmony with his divine will. Irving attributes this harmony of wills in Christ's person not to the hypostatic union but to the Holy Spirit's indwelling and empowerment of his humanity.[105] Christ cannot be said to be a sinful person like other human persons. Due to the Spirit's presence and activity in him, Christ's human nature is regenerated, and he is thus

---

[100]Ibid., 371.
[101]Jenkins, *Spirit Christology*, 9–11.
[102]Ibid., 11.
[103]Ibid., 142.
[104]Ibid., 145.
[105]Ibid., 146–7.

preserved from the original sin and guilt of Adam and from committing acts of disobedience.[106] In these assertions, Irving shows his concern for speaking of the Son's actions as "a true human obedience, determined not by necessity of nature, but by the choices of a willing individual."[107]

Irving conceives of three anointings in the life of Jesus. The Spirit first anointed Jesus from conception to sanctify his soul, but also at the Jordan with gifts for his prophetic office and to make him the baptizer with the Spirit.[108] Because the Son assumed our fallen flesh, he did not avoid death "through the assumption of an inherently immortal and incorruptible human nature" but came out of death by "being raised into immortality and incorruptibility by the power of the Holy Spirit."[109] This is the third Spirit-anointing of Jesus. Moreover, in Christlike fashion, human persons are empowered to triumph over their sin "in and through the same Holy Spirit that was triumphant in Jesus Christ."[110] Jenkins asserts that Irving's idea that a believer may live without sin in this life due to the Spirit's activity in him not only aligns with the Pentecostal teaching of "entire sanctification" but is an "advantage" that follows from a Spirit Christology in which "such holiness is possible, not just in theory, but in actuality because Jesus Christ actually accomplished it through the Spirit."[111] Similar to Habets's retrieval of Owen, Jenkins's appropriation of Irving adopts a concern for highlighting the true human life and obedience of the Son, a view of the incarnation in which the Spirit is the immediate agent of the Son's human and saving acts, and a strong sense of human cooperation with the same Spirit in whom the Son was empowered to live in obedience to the Father.

To substantiate his thesis that the Son assumes a *fallen* human nature that is sanctified and empowered by the Holy Spirit, Jenkins adopts Dunn's distinction in the Pauline corpus between being "in the flesh" and living "according to the flesh." As the representative of sinful humanity, Jesus assumes life in the flesh of Adam but does not personally sin according to the flesh or in opposition to God.[112] Although Jesus was subject to "sin as a power" and thus to temptation, corruption, and death because he assumed the fallen nature of Adam, he is not "guilty of sin" because, as the last Adam,

---

[106]Ibid., 148–9.
[107]Ibid., 151.
[108]Ibid., 152.
[109]Ibid., 152–3.
[110]Ibid., 153.
[111]Ibid., 167–8.
[112]Ibid., 187.

he does not commit "personal acts of disobedience;" instead, he defeats sin through his act of obedience unto death and resurrection.[113] Jesus' righteous obedience as the last Adam, which brings the end of death and the start of new eschatological life in his resurrection, takes place under the inspiration and power of the Holy Spirit.[114] As we noted in Chapter 2, Dunn's presentation of Jesus' identity as Son, Spirit bearer, and last Adam invites theologians to offer a synthesis of incarnational (Logos), resurrection (Adam), and Spirit Christologies. Jenkins sees in Irving's Christology the building blocks for this synthesis. Even though Jenkins finds helpful Barth's assertion that the Son assumed our fallen flesh without becoming a sinful man, he does not agree with Barth's attribution of Jesus' sinless human nature and life to the Word's assumption of the flesh at the personal union.[115] The rationale for disagreeing with Barth on this point is that such attribution not only fails to account for the important place Scripture gives the Holy Spirit in Jesus' life of obedience but also highlights the "radical discontinuity" between Jesus' human obedience and that of his disciples.[116]

Part of the problem lies in that Barth ontologizes Jesus' human obedience, seeing it as a manifestation in history of the divine Word's eternal obedience in relation to the Father within the Godhead.[117] Barth makes the Son's obedience (a human act) into a divine attribute and, in doing so, underplays his true humanity and the possibility for his disciples to share in such obedience by the Spirit's power. The solution to Barth lies in predicating Jesus' true human obedience "not upon his hypostatic identity as eternal Son, but rather upon the action and activity of the Holy Spirit."[118] Ultimately, Jenkins

---

[113] See ibid., 188, 190–1.
[114] See ibid., 192, 195–6.
[115] Ibid., 200–1.
[116] Ibid., 201; cf. 205.

> For him [Barth], it is enough simply to say that Jesus was the obedient man in virtue of his own Godhead, even if other human beings are so by virtue of the Godhead in the mode of being the Spirit. Is it enough, however, to say that all human obedience is a function of Godhead power: in us, it is the inhabiting power of the Holy Spirit; in Christ, it is Godhead power instantiated in human nature as the divine Word. Authentic human action, even as obedient human action empowered by the Spirit, is missing in Barth's theology. Even though Barth suggested at the end of his life that dogmatic theology could begin from the standpoint of the third article of the creed (i.e., from the Holy Spirit), the Spirit is woefully absent here, such that even Jesus' obedience is a function of the obedience of the eternal Son. (204)

[117] Jenkins, *Spirit Christology*, 204–5.
[118] Ibid., 217. After drawing attention to Barth's seemingly contradictory assertions that the Son's obedience is "a divine work not a human work," and yet he needs an anthropological "means"

considers Dunn's contributions—his distinction between living "in the flesh" and "according to the flesh," and his keen sense of Jesus' eschatological dependence on the Spirit—as more congenial to Irving's theology and his own proposal for an incarnational Spirit Christology. For Jesus to be truly human and for us to truly follow in his steps by the Spirit' power, one must posit Jesus' "real struggle and real possibility for disobedience."[119] Jenkins wants to affirm this possibility even if such struggle is completely overcome by Christ's human obedience acting in harmony with his divine will and in cooperation with the Spirit who dwells in him. Jenkins's interest in accounting for the Spirit's empowerment and sanctification of the Son as a progressive reality in which the Son and the Spirit constantly cooperate with one another has several advantages. It asserts the mutuality of the missions of the Son and the Holy Spirit in the mystery of the incarnation, while acknowledging the Son's true human acts empowered by the Spirit in their historical trajectory, and the possibility of believers' mutual cooperation with the Spirit in their sanctification.

Ecumenical Exchanges in Spirit Christology: Jenkins's Dialogue with Habets and Sánchez

Jenkins's work represents one of the latest attempts at an incarnational Spirit Christology that seeks to be both intelligible to the author's own theological tradition and to the wider church. In terms of its ecumenical significance, Jenkins, like other authors working in the field in the English-speaking world, draws significantly from David Coffey's work described in the previous chapter. Moreover, Jenkins interacts with Habets's and my appropriations of a Spirit Christology. Jenkins appreciates both authors'

---

to enact such obedience, Jenkins continues: "Nonetheless, I agree with Barth that Jesus Christ, as the incarnate Son, should have the *means* to obey. ... The *means* of Jesus' obedience is the Holy Spirit empowering and inspiring his life ... the obedience of the man Jesus is a function of his responsiveness to the Holy Spirit in and on his life" (215); McCormack rehabilitates Barth's pneumatic deficit through a Chalcedonian Spirit Christology, according to which not the Logos but the human Jesus acting in the Spirit's power is the "performative agent" of the God-human actions. On the basis of Phil. 2:7, he suggests that the Logos becomes receptive to the (Father's) Spirit in his humility, mirroring his own receptivity in relation to the Father in the Trinity. See Bruce McCormack, "The Spirit of the Lord is Upon Me: Pneumatological Christology with and beyond Barth," *Zeitschrift für Dialektische Theologie* 34, no. 1 (2018): 104–17.

[119] Jenkins, *Spirit Christology*, 216.

focus on the Spirit's constitutive role in Jesus' identity and in the various episodes of his life and mission, including his acts of obedience for the sake of our salvation. He also offers some important critiques, especially in terms of the integration of Spirit Christology with a fuller Trinitarian theology. He worries that Habets's apparent understanding of the incarnate Son's obedience as "a reflection of an immanent obedience to the Father" will lead to "an inappropriate transposition" of the economic into the immanent Trinity.[120] On this point, Jenkins's critique of Habets aligns with his critique of Barth. However, Habets sees his position as being more in line with T. F. Torrance's idea that, because of the incarnation, none other than the divine Son himself is obedient unto death, but not in a way that he loses his impassibility or transcendence.[121]

Somewhat similarly, Jenkins feels that my use of the language of the Spirit's perfecting of the Father's love for the Son seems to point to "an inappropriate extension of economic function into the immanent life of God."[122] My answer to Jenkins on this point is simply to note that perfection in this context should not be understood in the sense of "making better," which would clearly be "a signal of deficiency" in God's eternal love.[123] Rather, the term "perfection" is meant simply in the sense of "bringing to its proper term" the Father's love for the Son, which the Son then reciprocates. While I agree that the language of perfection, completion, and fulfillment can be misunderstood and it applies most clearly to the economy Trinity, I still want to affirm the potential though imperfect analogical use of this language to speak of the Spirit's personal identity in the immanent Trinity. Having said that, my main point is simply that the Holy Spirit is the personal love in whom the Father and the Son love another—or that the Father and the Son love each other in the Spirit (*in spiritu*)—and that this reality is both grounded in their intradivine life and manifested in the economy of salvation.[124]

---

[120]Ibid., 324.

[121]In a conversation with Habets, he noted he aligns with Torrance over Barth on this point. See Paul D. Molnar, "The Obedience of the Son in the Theology of Karl Barth and of Thomas F. Torrance," *SJT* 67, no. 1 (2014): 50–69; Habets has also criticized moves that read the cross into the immanent Trinity. See Myk Habets, "Putting the 'Extra' Back into Calvinism," *SJT* 62, no. 4 (2009): 441–56.

[122]Jenkins, *Spirit Christology*, 328.

[123]Ibid.

[124] The Holy Spirit is the hypostasized love, in whom God the Father and the Son mutually love one another and in whom their common love finds its perfection and reaches its fulfillment. ... To sum up, the dynamic and ecstatic presence of the Spirit of the Father in the incarnate Son's human actions for us has its eternal ground in the divine Son's loving response in the Spirit to the Father's inexhaustible love for him in the Spirit. (Sánchez, *Receiver, Bearer, and Giver*, 167)

In terms of the economic Trinity, Jenkins draws attention to an apparent contradiction in my account of the sanctification of the Son's human nature, asking how I can assert that the Holy Spirit "instantaneously sanctifies the humanity of the Son at conception," while also saying that the incarnate Son "progresses in his sanctification."[125] The author feels that holding these assertions amounts to "an actualization in history of a sanctification already accomplished by the Spirit," which in turns suggests "an ontologization of an act of the Spirit on Christ rather than a synergism based on the mutuality of the Son and Spirit's economic missions."[126] Understandably, Jenkins's concern on this point follows from his desire to uphold Jesus' genuine growth in holiness and empowerment by and in cooperation with the Spirit during the whole span of his historic life and work. My response to Jenkins is that, although I could be clearer about this in my work, I am using sanctification in a twofold sense. In a somewhat static sense, sanctification simply means that the Holy Spirit dwells fully and without measure in the humanity of the Son from conception. In this sense, the Son's humanity is sinless or preserved from sin from the beginning of his human existence. But the beginning is not the whole span of the Son's human life. He still has to undergo a human life in his kenosis, in which he must actively choose to obey the Father in the Spirit over against the temptations of the evil spirit so that he might fulfill the Father's plan of salvation. In this dynamic sense, the term "sanctification" communicates not only the static presence but also the ongoing activity of the Holy Spirit in the progressive fulfillment of the Son's human life and mission. To return to Martin Chemnitz's Christology, it seems to me that this twofold sense of sanctification is congenial to his reflections on the role of the Spirit and habitual gifts in Christ's humanity. On the one hand, "the Holy Spirit in the act of conception so sanctified and purified [Christ's human nature] from the whole ruin of sin" (static sense).[127] On the other hand, Christ's humanity is said to be "formed and perfected so that it can be an instrument characteristic of, suitable for, and properly disposed for the deity, through which and in communion with and in cooperation with which the divine power of the Logos can exercise and carry out the workings of His divine majesty" (active sense).[128] In my appropriation of Chemnitz, these statements speak to the Spirit's full sanctifying presence

---

[125]Jenkins, *Spirit Christology*, 326.
[126]Ibid., 327.
[127]Chemnitz, *The Two Natures in Christ*, 57.
[128]Ibid., 248.

in the Son's humanity from conception and also to the Spirit's continuous sanctifying action in his humanity in cooperation with him. Notwithstanding theological differences among the theological traditions represented by Habets, Jenkins, and myself, all our works make room in our incarnational Spirit Christologies for the Son's cooperative relationship with the Spirit in the sanctification of his humanity, and see such relationship as defining for understanding Trinitarian theology, salvation in Christ, and human sharing in the Spirit whom Christ bears and gives.

Questions

(1) Van der Kooi describes substitute, alternative, and mutual complementarity positions on the relationship between Logos and Spirit Christologies today. Explain each approach in your own words and share some ideas or proposals by theologians writing in each category.

(2) Describe a Logos Christology. What potential problems does a Logos Christology present and what are some ways in which a Spirit Christology proposes to address them? Conversely, how does a Logos Christology assist a Spirit Christology?

(3) A number of theologians see the teaching concerning the unity of Jesus Christ's divine and human wills as a promising framework for integrating Logos and Spirit Christologies. Explain how authors in this chapter use this teaching to conceive the relationship between the Holy Spirit and Christ's obedience.

(4) Elaborate on at least one insight from Chemnitz, Owen, and Irving that can enhance Logos Christology with a Spirit-oriented element or trajectory.

6

Christlike Ways of the Spirit: Spirit Christology and Life in the World

One of the contributions of a Spirit Christology lies in showing how the Spirit's presence and work in and with Christ shape human lives. The relative continuity between the Spirit's activity in Christ and his disciples is axiomatic in the field. In previous chapters, we have seen how biblical, historical, and systematic theologians have reflected on this continuity in the context of their own disciplines and traditions. In the Catholic tradition, Cantalamessa has done much to distill and instill the wisdom of Scripture and early church theologians in service to spiritual formation.[1] In his treatise on the baptism of Jesus, he argues that an exploration of the meaning of the Spirit's anointing of Jesus opens up venues for thinking about how the Spirit anoints the church in the likeness of Jesus. Three levels of reflection open up the mystery of the anointing for the church: "To the *historical* plane (the baptism of Jesus in the Jordan) and to the *sacramental* plane (our baptism and confirmation) must be added the existential or *moral* plane."[2] In Chapter 3, we showed how patristic reflections on the anointing of Jesus yield much thought on the church's sharing in his anointing through baptism. Some work has been done on the implications of a Spirit Christology for a theology of the Eucharist.[3]

---

[1] See Gastón Lorenzo, "Cristo y el Espíritu: Algunos aspectos de la cristología en Raniero Cantalamessa," *Revista Teología* 61, no. 128 (2019): 119–35.
[2] Cantalamessa, *The Holy Spirit in the Life of Jesus*, 17.
[3] See Brian A. Gauthier, "Jesus *In, With, and Under* the Spirit: The Spirit's Presence and Activity in Christ in the Sacrament of the Altar" (PhD diss., Concordia Seminary, 2021); Maarten Wisse, "Christ's Presence through the Spirit in the Holy Supper: Retrieving Abraham Kuyper," in Gijsbert van den Brink, Eveline van Staalduine-Sulman, and Maarten Wisse, eds., *The Spirit Is Moving: New Pathways in Pneumatology* (Boston, MA: Brill, 2019), 331–45; Eugene F. Rogers Jr., "The Fire

The intersection of Spirit Christology and sacramental theology—including studies in worship, hymnody, and liturgical traditions—remains open for further research. In terms of the moral plane, the author develops a theology of the church's threefold anointing that aligns with Christ's anointing for his threefold office as king, prophet, and priest. Cantalamessa proposes "to find out from the Gospels just what the Holy Spirit prompted Jesus to do [in his three offices] during his life on earth, what steps he made him take, what choices: for he is prompting the Church to do exactly the same."[4] The assumption is that, since the Spirit whom the church bears is the Spirit of Christ, the promptings of the Spirit in us are properly discerned through a look at the urgings of the Spirit in Christ's life. The same Spirit who urges Jesus to fight against Satan (kingly office), preach the gospel or evangelize (prophetic office), and pray and offer his life to the Father for others (priestly office) urges his body, the church, to share in his anointing in order to do similar works in his name and by his Spirit's leading.[5]

In the spirit of Cantalamessa, this chapter explores more deeply how a Spirit Christology functions as a fruitful bridge between Christology and other theological disciplines concerned with the meaning, transformation, and flourishing of human life. We focus on systematic theologians inquiring into the implications of the field for practical theology. We will begin with US Mexican American theologian Sammy Alfaro's proposal for constructing a Pentecostal Christology through a constructive dialogue between Spirit Christology and US Hispanic/Latin American theologies. Next, we will share the contributions of English Evangelical theologian Lucy Peppiatt toward a theology of mission informed by critical interaction between the fields of Spirit Christology and missiology. Finally, I will reflect on my contributions to the application of a Spirit Christology toward a models-based account of sanctification. The aim of this chapter is not to be exhaustive but simply show the potential and productivity of the field for spiritual formation and ways of living in the world.

---

in the Wine: How Does the Blood of Christ Carry the Holy Spirit?," in *TAT*, 251-64; Neville S. Clark, "Spirit Christology in the Light of Eucharistic Theology," *HeyJ* 23, no. 3 (1982): 270-84; and Edward J. Kilmartin, "The Active Role of Christ and the Holy Spirit in the Sanctification of the Eucharistic Elements," *TS* 45 (June 1984): 225-53.

[4] Cantalamessa, *The Holy Spirit in the Life of Jesus*, 20.

[5] Ibid., 21-2. He develops this thesis in three chapters (20-63).

Sammy Alfaro on Spirit Christology in a US Latino/a Context

The growth of Pentecostalism worldwide has given rise to voices from the Global South. Among them, we have the contributions of immigrants and their children, who bring to their churches and communities a concern for a ministry that accounts for the healing of the whole person. In Latin American and US Hispanic contexts, theological reflection is often done in the midst of poverty and marginality, a hunger for justice in society, and a religious worldview in which spirituality touches all areas of life. A Mexican American organic intellectual working in academia and as a pastor, Sammy Alfaro brings these concerns to his articulation of "a Hispanic Pentecostal Christology that is rooted in the experience of the Hispanic community and developed with an interest toward a liberative praxis."[6] Although Alfaro agrees with the move among Pentecostals such as Steven M. Studebaker and Skip Jenkins toward a Trinitarian Spirit Christology as a complement to a Chalcedonian Logos Christology, he feels that this shift on its own does not yet address the realities of Latino/a churches. The field of Spirit Christology needs to interact with "the contextual/liberative hermeneutics of Latina/o theologies" so that a "Hispanic Pentecostal Christology … is grounded in the experience, faith, and worship of its community and oriented toward liberative praxis."[7]

Exploring the Ecumenical and Contextual Sensitivity of Spirit Christology

Alfaro shows how a Spirit Christology is congenial to early Pentecostal descriptions of Jesus' dependence on the Spirit for his perfect life of sanctification and empowerment for ministry.[8] The Spirit's active agency in Jesus' works serves as a hermeneutical lens to make sense of the Pentecostal fivefold faith in and worship of Jesus as Savior, Sanctifier, Baptizer, Healer, and Coming King.[9] The author reviews non-Pentecostal authors

---

[6] Alfaro, *Divino Compañero*, 5.
[7] Ibid., 13.
[8] Ibid., 17–29.
[9] Ibid., 29–46.

proposing "replacement" (Lampe, Newman, Dunn), "revisionist" (Haight, Schoonenberg), and "complementary" (Pinnock, Surmont) approaches to Spirit Christology.[10] After a brief description of emerging Pentecostal Spirit Christologies,[11] Alfaro shows ecumenical sensitivity and proposes the model's use as a potential tool for dialogue between Trinitarian and Oneness Pentecostals.[12] Although Oneness Pentecostals deny the identity of the one God in three distinct persons and the preexistence of the Son/Logos, they favor speaking of Jesus' identity from the perspective of God's presence as "Spirit" in his humanity (flesh). Alfaro cites David K. Bernard's Oneness view of Jesus from this pneumatic perspective: "The name *Jesus* refers to the eternal Spirit of God (the Father) dwelling in the flesh. We can use the name *Jesus* when describing either aspect or both. For example, when we say Jesus died on the cross, we mean His flesh died on the cross. When we say Jesus lives in our hearts, we mean his Spirit is there" (emphasis in the original).[13] While admitting that Trinitarian and Oneness views are significantly incompatible, he suggests that "the best way to understand Oneness Christology is by understanding God the Spirit as intrinsically joined to the humanity of Jesus" and hopes that "by reflecting on the meaning of the presence and power of the Spirit in the life of Jesus, intra-Pentecostal Christological dialogue might find a more fruitful harvest and mutual understanding."[14] Given the significant number of contemporary Spirit Christologies that operate as a replacement for Logos Christology, a need arises to find ways to enter into dialogue with these approaches.[15] This remains an area in the field that arguably requires further exploration.

For a Spirit Christology aligned with the fivefold description of Jesus to be a viable model in a US Latino/a context, it must interact with "the liberative Christological imagination of Latin American and Hispanic thinkers," which "aims to integrate faith and lived experience of Jesus in a context of economic hardship, transnational ambivalence, and continual marginalization."[16] Latin American liberation theology calls for a discipleship

---

[10] Ibid., 63–86.
[11] Ibid., 87–9 (cf. 8–9). At the time of Alfaro's writing, Skip Jenkins's *A Spirit Christology* (2018) and Frank D. Macchia's *Jesus the Spirit Baptizer* (2018) had not yet been published.
[12] Alfaro, *Divino Compañero*, 89–93 (cf. 50–1).
[13] Cited in ibid., 93.
[14] Ibid.
[15] For a Catholic perspective, see Ralph Del Colle, "Oneness and Trinity: A Preliminary Proposal for Dialogue with Oneness Pentecostalism," *JPS* 10 (1997): 85–110; cf. Del Colle, "Spirit-Christology: Dogmatics Foundations for Pentecostal-Charismatic Spirituality," *JPT* 3 (1993): 91–112.
[16] Alfaro, *Divino Compañero*, 14 (cf. 94).

based on Jesus' embodiment of a preferential option for the poor in his ministry, which inspires an ethical commitment to his preaching of the kingdom by changing structures of sin oppressing vulnerable neighbors.[17] Jesus' death means solidarity with those who, like him, are killed by their oppressors; yet his resurrection means the triumph of life over death, the hope of justice over injustice not only in the future but already now.[18] Among Hispanic theologians, Alfaro commends Virgilio Elizondo's reflections on Jesus' experience of marginality as a Galilean as a source for affirming his solidarity with the struggles of Mexican Americans and others with *mestizo* (mixed) identities in the United States.[19] He endorses Roberto Goizueta's "theology of accompaniment," which argues for a discipleship that identifies with the plight of the poor because it identifies with the God who in Christ became poor for us.[20] Drawing attention to Jesus' identity as the Word, which in Spanish is translated with the more dynamic noun *verbo* (Eng. Verb), Luis Pedraja argues for a relational Christology that highlights Jesus' being-in-action through acts of love and justice that his followers "embody" as they "denounce the injustices of this world and announce the justice of the reign of God."[21] Alfaro also finds inspiration in Ada María Isasi-Díaz's *mujerista* Christology with its emphasis on Jesus' identity as our brother in God's family or *kin*-dom, faithful companion (especially, of the needy), and the God who talks with us in everyday quotidian life (*lo cotidiano*).[22] Alfaro sees all these insights on the social location and praxis-oriented character of Christian theology as congenial to the articulation of a Pentecostal Christology in line with a holistic approach to ministry among Hispanics.

The author concludes this section with an excursus on the socioeconomic and political context in which Jesus lived and ministered.[23] It was a world in which most people did not own land, leased land arrangements often led to the exploitation of hired tenants and laborers, and the heavy burden of high taxation and indebtedness favored the ruling and commercial elites. Even though Alfaro does not deny Jesus' spiritual message, he adds that one should locate such message in the historical context of Jesus' and his family's own poverty, his message of good news to the poor, and his proclamation of

---

[17] Ibid., 95–104.
[18] Ibid., 104–6.
[19] Ibid., 107–9.
[20] Ibid., 110.
[21] Ibid., 111.
[22] Ibid., 113.
[23] Ibid., 114–27.

a kingdom completely different from any earthly kingdom—a kingdom in which God's justice would triumph over all injustice.

Jesus as Divine Companion in Migration, Song, Testimony, and Holistic Ministry

Members of Pentecostal churches often share the difficult socioeconomic conditions of the broader US Hispanic population, including immigrants. They express their faith amidst life struggles not through academic theology but through testimonies and the singing of hymns or *coritos*.[24] Alfaro argues that these sources offer an implicit Christology that aligns with the Pentecostal fivefold description of Jesus, and with a view of Jesus' identity as "El Divino Compañero—their Divine Companion—the one who walks with them in the midst of pain and struggle, and makes provision for their needs through his Spirit."[25] A sample of these *coritos* expresses a Hispanic Pentecostal spirituality that brings together themes, such as Jesus' power to heal the sick and drive out demons, his presence in the church through the Spirit, his solidarity with the human race and kenosis, and his redemption from personal sin and evil and their social manifestations.[26] Sharing three personal narratives shaped by his immigrant identity, the author adopts the Pentecostal use of testimonies (*testimonios*) to articulate how Jesus has been his family's Divine Companion (the title of a *corito*) in their pilgrimages. His experience of Christ as a companion in the journey of the migrant resonates with members of Hispanic congregations: "As in the stories of the Bible that reveal the providential care of God, the immigrants who come to the U.S. are not alone in their journeys. Christ is the Guide and Shepherd of those who make the dangerous journey to come to the U.S.; he is their Divine Companion."[27]

The author concludes his work by summing up the benefits for Pentecostal churches of a Spirit Christology developed in dialogue with US Hispanic theology. Such an approach will offer a less individualistic and more holistic interpretation of the fivefold view of Jesus, serve as a Christological balance to the risk of pneumatological excesses in church, offer a critique of the prosperity gospel for taking advantage of the poor, and advance an integral

---

[24] Ibid., 132, 136–8.
[25] Ibid., 134.
[26] Ibid., 138–43.
[27] Ibid., 146–7.

view of God's salvation that includes the healing of the whole person through evangelism and justice.[28] Alfaro's Spirit Christology embodies the shift in Christianity from North Atlantic to Global South concerns, including those of the children of immigrants living in North America and Europe. Global South theological approaches adopt a more immediate identification with the biblical worldview in which experiences of poverty and exile, healings and exorcisms, and strongly inculturated forms of worship are common.[29] Alfaro's work shows the catholic promise of a Spirit Christology in dialogue with and nourished by growing communities of Christians from across the globe who are often underrepresented in the field.[30] The interaction of the author's Spirit Christology with ecumenical concerns in the Pentecostal tradition at large and with the musical sources of worship flowing from Pentecostal churches shows how the field can interact with other areas of practical theology.

Lucy Peppiatt on Spirit Christology for the Church's Mission in Europe

Living in post-Christendom Western Europe, English theologian Lucy Peppiatt asks what the church's witness in such a context looks like. She proposes that a Trinitarian Spirit Christology offers a proper dogmatic

---

[28] Ibid., 147–50.
[29] On Global South Christianity, see Philip Jenkins, *The Next Christendom: The Coming of Global Christianity* (New York: Oxford University Press, 2002); and John L. Allen Jr., *The Future Church: How Ten Trends are Revolutionizing the Catholic Church* (New York: Doubleday, 2009).
[30] Other Spirit Christologies that incorporate these concerns include Christina Manohar, *Spirit Christology: An Indian Perspective* (Delhi: ISPCK, 2009); San-Ehil Han, "Journeying into the Heart of God: Rediscovering Spirit-christology and its Soteriological Ramifications in Korean Culture," *JPT* 15, no. 1 (2006): 107–26; and Rathan Nicholas Almeida, "Uniqueness and Universality of Jesus Christ Re-visited: An Encounter of Walter Cardinal Kasper's Spirit Christology with the Indian Theology in the Light of Ecclesia in Asia. An Attempt to Focus on and Deepen the Specificity of Jesus Christ in the Context of Religious Pluralism in India" (PhD diss., University of Vienna, 2016); Kombo notes that a programmatic Africanization of Trinitarian theology must include an account of the Holy Spirit's relation to Christ. See James Kombo, "The Trinity in Africa," *Journal of Reformed Theology* 3 (2009): 142. Although an African view of Jesus as a Divine Conqueror power over evil spirits could potentially benefit from an engagement with Spirit Christology, Agyarko suggests that at present such views have yet to deal adequately with the Nicene Christian tradition. It appears that an integration of Spirit and incarnational aspects merits more attention in an African context. See Robert Owusu Agyarko, "Divine Conqueror Christology: A Critique of an African Functional Christology in the Light of Nicene Christian Tradition," *Valley View University Journal of Theology* 4 (2017): 10–27.

foundation for a model of mission that addresses "the exigencies of contemporary culture and modern or postmodern lives."[31] Peppiatt sees Catholic theologian Ralph Del Colle's claim that a Spirit Christology can assist the church's witness in addressing anthropological issues dealing with human culture, social justice, and religious pluralism as an invitation to expand on these matters.[32] The first part of the dissertation explores how systematic theologians working in the field can inform missiology. Among these contributions, for example, she points to Spirit Christology's focus on the active role of the Spirit-anointed humanity of Christ in the Father's mission as a paradigm for "a strong account of human agency" in describing the church's cooperation or co-laboring with the Spirit in God's mission.[33] The second part of her work offers an assessment of theologies of mission from the perspective of Spirit Christology. Peppiatt agrees with missiologist David Bosch's description of the need for mission in a Western context "to be characterized by witness, invitation, response, dialogue, the primacy of people over institutions, contextual evangelism and the preaching and practice of justice."[34] A Spirit Christology explores how models of mission justify their proposals for addressing this context by asking, for instance, how the coinherent or reciprocal character of the missions of the Son and the Holy Spirit inform such proposals. In contrast to models that privilege either the Holy Spirit (Stephen Bevans) or the historical Jesus (Frost and Hirsch), Peppiatt proposes a model that presents the mission of God (Lat. *missio Dei*) with "a strong and equal emphasis on both 'incarnation' and 'anointing.'"[35] One notes how the Christological and Trinitarian tenets of Spirit Christology further ground, refine, or expand on Bosch's shift toward the *missio dei* as the starting point for contemporary missiology.

Seeing the Missionary God through a Trinitarian Spirit Christology

Peppiatt draws attention to how Del Colle's and Coffey's reflections on the complementarity of the missions of the Son and the Spirit set the stage for a Trinitarian account of human communion with God the Father. Coffey's

---

[31] Lucy Peppiatt, "Spirit Christology and Mission" (PhD diss., University of Otago, 2010), 3.
[32] Ibid., 7–8.
[33] Ibid., 10 (cf. 14).
[34] Ibid., 12 (cf. 38–43).
[35] Ibid., 14.

"return" model of the Trinity gets at the heart of mission. It shows that the New Testament bears witness to the Father's sending of the Son and the Holy Spirit to save the world ("mission" model) but also to Christ's "return," and ours with him, to the Father, in the power of the Spirit.[36] Del Colle explores how the distinct yet related missions of the Son and the Spirit help us to discern the "presence" of the divine persons among us today in faith, hope, and love.[37] Concerning faith, Christ's presence (Lat. *Christus praesens*) is known to us in the *bodily* proclamation of the Word, and in the materiality of the sacrament, through faith in him and the memory of his words. In the sacrament, the Spirit's presence (Lat. *Spiritus praesens*) is known to us in a more *anonymous* way, as the Spirit is invoked in prayer for faith and love. Christ's presence is also enacted among us in hope for his future visible coming at the *parousia*; and although the Spirit is present in us now as the firstfruits of our resurrection in Christ, we have yet to experience the fullness of the Spirit in the glorification of our bodies at the *parousia*. Finally, Christ is present among us in his self-giving love for the Father on the cross for us and in his self-giving love for the church in the sending of the Spirit to us. The Spirit makes us aware of such love and allows us to share in it through a Christlike life of love for the Father and the neighbor. Del Colle's use of a Spirit Christology to articulate a theology of presence provides Peppiatt a basis for a model of mission that is rooted in the "coinherent missions of the Son and the Spirit," promotes a transformative account of "conversion in terms of inclusion, obedience, and hope" (aligning with Del Colle's Spirit Christological reading of the theological virtues of faith, love, and hope), and fosters a "Christlike life of discipleship."[38] The author's interest lies in linking mission not only to its Trinitarian origin in a missionary God but also to its effect in nourishing a vibrant faith and life of discipleship in the world.

From Thomas Weinandy's model of the Trinity, which we described in Chapter 1, the author gathers further ideas for articulating a theology of mission. As an example, Weinandy reflects on our adoption into sonship (and daughterhood) by the Spirit of the Son (Rom. 8:14-17) as an icon of the Son's relation with his Father in or by the Spirit. Peppiatt sees this emphasis as congruent with a Spirit Christology's interest in the pneumatic continuity between Jesus and his disciples, and as aligning with the conviction that "the transformation and re-creation of humanity as sons and daughters of

---

[36] See ibid., 43–54 (cf. 114).
[37] See ibid., 61–2.
[38] Ibid., 63.

the Father is at the heart of any Trinitarian model of mission."[39] Through the experience of our adoption by grace into sonship and daughterhood, we come to know and pray to God as our gracious Father (Abba). As long as pneumatology does not collapse into anthropology, the author finds the emphasis on the experience of God through the Spirit as salutary for engaging mission theologically at a time when human experience is seen as more immediately authentic for a living spirituality than institutional affiliations.[40] By seeing the Holy Spirit not merely as a passive person who proceeds from the Father and the Son (or through the Son) but as an active person through or in whom the Father begets the Son and the Son is begotten, Weinandy offers a more social, nonhierarchical portrayal of the Trinitarian life. In Weinandy's argument that in the Trinity there is no sequence or priority of one person over another, since all the persons constitute one another in a perichoretic unity, Peppiatt sees a further basis for the primacy of people over institutions—a key sensibility to postmodern ears who are suspicious of hierarchical institutions and prefer to see life in terms of community.[41] Of particular interest is the author's use of Colin Gunton's study of John Owen and Edward Irving, which we described in Chapter 5, for the active role it gives the Holy Spirit in Christ's free human decisions and saving acts (Owen) and in the sanctification of fallen flesh assumed by Christ for the sake of restoring fallen humanity (Irving).[42] Receiving the Spirit of Christ by grace, disciples become responsive Spirit-anointed agents in Christ's mission. They are objects of salvation first and then instruments of God's saving mission in cooperation with his Spirit.

Spirit Christology and Human Participation in the Mission of God

A key insight for mission Peppiatt draws from Owen and especially Ivor Davidson lies in their understanding of human response to God's mission on the basis of Christ's free human response to the Father in the Spirit' power. As she puts it, "Spirit Christology not only lends theological significance to human being, but by acknowledging Jesus' existence and

---

[39] Ibid., 77.
[40] Ibid., 78–80.
[41] Ibid., 79–80.
[42] See ibid., 86–9, 94–6; in a conversation with Peppiatt, she notes a shift in her thinking toward Owen rather than Del Colle in more recent work. See Lucy Peppiatt, "Life in the Spirit: Christ's and

his humanity as prototypical, we also understand that the fulfilled human existence in Christ by the Spirit becomes the goal of the Christian life."[43] Davidson argues that the teaching of the enhypostatic union, according to which the assumed humanity subsists in the person of the Word, does not have to be understood in a way that such humanity is merely passive. If the Spirit is given a prominent place in Christ's assumed humanity, then, the theology of enhypostasis can make room for Christ's human freedom as he is led by the Spirit, while also seeing such freedom as possible on the basis of divine generosity.[44] This thesis of a Spirit-oriented enhypostasis serves as the Christological basis for an account of the church's Spirit-shaped embodiment of Christ in the world that avoids "ethical docetism while preserving the primacy of divine enabling" in ministry and mission.[45] Peppiatt believes that the heavy emphasis on human freedom and individuality in the West can benefit from a view of mission "in which human agency is held in dialectical tension with the grace and sovereignty of God and the empowering of the Spirit."[46]

Acknowledging what Charles Taylor calls the general shift toward disenchantment or the loss of transcendence and the supernatural in Western secular humanism, Peppiatt sees a paradoxical situation playing out in Western Europe where increasing secularism is accompanied by an increasing deference to and acceptance of religious pluralism.[47] Along with rising suspicion of truth claims and organized religion, we see interest in spirituality and a willingness to commit to smaller groups based on close friendships and justice causes worth fighting for such as decent work among the poor and marginalized.[48] Following Murray Williams, Peppiatt agrees that the church's loss of prominence in post-Christendom Europe has become a blessing in disguise for the church because it has taught her to deal with others not from a position of power but from one of marginality and humility.[49] The aforementioned features of the Western European situation in a secular, pluralistic, and post-Christian milieu calls for a dialogical approach to mission that

---

Ours," in Oliver D. Crisp and Fred Sanders, eds., *The Christian Doctrine of Humanity: Explorations in Constructive Dogmatics* (Grand Rapids, MI: Zondervan, 2018), 165–81.
[43] Peppiatt, "Spirit Christology and Mission," 126.
[44] Ibid., 127.
[45] Ibid., 128.
[46] Ibid., 129 (cf. 32).
[47] Ibid., 147–8.
[48] Ibid., 148–9.
[49] Ibid., 150–2.

emphasizes the primacy of people over institutions, the church as witness not judge, invitation rather than command ... the response of the invitation will be something we cannot control ... dialogue rather than monologue will be important ... evangelism will be in the context of the preaching and practicing of justice.[50]

At a time when suspicion about religious leaders and truth claims is high, and a preference for authenticity of life and caring for the poor in community is welcome, Peppiatt sees the need to place the preaching of the Word in the context of a more holistic or transformational approach to ministry. Doing so places the more Logos-oriented task of proclaiming the Word made flesh through words spoken and heard in a broader Spirit-oriented framework of lifelong discipleship in which the anointed speaker adorns his ministry with works of healing and justice, and a holy life.[51] The author sees this as one example of how the coinherence of the missions of the Son and the Spirit might interact in the church's practice of mission. Peppiatt warns, however, that being a disciple and ambassador of Christ in the Spirit's power will include not only miracles and signs such as healings but also a Spirit-led life marked by Christ's humility, vulnerability, and solidarity with suffering neighbors.[52] In these reflections, the author illustrates how a Spirit Christology informs a view of mission that does not merely present the truth as a propositional claim but embodies it as a way of life that is compelling and inviting to the postmodern mind.

Peppiatt compares her own Spirit Christology approach to mission to other models that are based either on Jesus or the Spirit alone. She commends the Christological approach of Frost and Hirsch for their starting point in the historical Jesus of the gospels and their focus on imitating him in works of justice on behalf of the poor and marginalized, but also criticizes their lack of engagement with the Logos Christology of the ecumenical councils and pneumatological deficit in their description of Christlike discipleship.[53] On the other hand, the author appreciates Stephen Bevans's theology of mission's focus on the Spirit as the forerunner of Christ's and the church's mission, as well as his call for discerning the Spirit in a holistic approach to mission that includes evangelism, justice, and the care of creation. However, calling for clearer ways of conceiving the distinction and integration of the

---

[50] Ibid., 153.
[51] Ibid., 166–8.
[52] Ibid., 172–3 (cf. 184).
[53] See ibid., 191–201.

missions of the Son and the Spirit, Peppiatt warns against the tendency in Bevans's and others' Spirit-oriented models of mission to disconnect the Spirit's universal presence and activity in creation from the particularity of Christ's unique work and his sending of the Spirit to the church for the sake of the world.[54]

In the final chapter of her work, Peppiatt brings together into a thematic and programmatic framework the implications of a Spirit Christology for mission. As mentioned above, she argues for a model that, while strongly emphasizing the divine initiative in mission, includes the church's sharing in the Spirit-anointed humanity of Christ as the paradigm of her human response of obedience to God's mission in the world. She adds that such sharing should not be reduced to a human-centered decision to imitate Jesus but seen as a faith response empowered by the indwelling Spirit which then leads to lifelong Christlike discipleship.[55] In its work of forming people to be Christlike, the Spirit transforms not only the individual but calls persons into communion with one another in the body of Christ. The relational orientation of the church's witness involves dialogue rather than imposition, as well as the authentication of the truth she proclaims by embodying a life that bears witness to the truth in self-sacrifice and solidarity with suffering neighbors.[56] Peppiatt argues that a Spirit Christology frames a theology of mission in a dialogical manner that can faithfully navigate the polarities of unity and diversity, universal and particular, and certitude and open-endedness. On the one hand, for instance, the Holy Spirit forms people into the likeness of Christ, who is the standard prototype of a new humanity. On the other hand, the Spirit conforms people to this Christlike pattern in a plurality of ways, without erasing the particularity of each person, her gifts, ethnic and linguistic diversity, and personality.[57] The universal Christological shape of human life is thus mediated by the Spirit through its created particularity, yielding a form of unity in Christ without homogeneity embodied in the life of the church and all her gifts. Because the gospel is rooted in the story of Christ, it offers certitude in its unified message; yet because this one gospel is embedded in a variety of cultures, there is an open-endedness to its particular shape in a context.[58]

---

[54] For Peppiatt's discussion of models of mission prioritizing the Spirit over the Son, see ibid., 202–17.
[55] Ibid., 219–20.
[56] Ibid., 220–1.
[57] Ibid., 231.
[58] Ibid., 234.

In bringing the one Christ to many people groups, the Spirit can surprise us and form indigenous churches that do not reflect in every way the church of the missionaries. Peppiatt suggests that a contemporary model of mission that actualizes the universal mission of Christ in a way that celebrates creaturely diversity in a process of dialogue and relationship-building is more effective in the context of a Western European pluralistic society. This is especially true if one considers that people in the West are often deeply suspicious about the church's imperialistic past, monologue-style approaches to evangelism, and occasional attempts at dismissing cultural differences. Peppiatt shows the possibilities of the use of Spirit Christology as a theological lens for engaging missiology, an important area of practical theology, with a sensitivity to issues touching on the missionary's Christlike formation, modes of communicating the gospel, and the cultural milieu of the hearers of the message.

Leopoldo Sánchez on Spirit Christology and Sanctification in North America

When a Methodist colleague of mine heard I was writing on sanctification, he looked at me and, somewhat surprised, said: "A Lutheran writing on sanctification?" He was a little perplexed. He added: "Shouldn't you be writing about justification?" As a Lutheran theologian, I come from a tradition in which justification by faith is spoken of as the article on which the church stands or falls. The sheer giftedness of God's favor in Christ on behalf of sinners is the material principle of theology, the hermeneutical lens to interpret God's character and his dealings with creation. Carter Lindberg once asked if Lutherans shouted justification but whispered sanctification.[59] The answer is not that Lutherans have nothing to say about sanctification but that sanctification is indissolubly linked to justification. Lutherans have various ways of framing this indivisible nexus. For instance, Gerhard Forde speaks of sanctification as "getting used to justification," and Oswald

---

[59] Carter Lindberg, "Do Lutherans Shout Justification but Whisper Sanctification?," *Lutheran Quarterly* 13 (1999): 1–20.

Bayer speaks of it as the "institutional side" of justification.[60] Although correct at some level, these ways of speaking are largely conceptual. They tell us what sanctification is not: Not justification! They can also tell us what sanctification is, namely, inner renewal and outward works that flow from justifying faith—or more simply, living by faith. Sanctification is described positively in relationship to justification. There are historical and pastoral reasons for framing holiness in relation to God's justification of the sinner in Christ. The Lutheran confessors in the sixteenth century wished to stress the gratuity of God's forgiveness apart from human works and console consciences with the Gospel of God's grace alone by faith in Christ alone.

Yet to know what something is not or what it is at a conceptual level does not necessarily tell us what it looks like in everyday life. What does sanctification in living color look like? To explore this question, I draw from the church's devotional language, attempting to move from concept to image, from idea to story or narrative. I paint vivid pictures of the sanctified life with the help of biblical writers, church fathers (especially from the fourth century), Martin Luther as an example of a Reformation voice, and other contemporary theologians. The church's language has always had both modes of discourse, the philosophical and the devotional, systematics and practical theology, the language of argument and the language of prayer. My work on sanctification seeks to integrate these modes of discourse into the systematic framework of a Nicene (or Chalcedonian) Spirit Christology in order to portray life in the Spirit in ways that inform spiritual growth and embodied witness in the world—a concern to bring theology and spirituality into dialogue with one another.

Given my own ecclesial background, I want to dispel the myth that Lutherans have little to nothing to say about the Holy Spirit or sanctification. I do so by reintroducing Luther to the ecumenical scene, not for his contributions to the theology of justification but as a teacher and preacher of sanctification—a legacy that, in my opinion, is not appreciated enough by Lutherans themselves! Traditionally, Lutheran piety emphasizes the self-effacing character of the Spirit, who is always shining the spotlight on the Son. The Spirit points us not to its own person but to faith in Christ who is the way to the Father. I myself have spoken, by way of analogy, of a sort

---

[60] Gerhard O. Forde, "The Lutheran View," in Donald L. Alexander, ed., *Christian Spirituality: Five Views of Sanctification* (Downers Grove, IL: InterVarsity Press, 1988), 13; Oswald Bayer, *Living by Faith: Justification and Sanctification*, trans. Geoffrey W. Bromiley (Grand Rapids, MI: Eerdmans, 2003), 59.

of modesty or kenosis of the Spirit, according to which the Spirit humbly works like a behind-the-scenes director working hard to connect people to the Son as the main actor in God's economy of salvation.[61] Granted, the language of self-effacement has its purposes, but one cannot say that all the time about the Spirit and its work in our lives. At some point, one has to deal more robustly with the richness of the Scriptures and the Great Christian Tradition's ecumenical treasure of teaching on the Spirit in its inseparable link to the Son and through him to us.

A Spirit Christology offers a conceptual framework to explore how the Spirit makes us certain kinds of persons. Moreover, it allows us to ground sanctification not in a general human experience or spiritual feeling but in a human participation by grace in the same Spirit whom the Son bears in his life and mission, and then upon completion of his paschal mystery gives to others. Spirit Christology is a means to make the doctrine of the Trinity practical by locating it in the economy of God's action by his Spirit in the life of his Son and in our lives. In terms of dealing specifically with the methodological Trinitarian and Christological issues laid out in Chapters 4 and 5, Spirit Christology has in a sense come of age. Of course, there is always room for adjustment, clarification, and extension of ideas in these matters. But it is generally agreed upon by writers in the field that more needs to be done to explore the productivity of Spirit Christology for dealing with reflection on and formation in Christian practices such as preaching, prayer, sanctification, worship, mission, ecumenism, and social justice.[62] Alfaro, Peppiatt, and myself represent voices that have full works dedicated to the

---

[61] Similarly, or in an analogous way, the Holy Spirit undergoes a sort of humble or modest demeanor—a form of humiliation or *kenosis*, if you will—which in His particular case means basically His desire not to draw attention to Himself or to His presence in the saints, but rather to the Son and through Him to the Father as well as to our neighbor. (Sánchez, "Pneumatology: Key to Understanding the Trinity," 124)

[62] Over the years, I have attempted to test the fruitfulness of Spirit Christology to address a number of issues in practical theology and foster spiritual practices. On proclamation, prayer, and sanctification, see Sánchez, *Receiver, Bearer, and Giver*, 181–237; on immigration, see Sánchez, "Living among Immigrant Neighbors: How a Lutheran Theology of Sanctification Can Inform Our Witness," *Lutheran Mission Matters* 28, no. 1 (May 2020): 46–53; on ecumenism, see Sánchez, "More Promise Than Ambiguity: Pneumatological Christology as a Model for Ecumenical Engagement," in Alberto García and Susan K. Wood, eds., *Critical Issues in Ecclesiology: Essays in Honor of Carl E. Braaten* (Grand Rapids, MI: Eerdmans, 2011), 189–214; on labor and prayer, see Sánchez, "Individualism, Indulgence, and the Mind of Christ: Making Room for the Neighbor and the Father," in Robert Kolb, ed., *The American Mind Meets the Mind of Christ* (St. Louis, MO: Concordia Seminary Press, 2010), 54–66; on missions, see Sánchez, "A Missionary Theology of the Holy Spirit: The Father's Anointing of Christ and Its Implications for the Church in Mission," *Missio Apostolica* 14, no. 1 (2006): 28–40. Other authors have offered thoughts on the applicability of the field to practical issues, usually as a chapter in their monographs. On

intersection of Spirit Christology and some of these areas. Bringing the rigor of a Spirit Christology to bear on sanctification, my thesis is that the same Spirit in whom Christ lived his life shapes the lives of his disciples today—a basic tenet of Spirit Christology—in ways that can be described through a variety of models of sanctification. The image of the Spirit as a sculptor allows me to stress the divine initiative in sanctification, locating holiness in an account of divine agency, but also to highlight the Spirit's formative work in and through human persons who cooperate or collaborate with the Spirit in sanctification.

Models of Sanctification from Spirit Christology

Without attempting to be exhaustive, I argue that a Spirit Christology yields five models of sanctification, five ways in which the Spirit sculpts us after the image of Christ. Each model inhabits a set of narratives and images from Scripture, early church fathers, Martin Luther, and contemporary theologians that invite us to revel in the Spirit's work in and through us. My work is intended not only as an open-ended exploration of such models, but also as an invitation for others to suggest other potential models. Each model offers a description of the Christian life, the work of the Spirit, and the biblical pictures and catechetical images that accompany the model. A payoff of this models-based approach is that each model deals with particular issues in the Christian life, views growth in sanctification differently, and fosters various spiritual disciplines. My approach contests the idea that there is a single, homogeneous way of speaking about sanctification or holiness. Instead, sanctification describes a rich, colorful tapestry of ways of living in the Spirit, acknowledging not

---

culture and experience, social justice, and interreligious dialogue, see Del Colle, *Christ and the Spirit*, 195–216; on issues in ministry and mission (including ecumenism and discipleship), see Habets, *The Anointed Son*, 258–80; on nonviolence, contentment and sharing, and racial unity, see Snavely, *Life in the Spirit*, 154–89; on ecclesiology, see Gregory J. Liston, *The Anointed Church: Toward a Third Article Ecclesiology* (Minneapolis, MN: Fortress, 2015), and his article "Where the Love of Christ is Found: Toward a Third Article Ecclesiology," in *TAT*, 321–45; on preaching, see Jonathan W. Rusnak, "Shaped by the Spirit: Spirit Christology as a Framework for Preaching Sanctification" (STM thesis, Concordia Seminary, 2014); on discipleship, see Jeff B. Phillips, "Discipleship in the Spirit of Jesus: Reflections on Spirit Christology" (MA thesis, Abilene Christian University, 1999).

only the complexity of life itself but also the Spirit's lavish generosity in our lives. The five models of sanctification are:[63]

(1) *Renewal*: Dying to sin and being raised with Christ to new life through daily repentance, and practices of reconciliation. Due to its cyclical view of life in the Spirit, the model especially avoids perfectionistic and fatalistic views of sanctification, redirecting people to an identity rooted in daily contrition and forgiveness.
(2) *Dramatic*: Vigilance in the desert amidst temptation and testing through the Word, prayer, and support groups in the company of saints. The model acknowledges that everyone has a desert she is vulnerable to and addresses the human need for security in a world full of struggles.
(3) *Sacrificial*: Sharing in Christ's servanthood by dying to self in order to make room for neighbors in an interdependent community, where people share in each other's joys and burdens. The model deals especially with the problem of individualism and the need for community.
(4) *Hospitality*: Working from and toward the margins among excluded neighbors, bringing the kingdom to strangers and other marginal characters. The model addresses the human need for belonging and proposes an ethic that does not merely love those whom we like but also the unlovable.
(5) *Devotional*: Living a devoted life as God's human creatures in the rhythm of repose and movement, attending not only to labor but also to rest (or Sabbath) and even play. The model acknowledges the need for balance in life and deals with issues such as idleness and burnout.

The diversity of models reminds us that people are going through different issues in their lives, and proper spiritual care requires a toolbox of resources to assist them in discerning the Spirit in their own spiritual journey. I once presented three of these models of sanctification at a parish and then asked participants to reflect on which model they especially related to. I got three different responses. One sister was dealing with guilt for not measuring up to God's will. A brother was feeling under spiritual attack as he struggled with trust in God's faithfulness amidst his struggles with unemployment. Another person was more concerned about needy neighbors, asking about

---

[63] The following list is an adaptation of Sánchez, *Sculptor Spirit*, 235–6.

ways he could serve people in the community. Their answers reinforced the idea that sanctification is a multidimensional reality, addressing different issues, needs, and struggles.

Why a "Spirit Christology" approach to sanctification? Why not just "Christology"? There are at least two reasons for making this move. First, as we have noted in earlier chapters, Spirit Christology in contemporary theology is often argued either as a replacement for or complement to the Logos Christology of the church councils. Logos Christology focuses on the identity of Jesus as the Word (Logos) made flesh, highlighting the unity of the Son with the Father (against Arianism) and the unity of the person or hypostasis of the Son (against Nestorianism). As a result, the emphasis falls on the discontinuity between Jesus and us. He is God. We are not. He is God made flesh. We are not. Without denying Logos Christology, its legitimate apologetic ends, and the discontinuity it accents between Jesus and us, a Spirit Christology highlights the relative continuity between Jesus and us, which allows us to ask questions about the modes of our sharing by grace in the Spirit-anointed humanity of the Son. We can thus ask questions about how our lives reflect Christ's life in a way that is appropriate to human persons. A second reason for using a Spirit Christology as a framework for sanctification lies in my interest to move from an imitation to a formation approach to Christlikeness. I am not against the notion of *imitatio Christi* per se, but I am aware that at times this language can make Christlikeness solely our human responsibility. For this reason, I prefer to speak of *conformitas Christi*, of the Spirit's sculpting work of conforming humans to Christ's life. As new creatures in Christ, we are called to cooperate with the Spirit, but always under the Spirit's ongoing initiative and action in our lives. Imitation language could call us to be like a Jesus that is "out there" somewhere, and the move is then for humans to bridge this gap between us and "that" Jesus. The more formative language of conformation accents how the Spirit bridges this gap between Jesus "out there" and us "over here" by working Christ's life "in here," that is, in and through us. So we are dealing here with a difference between imitating Christ out there or being conformed to Christ in here.[64]

---

[64] I share McGarry's (citing Hughes) critique of theologies of formation in character and virtues that, by lacking a pneumatological component, tend to reduce character formation to the human will's role in moral progress. See McGarry, "Formed by the Spirit," 285–8.

Spirit Christology as a Story to Discern Spiritual Needs and Journeys

The models-based approach to sanctification has centripetal and centrifugal goals. It exhorts Christians to grow in a deeper appreciation of the Spirit's manifold works in their lives by giving them a pneumatological grammar to discern the Spirit's presence, describe their own spiritual journeys, and have a language to pray in and to the Spirit. Spirit Christology becomes an invitation to discern, journey with God, and pray. Centrifugally, my intent is to give the church an opportunity to hear out other neighbors, such as millennials, Nones (religiously unaffiliated), and Hispanics or Latino/as, who have struggles and needs not unlike those of the rest of the human family. These include the need for identity, reconciliation, security, meaning, community, belonging, and balance in life—needs that models of sanctification address in various ways. Spirit Christology becomes a way to give Christians a language to engage other neighbors (Christian or not) on the spiritual life through dialogue, modeling, and invitation. These practical goals are the ecclesial and missional payoffs of my work, and align in many ways with Alfaro's and Peppiatt's uses of Spirit Christology to engage culturally and religiously diverse contexts and communities. Having Hispanic millennial (and postmillennial) children with friends who are Nones made me aware of the need for thinking through issues of importance to them such as community, hospitality, and belonging, as well as their preference for religious leaders who not only talk the talk but walk the walk, that is, for religious leaders who embody the spiritual life in compelling and inviting ways.

One of the things we learn from surveys on spirituality by sociologists of religion is that North Americans are looking for cohesive and compelling stories that give meaning and purpose to their lives, provide a framework for them to describe their spiritual journey, its beginnings and purpose, including its high and low points.[65] Yielding a plurality of models of the sanctified life, a Spirit Christology paints for us a rich tapestry of portrayals of God's work in Christ and his saints by the Spirit. Each of these models offers distinct yet often related and simultaneous narratives and images that help us articulate our spiritual journeys, their corresponding purposes and struggles or crisis moments, and foster spiritual disciplines. The renewal

---

[65] The rest of this section is from Sánchez, *Sculptor Spirit*, 204–6.

model frames life as a journey of death leading to resurrection, the dramatic one as a wilderness pilgrimage, and the sacrificial one as a life of service and communal sharing. The hospitality model paints the Christian journey as a move from the center to the margins, a posture of welcome toward the forgotten and excluded "other," and a vision of shared life in God's kingdom with the unlovable of our day. In the devotional model, God's people rediscover and embrace their creatureliness as they journey toward final communion with God in Paradise, a new heaven and earth, where humans talk with and praise their creator. In that pilgrimage, we learn to live according to God's designed rhythm of movement and repose, work and rest. Each of these spiritual walks through life has its lows and highs, its times of suffering and hope. There is a cruciform orientation to life in the Spirit. Humans face a struggle, crisis, or conflict before they experience a resolution, transformation, or newness of life by the Spirit's power. For example, in the renewal model, the pain of sins is met with the sweetness of pardon. In the dramatic model, the disappointment of falling trapped under Satan's seductions leads to increased dependence on God's Word and prayer. Under the sacrificial model, an unfulfilling search for significance focused on self-fulfillment or having more things gives way to a review of life's priorities that finds sharing one's gifts and lives with others rewarding. Experiences of marginality lead to solidarity with vulnerable neighbors (hospitality). A restless body and mind receives the gifts of leisure with family and friends and time with God (devotional).

Certain disciplines or practices correspond with each description of the spiritual journey: confession and absolution under the renewal model, prayer for the Spirit's deliverance from evil in the dramatic model, and engaging in "happy exchanges" where each other's strengths and gifts contribute to each other's weaknesses and needs in an intercommunion of love (sacrificial model). Cross- and intercultural exchanges with neighbors different from us often come from a recognition of one's own marginality and a welcoming spirit (hospitality). Restoring balance to life in the face of spiritual or literal idleness and weariness includes an appreciation for cultivating the garden God has given us through our labors and vocations and for honoring the day of rest through reception of God's Word, prayer, sleep, and play (devotional). All these practices assume an opposite, life-denying way of being that the Spirit has to move humans out of, so that the Spirit can shape the mind of Christ in them. The Spirit moves the sinner from guilt to forgiveness, from vulnerability to vigilance and resistance, and from self-centeredness (or conversely, the loss of self) to a communion that embodies a diversity of gifts (and burdens). The Spirit moves humans from the shame of marginality and exclusion to the joy of belonging in God's kingdom and reaching out to others in the margins who have yet to experience such divine embrace. The Spirit also moves weary souls from the restlessness of the idolatry of work and spiritual idleness to an embrace of their creatureliness through devotion to God in the healthy rhythm of activity, rest, and play.

Questions

(1) Alfaro notes that a Spirit Christology on its own does not necessarily address the needs or situations of marginalized neighbors. What insights does he draw from US Latina/o theologians to assist in a contextualization of Spirit Christology? Can you name some examples of biblical narratives, hymns, or personal stories that speak to the Spirit's role in Christ's or the church's ministry to marginal neighbors?

(2) What does Peppiatt mean by a dialogical model of mission? Describe two or three insights from Spirit Christology that, according to the author, can assist in promoting this model of mission in a Western post-Christian context.

(3) Sánchez suggests five models of sanctification. Which model(s) do you identify with the most at this particular time in your life? Explain. Suggest one or two ways in which any of the five models can be embodied in inviting ways in your family, church, or community.

Conclusion

We began our journey into Spirit Christology with Justin's burden: How do we reconcile the confession that Jesus is truly God and truly a man in whom the Holy Spirit dwells? The question comes up, explicitly or implicitly, at various times in church history. Spirit Christology provides the best contemporary framework to lift the burden. With the major exception of post-Nicene (post-Chalcedonian) proposals, and Schoonenberg's model in which Spirit Christology stands as an alternate parallel to a Logos Christology, a growing number of theologians have opted for a Nicene (Chalcedonian) approach. All contemporary types of Spirit Christology agree on the major questions raised in the field. They explore what a Spirit-oriented reading of Jesus' identity tells us about (1) Jesus and salvation in him, (2) God, and (3) a human life shaped by Jesus' Spirit. The answers, of course, differ substantially depending on what "Spirit" means, yielding non-Trinitarian and Trinitarian narratives. To what extent the post-Nicene and Nicene approaches can enter into further dialogue with one another remains to be seen. Some guideposts for such dialogue may be gathered from the type of sustained engagement between systematic theologians and biblical scholar J. D. G. Dunn's work. Over many years, this exchange fostered theologians' appreciation of Dunn's eschatological framing of Jesus' experience in terms of the Spirit and also led to Dunn's own growing appreciation for the value of integrating the incarnational and pneumatic aspects of Jesus' identity.

Theologians working in a Nicene paradigm can differ in their approaches and answers to the major questions above. Yet the consensus is greater than the differences because they operate with what Ayres calls a Nicene logic. In a way similar to the situation of the fourth century, Spirit Christology today allows for a spectrum of legitimate solutions within a unified commitment to the Nicene faith and the subsequent councils it inspired. In terms of method, scholars in the field begin "from below," speaking of the man Jesus in whom the Spirit dwells, and then integrate this starting point in various ways with a Logos Christology and Trinitarian theology "from above." The move from below seeks a solution in the spirit of Bobrinskoy's call for a balanced Syriac-Antiochene route, one that moves beyond the Alexandrian shyness to talk about the Logos' ongoing dependence on the Spirit according to the flesh but avoids Theodore of Mopsuestia's tendency to speak of the man Jesus being filled with the Spirit as a power external to him. Theologians have moved in the direction of enriching a Logos Christology with a biblically informed account of the Spirit's active role in Christ that accents the historical particularity and progression of his human life and mission. The reasons for moving in this direction include accounting for the Scripture's robust witness to the Spirit in the gospels, mitigating against a perceived danger of Apollinarianism in Christology, and the desire to make Christ intelligible at a time when people are more historically conscious and think of the human person as a self-conscious agent who relates to another. The man Jesus is thus not seen as a human nature but as a human person. This focus at times leads to disjointed expressions in the literature that refer to Jesus and the Logos as seemingly parallel realities, raising questions about the full integration of the unity of Christ's person into a Spirit Christology. To handle this issue, the consensus has been in part to retrieve the teaching of the communion of divine and human wills in the person of Christ, accenting the cooperation between Christ's divine will and Spirit-led human will in all his works of salvation.

Drawing attention to the Holy Spirit's defining role in Jesus' life and work has led to models of the Trinity that account not only for the Father's sending of the Spirit through the Son (Father-Son-Spirit) but also for the Father's sending of the Spirit upon the Son (Father-Spirit-Son). Seeking to express these biblical patterns in the context of the correspondence between the divine persons in their relationship to us (economic Trinity) and to one another (immanent Trinity), theologians have sought to highlight the Holy Spirit's active personhood in the Trinitarian life. The consensus in the field has been to move toward a perichoretic model of Trinitarian relations that posits the equality of the persons in their simultaneous and mutual indwelling. Yet proposals in this direction have attempted to integrate the perichoretic accent without giving up on the more traditional mission and procession models of the Trinity (based on the order Father-Son-Spirit). In the case of Moltmann, who seeks to transcend the distinction between the economic and the immanent Trinity and speaks only of a doxological Trinity at the end of history, there is still a recognition of various models of the Trinity at work in biblical narrative (including those aligning with the traditional order). Overall, Spirit Christology has enriched Trinitarian theology, seeking to integrate some perichoretic form of an *in spiritu* model into the classic processional *filioque* or *per filium* models of the Trinity. The Holy Spirit proceeds from the Father and (or through) the Son (*filioque, per filium*) as the one in whom the Father and the Son exist for one another (*in spiritu*). Or in the language of the West: The Holy Spirit proceeds from the Father and the Son as the Love in whom the Father and the Son love one another. As in the complementarity approach to Spirit and Logos Christologies, the attempt has been to integrate social and procession aspects.

Finally, Spirit Christology has brought the Spirit back into an account of salvation in Christ, which includes the Spirit's role in all major events of his life, from his receiving and bearing of the Spirit to his giving of the Spirit to others. The consensus remains that, despite Christ's uniqueness as bearer and giver of the Spirit, humans can participate by the grace of adoption in the same Spirit who dwells in Christ's humanity. The field is still wide open to explore what such Christlike participation means for areas such as anthropology, ecclesiology, and public theology. Some work is already underway engaging the intersection between Spirit Christology and theological reflections dealing with interculturality, missiology, and spiritual formation in North Atlantic and Global South contexts. We pray for the Spirit of Christ to bless us with an even greater global harvest for years to come. *Come, Holy Spirit!* ¡*Ven, Espíritu Santo!*

Glossary

Adoptionism (see docetism): Jesus is a mere man adopted as God's son by grace or by receiving his Spirit. This position denies that Jesus is true God.

Anhypostatic union (see enhypostatic union): Christ's assumed humanity does *not* subsist as its own person or hypostasis (*an*-hypostatic). The man Jesus does *not* have an independent existence from the Logos because he is the incarnate Logos.

Anointing (of Christ): The Father's sending of the Spirit (= anointing) on the incarnate Son at his baptism for his mission (*historical anointing*). The Son's communication of his divinity (= anointing) to his human nature in the personal union (*incarnational anointing*). The Father's begetting of the Son in eternity in view of his creation of the world (*cosmic anointing*).

Apatheia (see pneumatology of the cross): God is impassible (cannot suffer). Among orthodox and heterodox theologians in the early church, the idea functions to preserve the distinction between God (impassible) and creation (passible). In contemporary theology, there are theologians who locate suffering in God's own Trinitarian being (Dabney, Moltmann).

Apollinarism (see docetism): At the incarnation, the divine Logos takes the place of Christ's human soul. The Logos does not assume a complete humanity. Against this idea, Gregory of Nazianzus taught that the Logos cannot save what he has not assumed, and the Council of Chalcedon (AD 451) confesses Christ to be truly human, of a rational soul and body.

Appropriation (see *proprium*): Although all persons of the Trinity share the same works in common because of their indivisible unity, some works can be especially appropriated or attributed to one of the divine persons (e.g., creation to the Father, redemption to the Son, and sanctification to the Holy Spirit).

Arianism (see adoptionism): The Son is a special creature of God, who becomes deified (godlike) on the basis of his works. The position denies that Jesus is Son of God by nature. Against this idea, Athanasius taught that Jesus is not a man who becomes defied, but the divine Word who became flesh in order to deify the flesh.

Deification: The Holy Spirit's work of sanctifying human persons to make them sharers by grace in God's life through union with Christ. The creature does not become God by nature, but a son (daughter) of God by the grace of adoption or by sharing in the Spirit of Christ.

Docetism (see adoptionism, Apollinarism): The Son is divine but only seems to be (Gk. *dokéō*) human. The position denies that Jesus is true man.

Economic Trinity (see immanent Trinity): The persons of the Trinity as they relate to us in creation for our salvation.

Enhypostatic union (see anhypostatic union): Christ's assumed humanity subsists *in* the person or hypostasis (*en*-hypostatic) of the Logos.

Eutychianism (see Nestorianism): After the incarnation, the Logos has only one (divine) nature. Against this idea, the Council of Chalcedon (AD 451) confesses the one person of Christ in *two* natures "without confusion, without change."

Filioque (see *per filium*): The Holy Spirit proceeds from the Father "and the Son" (Lat. *filioque*) as from a single principle. The *filioque* clause is a Western addition to the Nicene Creed.

Flesh: A reference to Christ's human nature, which he shares with the rest of humanity. The Son assumes the flesh (human nature) in order to save the flesh (humanity). It can also refer, more narrowly, to the Son's assumption of fallen human nature in order to save fallen humanity (Irving). The Son lives "in the flesh" but does not sin or act "according to the flesh" (Dunn).

Genera: The kinds (Lat. *genera*) of communication of divine and human attributes in the person of Christ. Lutheran Christology includes three genera (see *genus apotelesmaticum, genus idiomaticum, genus maeistaticum*).

Genus apotelesmaticum: The person of Christ does all his works (Gk. *apotelesmata*) through both natures, each nature working with the other according to what is proper to each. This *genus* is especially helpful to talk about the communion of divine and human wills in Christ. The Logos works in cooperation with his Spirit-anointed humanity.

Genus habitualis (see *genus pneumatikon*, habitual grace): Christ's human nature receives the Holy Spirit's supernatural created (habitual) gifts for his work of salvation (Sánchez).

Genus idiomaticum: The attributes or properties (Gk. *idiomata*) of the divine and human natures are attributed to the person of Christ.

Genus maiestaticum: The attributes or properties of the Logos' divine nature are communicated to or displayed through his human nature.

Genus pneumatikon (see *genus habitualis*): The Holy Spirit's supernatural presence and activity in, with, and through the Logos' human nature and history (Sánchez).

Gnosticism: Since the material world is evil and the flesh cannot be redeemed, salvation is reduced to a spiritual reality. Against this idea, Irenaeus defended the creation, incarnation, and resurrection of the flesh as God's work through his two hands (the Son and the Spirit).

Gratia habitualis (see *gratia unionis*): Habitual grace. A Western scholastic term that refers to the special holiness of Christ or to the Holy Spirit's role in the sanctification of the humanity of Christ and saints.

Gratia unionis (see *gratia habitualis*): Grace of union. A Western scholastic term that refers to the Logos' assumption of a human nature unto his person (incarnation, personal union).

Immanent Trinity: The persons of the Trinity as they relate to one another in the Godhead.

In spiritu: The Son is begotten of the Father "in the Spirit." The expression is used implicitly or explicitly by some contemporary authors (Weinandy, Coffey, Habets, Sánchez) to accent the Holy Spirit's role in the relationship between the Father and the Son. The expression is generally not used in opposition to but as a complement to the processional model.

Inverted enhypostasis (see reciprocal enhypostasis): The divine Logos subsists in the human person Jesus (Schoonenberg).

Kenotic Christology (see *apatheia*): Without ceasing to be God, the Son undergoes a kenosis (condescension, humiliation) as the Servant, becoming dependent on the Spirit for guidance and empowerment, so that he might take upon himself our sinful flesh and carry out his work of salvation.

Logos Christology: Jesus is the God-man or the divine Word made flesh. Against Arianism, it defends the unity of the Son and the Father, or the Son's consubstantiality (*homoousios*) with the Father. Against Nestorianism, it defends the unity of the person of Christ in two natures.

Mutual Love Theory (see processional model, return model): A model of the Trinity based on Augustine's description of the Holy Spirit as the mutual love or bond of communion between the Father and the Son. Some contemporary theologians see this model as a complement to the processional model of the Trinity.

Nestorianism (see Eutychianism): The humanity of Christ is born of Mary but not the impassible Logos. This position denies the communion of properties in the one person of Christ. Against this idea, the Council of

Chalcedon (AD 451) confesses the *one* person of Christ in two natures "without division, without change" and warns against dividing Christ "into two persons."

Nicene faith (logic): The general Trinitarian consensus held in the fourth century that laid the basis for and inspired the subsequent pneumatological and Christological formulations of councils after Nicaea such as Constantinople I (AD 381) and Chalcedon (AD 451). Such consensus includes the understanding of the Son's begetting from the Father in the context of the unity of the incomprehensible God, the distinction between nature and person, and the indivisibility of the persons in their works (Ayres).

Per filium (see *filioque*): The Holy Spirit proceeds from the Father "through the Son." A model of the Trinity that the East prefers over the Western *filioque* because it highlights that the Holy Spirit proceeds from the Father uniquely as the ultimate origin, source, and cause of the Son and the Holy Spirit, while allowing the Son a place in the Spirit's procession.

Perichoresis: In Trinitarian theology, a way to express the unity of God by highlighting how the divine persons relate to one another in a reciprocal or mutual manner. In Christology, a way to express the unity of Christ by highlighting how the divine and human properties of Christ relate to one another without confusion or change.

Pneumatology of the cross (see *apatheia*, kenotic Christology): The Spirit conforms sinners to Christ's death and resurrection (Luther). In contemporary theology, the idea that the Spirit undergoes a kenosis because he accompanies Jesus on the cross and sustains him and his disciples in their suffering (Moltmann, Dabney).

Processional model (see return model, *filioque*, *per filium*): The Holy Spirit proceeds from the Father "and the Son" (*filioque*) or from the Father "through the Son" (*per filium*).

Proprium (see appropriation): A divine person's proper work. That which is proper and not only appropriated to each person of the Trinity in the economy of salvation (e.g., only the Son becomes incarnate).

Reciprocal enhypostasis (see inverted enhypostasis): The divine Logos subsists in the human person Jesus (inverted enhypostasis) and the human person Jesus subsists in or is sustained by the divine Logos (Schoonenberg).

Return model (see processional model): A comprehensive model of the Trinity that highlights the Holy Spirit's active role in the incarnate Son's and the adopted sons' return to the Father (Coffey).

Spirit Christology (see Logos Christology): Jesus is the receiver, bearer, and giver of God's Spirit. A Nicene (or Chalcedonian) Spirit Christology understands Jesus' identity in the Spirit in a Trinitarian perspective and as a complement to Logos Christology. Replacing a Nicene Spirit Christology, a post-Nicene Spirit Christology understands "Spirit" not as a person of the Trinity but more generally as God's general presence in the man Jesus. Finally, some church fathers work with a pre-Nicene Spirit Christology, which understands "Spirit" as the divine element in the Logos.

Bibliography

Agyarko, Robert Owusu. "Divine Conqueror Christology: A Critique of an African Functional Christology in the Light of Nicene Christian Tradition." *Valley View University Journal of Theology* 4 (2017): 10–27.

Alfaro, Sammy. *Divino Compañero: Toward a Hispanic Pentecostal Christology*. Princeton Theological Monograph Series 147. Eugene, OR: Pickwick, 2010.

Allen Jr., John L. *The Future Church: How Ten Trends Are Revolutionizing the Catholic Church*. New York: Doubleday, 2009.

Almeida, Rathan Nicholas. "Uniqueness and Universality of Jesus Christ Re-visited: An Encounter of Walter Cardinal Kasper's Spirit Christology with the Indian Theology in the Light of Ecclesia in Asia. An Attempt to Focus on and Deepen the Specificity of Jesus Christ in the Context of Religious Pluralism in India." PhD diss., University of Vienna, 2016.

Anatolios, Khaled. *Retrieving Nicaea: The Development and Meaning of Trinitarian Doctrine*. Grand Rapids, MI: Baker Academic, 2011.

Antón, Ángel. "El Espíritu Santo y la Iglesia: En busca de una fórmula para el misterio de la Iglesia." *Greg* 47, no. 1 (1966): 101–13.

Athanasius. *Letters to Serapion on the Holy Spirit*. In *Works on the Spirit: Athanasius the Great and Didymus the Blind*, translated with an introduction and annotations by Mark DelCogliano, Andrew Radde-Gallwitz, and Lewis Ayres, 51–137. Crestwood, NY: St. Vladimir's Seminary Press, 2011.

Ayres, Lewis. *Nicaea and Its Legacy: An Approach to Fourth-Century Trinitarian Theology*. New York: Oxford University Press, 2004.

Badcock, Gary D. *Light of Truth and Fire of Love: A Theology of the Holy Spirit*. Grand Rapids, MI: Eerdmans, 1997.

Bauckham, Richard. *God Crucified: Monotheism and Christology in the New Testament*. Grand Rapids, MI: Eerdmans, 1998.

Bayer, Oswald. *Living by Faith: Justification and Sanctification*. Translated by Geoffrey W. Bromiley. Grand Rapids, MI: Eerdmans, 2003.

Berkhof, Hendrikus. *The Doctrine of the Holy Spirit*. Richmond, VA: Knox, 1964.

Bernard, David K. *The Oneness View of Jesus Christ*. Hazelwood, MO: Word Aflame, 2000.

Bobrinskoy, Boris. "The Indwelling of the Spirit in Christ: 'Pneumatic Christology' in the Cappadocian Fathers." *St. Vladimir's Theological Quarterly* 28, no. 1 (1984): 49–65.

Bobrinskoy, Boris. *The Mystery of the Trinity: Trinitarian Experience and Vision in the Biblical and Patristic Tradition*. Translated by Anthony P. Gythiel. Crestwood, NY: St. Vladimir's Press, 1999.

Borg, Marcus J. *Jesus, A New Vision: Spirit, Culture, and the Life of Discipleship*. San Francisco, CA: Harper & Row, 1987.

Bryant, Herschel Odell. *Spirit Christology in the Christian Tradition: From the Patristic Period to the Rise of Pentecostalism in the Twentieth Century*. Cleveland, TN: CPT Press, 2014.

Bulgakov, Sergius. *The Comforter*. Translated by Boris Jakim. Grand Rapids, MI: Eerdmans, 2004.

Cantalamessa, Raniero. *The Holy Spirit in the Life of Jesus: The Mystery of Christ's Baptism*. Translated by Alan Neame. Collegeville, MN: Liturgical Press, 1994.

Cantalamessa, Raniero. "The Incarnation and the Mystery of the Anointing: Christology and Pneumatology in the Early Centuries of the Church." In *TAT*, 175–92.

Catechism of the Catholic Church. 2nd ed. New York: Doubleday, 1995.

Cavadini, John C. *The Last Christology of the West: Adoptionism in Spain and Gaul*. Philadelphia: University of Pennsylvania Press, 1993, 785–820.

Chemnitz, Martin. *De Duabis Naturis in Christo*. 1653. Reprint, Chelsea, MN: Lutheran Heritage Foundation/Sheridan, 2000.

Chemnitz, Martin. *The Two Natures in Christ*. Translated by J. A. O. Preus. St. Louis, MO: Concordia, 1971.

Clark, Neville S. "Spirit Christology in the Light of Eucharistic Theology." *HeyJ* 23, no. 3 (1982): 270–84.

Claunch, Kyle David. "The Son and the Spirit: The Promise of Spirit Christology in Traditional Trinitarian and Christological Perspective." PhD diss., The Southern Baptist Theological Seminary, 2017.

Coffey, David. *Deus Trinitas: The Doctrine of the Triune God*. New York: Oxford University Press, 1999.

Coffey, David. *"Did You Receive the Holy Spirit When You Believed?" Some Basic Questions for Pneumatology*. The Pere Marquette Lecture in Theology 2005. Milwaukee, WI: Marquette University Press, 2005.

Coffey, David. "The Method of Third Article Theology." In *TAT*, 21–36.

Coffey, David. "Spirit Christology and the Trinity." In *Advents of the Spirit: An Introduction to the Current Study of Pneumatology*, edited by Bradford E. Hinze and D. Lyle Dabney. Milwaukee, WI: Marquette University Press, 2001, 315–38.

Congar, Yves. *I Believe in the Holy Spirit*. Translated by David Smith. 3 vols. New York: Crossroad, 1997.

Congar, Yves. *The Word and the Spirit*. Translated by David Smith. San Francisco, CA: Harper & Row, 1986.

Congregation for the Doctrine of the Faith, "Notification on the Book 'Jesus Symbol of God' by Father Roger Haight D.J." December 13, 2004. www.vatican.va/roman_curia/congregations/ cfaith/documents/ rc_con_cfaith_doc_20041213_notification-fr-haight_en.html.

Crisp, Oliver D. *Revisioning Christology: Theology in the Reformed Tradition*. Farnham: Ashgate, 2011.

Cyril of Alexandria. *Commentary on John*. Translated by David R. Maxwell, vol. 1. Downers Grove, IL: IVP Academic, 2013.

Dabney, D. Lyle. "The Advent of the Spirit: The Turn to Pneumatology in the Theology of Jürgen Moltmann." *Asbury Theological Journal* 48, no. 1 (1993): 81–107.

Dabney, D. Lyle. *Die Kenosis des Geistes: Kontinuität zwischen Schöpfung und Erlösung im Werk des Heiligen Geistes*. Neukirchen-Vluyn: Neukirchener Verlag, 1997.

Dabney, D. Lyle. "*Pneumatologia Crucis*: Reclaiming *Theologia Crucis* for a Theology of the Spirit Today." *SJT* 53, no. 4 (2000): 511–24.

Day, Adrian Davis. "The Spirit in the Drama: Balthasar's 'Theo-Drama' and the Relationship Between the Son and the Spirit." PhD diss., Marquette University, 2001.

Del Colle, Ralph. "A Response to Jürgen Moltmann and David Coffey." In *Advents of the Spirit: An Introduction to the Current Study of Pneumatology*, edited by Bradford E. Hinze and D. Lyle Dabney, 339–46. Milwaukee, WI: Marquette University Press, 2001.

Del Colle, Ralph. *Christ and the Spirit: Spirit-Christology in Trinitarian Perspective*. New York: Oxford University Press, 1994.

Del Colle, Ralph. "Oneness and Trinity: A Preliminary Proposal for Dialogue with Oneness Pentecostalism." *JPS* 10 (1997): 85–110.

Del Colle, Ralph. "Spirit-Christology: Dogmatics Foundations for Pentecostal-Charismatic Spirituality." *JPT* 3 (1993): 91–112.

De la Potterie, Ignace. "L'onction du Christ. Étude de théologie biblique." *Nouvelle revue théologique* 80, no. 3 (1958): 225–52.

Dorman, David A. "The Spirit Christology of Geoffrey Lampe: A Critical Analysis." PhD diss., Fuller Theological Seminary, 1992.

Dunn, James D. G. *Christology*. Vol. 1 of *The Christ and the Spirit*. Grand Rapids, MI: Eerdmans, 1998.

Dunn, James D. G. *Jesus and the Spirit: A Study of the Religious and Charismatic Experience of Jesus and the First Christians as Reflected in the New Testament*. Grand Rapids, MI: Eerdmans: 1997.

Dunn, James D. G. *Pneumatology*. Vol. 2 of *The Christ and the Spirit*. Grand Rapids, MI: Eerdmans, 1998.

Flannery, Austin, ed. *Vatican Council II: The Conciliar and Post Conciliar Documents*. Vol. 1 of *Vatican Collection*. New rev. ed. New York: Costello, 1992.

Forde, Gerhard O. "The Lutheran View." In *Christian Spirituality: Five Views of Sanctification*, edited by Donald L. Alexander. Downers Grove, IL: InterVarsity Press, 1988.

García-Moreno, Antonio. "El Espíritu Santo, fruto de la Cruz." In *El Espíritu Santo y la Iglesia*, edited by Pedro Rodríguez, José R. Villar, Ramiro Pellitero, José Luis Gutiérrez, and José Enériz, 71–7. Pamplona: Universidad de Navarra, 1999.

Gašpar, Veronika. *Cristologia Pneumatologica in alcuni autori postconciliari (1965-1995): Status quaestionis e prospettive*. Roma: Gregoriana, 2000.

Gauthier, Brian A. "Jesus In, With, and Under the Spirit: The Spirit's Presence and Activity in Christ in the Sacrament of the Altar." PhD diss., Concordia Seminary, 2021.

Gorman, Michael J. "The Spirit, the Prophets, and the End of the 'Johannine Jesus.'" *JTI* 12, no. 1 (2018): 3–23.

Greene, Joseph R. "Integrating Interpretations of John 7:37–39 into the Temple Theme: The Spirit as Efflux from the New Temple." *Neotestamentaria* 47, no. 2 (2013): 333–53.

Grillmeier, Aloys. *From the Apostolic Age to Chalcedon (451)*. Vol. 1 of *Christ in Christian Tradition*. 2nd rev. ed. Atlanta: John Knox, 1975.

Gunton, Colin. "Two Dogmas Revisited: Edward Irving's Christology." *SJT* 41 (1988): 359–76.

Habets, Myk. *The Anointed Son: A Trinitarian Spirit Christology*. Eugene, OR: Pickwick, 2010.

Habets, Myk. "Jesus, the Spirit, and the Unforgivable Sin: A Contribution from Spirit Christology." *JTI* 12, no. 1 (2018): 39–57.

Habets, Myk. "Prolegomenon: On Starting with the Spirit." In *TAT*, 1–19.

Habets, Myk. "Putting the 'Extra' Back into Calvinism." *SJT* 62, no. 4 (2009): 441–56.

Habets, Myk. "Spirit Christology: Seeing in Stereo." *JPT* 11, no. 2 (2003): 199–234.

Habets, Myk. "Spirit Christology: The Future of Christology?" In *TAT*, 207–32.

Habets, Myk, ed. *Third Article Theology: A Pneumatological Dogmatics*. Minneapolis, MN: Fortress, 2016.

Habets, Myk, and Leopoldo A. Sánchez M. "Introduction: Spirit Christology and the Theological Interpretation of Scripture." *JTI* 12, no. 1 (2018): 1–2.

Haight, Roger. *Jesus: Symbol of God*. Maryknoll, NY: Orbis, 1999.

Haight, Roger. "The Case for Spirit Christology." *TS* 53 (1992): 257–87.

Hansen, Olaf. "Spirit-Christology: A Way Out of Our Dilemma?." In *The Holy Spirit in the Life of the Church: From Biblical Times to the Present*, edited by Paul D. Opsahl, 172–203. Minneapolis: Augsburg, 1978.

Hawthorne, Gerald F. *The Presence and the Power: The Significance of the Holy Spirit in the Life and Ministry of Jesus*. Eugene, OR: Wipf & Stock, 1991.

Hook, Norman. "A Spirit Christology." *Theology* 75, no. 623 (1972): 226–32.

Hunter, Harold. "Spirit Christology: Dilemma and Promise (1)." *HeyJ* 24 (1983): 127–40.

Hunter, Harold. "Spirit Christology: Dilemma and Promise (2)." *HeyJ* 24 (1983): 266–77.

Hurtado, Larry W. *Lord Jesus Christ: Devotion to Jesus in Earliest Christianity*. Grand Rapids, MI: Eerdmans, 2003.

Imbelli, Robert P. "The New Adam and Life-Giving Spirit: The Paschal Pattern of Spirit Christology." *Communio* 25 (1998): 233–52.

Irving, Edward. Vol. 5 of *The Collected Writings of Edward Irving in Five Volumes*, edited by G. Carlyle. London: Alexander Strachan, 1865.

Jenkins, Philip. *The Next Christendom: The Coming of Global Christianity*. New York: Oxford University Press, 2002.

Jenkins, Skip. *A Spirit Christology*. New York: Peter Lang, 2018.

Johnson, Andy. " 'You Wonder Where the Spirit Went': The Spirit and the Resurrection of the Son in Matthew and John." *JTI* 12, no. 1 (2018): 58–75.

Jüngel, Eberhard. *God as the Mystery of the World*. Translated by Darrell L. Guder. Edinburgh: T&T Clark, 1983.

Kasper, Walter. *Jesus the Christ*. Translated by V. Green. New York: Paulist, 1976.

Keating, Daniel A. " 'For as Yet the Spirit Had Not Been Given': John 7:39 in Theodore of Mopsuestia, Augustine, and Cyril of Alexandria." In *Studia Patristica* 39, edited by F. Young, M. Edwards, and P. Parvis, 233–8. Leuven: Peeters, 2006.

Kelly, J. N. D. *Early Christian Creeds*. 3rd ed. New York: Longman, 1972.

Kelly, J. N. D. *Early Christian Doctrines*, 5th rev. ed. London: A.&C. Black, 1977, 144–5.

Kilmartin, Edward J. "The Active Role of Christ and the Holy Spirit in the Sanctification of the Eucharistic Elements." *TS* 45 (June 1984): 225–53.

Kolb, Robert, and Timothy J. Wengert, eds. *The Book of Concord: The Confessions of the Evangelical Lutheran Church*. Minneapolis, MN: Fortress, 2000.

Kombo, James. "The Trinity in Africa." *Journal of Reformed Theology* 3 (2009): 125–43.

Ladaria, Luis F. "Cristología del Logos y cristología del Espíritu." *Greg* 61 (1980): 353–60.

Ladaria, Luis F. *El Dios vivo y verdadero: El misterio de la Trinidad.* Salamanca: Secretariado Trinitario, 1998.

Ladaria, Luis F. "El Espíritu Santo en San Hilario de Poitiers." Vol. 1 of *Credo*, 1983, 243–53.

Ladaria, Luis F. "El P. Antonio Orbe: La gnosis y la teología prenicena." *Revista española de teología* 67, no. 4 (2007): 417–36.

Ladaria, Luis F. *La Trinidad, misterio de comunión.* Salamanca: Secretariado Trinitario, 2002.

Ladaria, Luis F. "La unción de Jesús y el don del Espíritu." *Greg* 71 (1990): 547–70.

Lampe, G. W. H. *God as Spirit.* Oxford: Clarendon Press, 1977.

Lampe, G. W. H. "The Holy Spirit and the Person of Christ." In *Christ, Faith, and History*, edited by S. W. Sykes and J. P. Clayton, 111–30. London: Cambridge University Press, 1972.

Laytham, D. Brent. "'But if … by the Spirit of God': Reading Matthew's Lord's Prayer as Spirit Christology." *JTI* 12, no. 1 (2018): 24–38.

Lindberg, Carter. "Do Lutherans Shout Justification but Whisper Sanctification?" *Lutheran Quarterly* 13 (1999): 1–20.

Liston, Gregory J. "A 'Chalcedonian' Spirit Christology." *Irish Theological Quarterly* 81 (2016): 75–93.

Liston, Gregory J. *The Anointed Church: Toward a Third Article Ecclesiology.* Minneapolis, MN: Fortress, 2015.

Liston, Gregory J. "Where the Love of Christ is Found: Toward a Third Article Ecclesiology." In *TAT*, 321–45.

Lodahl, Michael E. *Shekinah/Spirit: Divine Presence in Jewish and Christian Traditions.* Eugene, OR: Wipf & Stock, 1992.

Lorenzo, Gastón. "Cristo y el Espíritu: Algunos aspectos de la cristología en Raniero Cantalamessa." *Revista Teología* 61, no. 128 (2019): 119–35.

Macchia, Frank. *Jesus the Baptizer: Christology in Light of Pentecost.* Grand Rapids, MI: Eerdmans, 2010.

Madonia, Nicolò. *Cristo siempre vivo en el Espíritu: Fundamentos de cristología pneumática.* Translated by Fernando Torres Antoñazas. Salamanca: Secretariado Trinitario, 2006.

McCormack, Bruce L. *For Us and Our Salvation: Incarnation and Atonement in the Reformed Tradition*, Studies in Reformed Theology and History, vol. 1, no. 2. Princeton, NJ: Princeton Theological Seminary, 1993.

McCormack, Bruce L. "The Spirit of the Lord is Upon Me: Pneumatological Christology with and beyond Barth." *Zeitschrift für Dialektische Theologie*, 34, no. 1 (2018): 104–17.

McDonnell, Kilian. *The Baptism of Jesus in the Jordan: The Trinitarian and Cosmic Order of Salvation.* Collegeville, MN: Liturgical Press, 1996.

McDonnell, Kilian. "The Determinative Doctrine of the Holy Spirit." *Theology Today* 39 (1982): 142–61.

McDonnell, Kilian. *The Other Hand of God: The Holy Spirit as the Universal Touch and Goal*. Collegeville, MN: Liturgical Press, 2003.

McGarry, Joseph. "Formed by the Spirit: A Third Article Theology of Christian Spirituality." In *TAT*, 283–96.

McGukin, Paul. "Spirit Christology: Lactantius and His Sources." *HeyJ* 24 (1983): 141–8.

Molnar, Paul D. "The Obedience of the Son in the Theology of Karl Barth and of Thomas F. Torrance." *SJT* 67, no. 1 (2014): 50–69.

Moltmann, Jürgen. *Crucified God: The Cross of Christ as the Foundation and Criticism of Christian Theology*. Translated by Margaret Kohl. Minneapolis, MN: Fortress, 1993.

Moltmann, Jürgen. *The Source of Life: The Holy Spirit and the Theology of Life*. Minneapolis, MN: Fortress, 1997.

Moltmann, Jürgen. *The Spirit of Life: A Universal Affirmation*. Translated by Margaret Kohl. Minneapolis, MN: Fortress, 1992.

Moltmann, Jürgen. "The Trinitarian History of God." *Theology* 78 (1975): 632–46.

Moltmann, Jürgen. *The Trinity and the Kingdom: The Doctrine of God*. Translated by Margaret Kohl. Minneapolis, MN: Fortress, 1993.

Moltmann, Jürgen. *The Way of Jesus Christ: Christology in Messianic Dimensions*. Translated by Margaret Kohl. Minneapolis, MN: Fortress, 1993.

Mühlen, Heribert. *Der Heilige Geist als Person: In der Trinität, bei der Inkarnation und im Gnadenbund: Ich-Du-Wir*. 2nd ed. Münster: Aschendorff, 1966.

Mühlen, Heribert. "El acontecimiento Cristo como acción del Espíritu Santo." In *Mysterium Salutis*, edited by J. Feiner and M. Löhrer and translated by Guillermo Aparicio and Jesús Rey, vol. 3, 960–84. Madrid: Cristiandad, 1992.

Mühlen, Heribert. *Una Mystica Persona: Die Kirche als das Mysterium der Identität des Heiligen Geistes in Christus und die Christen: Eine Person in Vielen Personen*. 2nd ed. Münich: Schöningh, 1967.

Newman, Paul W. *A Spirit Christology: Recovering the Biblical Paradigm of Christian Faith*. Lanham, MD: University Press of America, 1987.

Nissiotis, Nikos A. "Pneumatological Christology as a Presupposition of Ecclesiology." In *Oecumenica: An Annual Symposium of Ecumenical Research*, edited by Friedrich Wilhelm Kantzenbach and Vilmos Vajta, 235–52. Minneapolis, MN: Augsburg, 1967.

O'Byrne, Declan J. "Spirit Christology and the Trinity in the Theology of David Coffey." PhD diss., Dublin City University, 2009.

Odero, José Miguel. "La unción de Cristo según S. Cirilo Alejandrino." Vol. 1 of *Credo*, 1983, 203–8.

O'Donnell, John J. "In Him and Over Him: The Holy Spirit in the Life of Jesus." *Greg* 70 (1989): 25–45.

Orbe, Antonio. "El Espíritu Santo en el bautismo de Jesús (*en torno a San Ireneo*)." *Greg* 76, no. 4 (1995): 663–99.

Orbe, Antonio. *La unción del Verbo*. Vol. 3 of *Estudios valentinianos*. Roma: Università Gregoriana, 1961.

Owen, John. *The Holy Spirit*. Grand Rapids, MI: Sovereign Grace, 1971.

Peñamaría de Llano, Antonio. "'Espíritu' en la Cristología de los Padres: ¿Binitarismo o Trinitarismo?" *Recherches Augustiniennes* 21 (1986): 55–84.

Peppiatt, Lucy. "Life in the Spirit: Christ's and Ours." In *The Christian Doctrine of Humanity: Explorations in Constructive Dogmatics*, edited by Oliver D. Crisp and Fred Sanders, 165–81. Grand Rapids, MI: Zondervan, 2018.

Peppiatt, Lucy. "Spirit Christology and Mission." PhD diss., University of Otago, 2010.

Petriano, Thomas I. "Spirit Christology or Son Christology? An Analysis of the Tension Between the Two in the Theology of Walter Kasper." PhD diss., Fordham University, 1998.

Phillips, Jeff B. "Discipleship in the Spirit of Jesus: Reflections on Spirit Christology." MA thesis, Abilene Christian University, 1999.

Pikaza, Xabier. *El Espíritu Santo y Jesús: Delimitación del Espíritu Santo y relaciones entre Pneumatología y Cristología*. Salamanca: Secretariado Trinitario, 1982.

Pinnock, Clark H. *Flame of Love: A Theology of the Holy Spirit*. Downers Grove, IL: IVP Academic, 1996.

Pinnock, Clark H. "The Recovery of the Holy Spirit in Evangelical Theology." *JPS* 13, no. 1 (October 2004): 3–18.

Pinnock, Clark H. "The Work of the Spirit in the Interpretation of Holy Scripture from the Perspective of a Charismatic Biblical Theologian." *JPS* 18, no. 2 (April 2009): 157–71.

Porsch, Felix. *El Espíritu Santo, defensor de los creyentes: la actividad del Espíritu según el evangelio de san Juan*. Translated by Severiano Talavero Tovar. Salamanca: Secretariado Trinitario, 1983.

Rahner, Karl. *The Trinity*. Translated by Joseph Donceel. With an introduction, index, and glossary by Catherine Mowry LaCugna. New York: Herder & Herder, 1970. Reprint, Crossroad, 1998.

Ribeiro Santana, Luiz Fernando. "O Espírito Santo na vida de Jesus: Por uma Cristologia Pneumática." *Atualidade Teológica* 14, no. 36 (2010): 265–92.

Rogers, Eugene F. *After the Spirit: A Constructive Pneumatology from Resources Outside the Modern West*. Grand Rapids, MI: Eerdmans, 2005.

Rogers, Eugene F. "The Fire in the Wine: How Does the Blood of Christ Carry the Holy Spirit?" In *TAT*, 251-64.

Rosato, Philip J. "Spirit Christology: Ambiguity and Promise." *TS* 38 (1977): 423-49.

Rusnak, Jonathan W. "Shaped by the Spirit: Spirit Christology as a Framework for Preaching Sanctification." STM thesis, Concordia Seminary, 2014.

Sánchez M., Leopoldo A. "A Missionary Theology of the Holy Spirit: The Father's Anointing of Christ and Its Implications for the Church in Mission." *Missio Apostolica* 14, no. 1 (2006): 28-40.

Sánchez M., Leopoldo A. "The Holy Spirit and the Son's Glorification: Spirit Christology as a Lens for Interpreting John 7:37-39." *JTI* 12, no. 1 (2018): 76-89.

Sánchez M., Leopoldo A. "The Holy Spirit in Christ: Pneumatological Christology As a Ground for a Christ-Centered Pneumatology." In *Propter Christum: Christ at the Center*, edited by Scott R. Murray, Aaron M. Moldenhaeur, Carl D. Roth, Richard A. Lammert, Martin R. Noland, Charles L. Cortright, and Michael J. Albrecht, 343-56. St. Louis, MO: Luther Academy, 2013.

Sánchez M., Leopoldo A. "Individualism, Indulgence, and the Mind of Christ: Making Room for the Neighbor and the Father." In *The American Mind Meets the Mind of Christ*, edited by Robert Kolb, 54-66. St. Louis, MO: Concordia Seminary Press, 2010.

Sánchez M., Leopoldo A. "Living among Immigrant Neighbors: How a Lutheran Theology of Sanctification Can Inform Our Witness." *Lutheran Mission Matters* 28, no. 1 (May 2020): 46-53.

Sánchez M., Leopoldo A. "More Promise Than Ambiguity: Pneumatological Christology as a Model for Ecumenical Engagement." In *Critical Issues in Ecclesiology: Essays in Honor of Carl E. Braaten*, edited by Alberto García and Susan K. Wood, 189-214. Grand Rapids, MI: Eerdmans, 2011.

Sánchez M., Leopoldo A. "Pneumatology: Key to Understanding the Trinity." In *Who Is God?: In the Light of the Lutheran Confessions*. Papers presented at the 2009 Congress on the Lutheran Confessions, edited by John A. Maxfield, 137-9. St. Louis, MO: Luther Academy, 2012.

Sánchez M., Leopoldo A. *Receiver, Bearer, and Giver of God's Spirit: Jesus' Life in the Spirit as a Lens for Theology and Life*. Eugene, OR: Pickwick, 2015.

Sánchez M., Leopoldo A. "Sculpting Christ in Us: Public Faces of the Spirit in God's World." In *TAT*, 297-318.

Sánchez M., Leopoldo A. *Sculptor Spirit: Models of Sanctification from Spirit Christology*. Downers Grove, IL: IVP Academic, 2019.

Saraiva Martins, José, ed. *Credo in Spiritum Sanctum: Atti del Congresso Teologico Internazionale di Pneumatologia*. 2 vols. Vatican City: Libreria Editrice Vaticana, 1983.

Schoonenberg, P. J. A. M. *El Espíritu, la Palabra y el Hijo: Reflexiones teológicas sobre una cristología del Espíritu. Cristología del Logos. Lectura Trinitaria*. Translated by Ramon Puig Massana. Salamanca: Ediciones Sígueme, 1998.

Schoonenberg, P. J. A. M. "Spirit Christology and Logos Christology." *Bijdragen* 38 (1977): 350–75.

Simonetti, Manlio. "Note di cristologia pneumatica." *Augustinianum* 12 (1972): 201–32.

Snavely, Andréa. *Life in the Spirit: A Post-Constantinian and Trinitarian Account of the Christian Life*. Eugene, OR: Pickwick, 2015.

Sosa Siliezar, Carlos Raúl. *La Condición Divina de Jesús: Cristología y Creación en el Evangelio de Juan*. Salamanca: Ediciones Sígueme, 2016.

Spence, Alan. "Christ's Humanity and Ours: John Owen." In *Persons, Divine and Human: King's College Essays in Theological Anthropology*, edited by Christoph Schwöbel and Colin E. Gunton, 74–97. Edinburgh: T&T Clark, 1991.

Studebaker, Steven M. "Integrating Pneumatology and Christology: A Trinitarian Modification of Clark H. Pinnock's Spirit Christology." *Pneuma* 28, no. 1 (Spring 2006): 5–20.

Theodore of Mopsuestia. *Commentary on the Gospel of John*. Translated by Marco Conti. Downers Grove, IL: IVP Academic, 2010.

Theodore of Mopsuestia. *Commentary on the Nicene Creed*. Translated by Alphonse Mingana. http://www.tertullian.org/fathers/theodore_of_mopsuestia_nicene_02_text.htm#C10.

Van de Kamp, Gerrit. "De pneumatologische christologie van David Coffey." *The Australian Catholic Record* 92, no. 1 (2015): 67–80.

Van der Kooi, Cornelis. "On the Identity of Jesus Christ: Spirit Christology and Logos Christology in Converse." In *TAT*, 193–206.

Van der Kooi, Cornelis. *This Incredible Benevolent Force: The Holy Spirit in Reformed Theology and Spirituality*. Grand Rapids, MI: Eerdmans, 2018.

Vanhoye, A. "L'azione dello Spirito Santo nella passione di Cristo secondo l'epistola agli Ebrei." Vol. 1 of *Credo*, 1983, 759–73.

Weinandy, Thomas G. "The Case for Spirit Christology: Some Reflections." *The Thomist* 59, no. 2 (1995): 173–88.

Weinandy, Thomas G. *The Father's Spirit of Sonship: Reconceiving the Trinity*. Edinburgh: T&T Clark, 1995.

Wisse, Maarten. "Christ's Presence through the Spirit in the Holy Supper: Retrieving Abraham Kuyper." In *The Spirit Is Moving: New Pathways in Pneumatology*, edited by Gijsbert van den Brink, Eveline van Staalduine-Sulman, and Maarten Wisse, 331–45. Boston, MA: Brill, 2019.

Wong, Joseph H. P. "The Holy Spirit in the Life of Jesus and of the Christian." *Greg* 73, no. 1 (1992): 57–95.

Wright, John H. "Roger Haight's Spirit Christology." *TS* 53 (1992): 729–35.

Zizioulas, John D. *Being as Communion: Studies in Personhood and the Church.* Crestwood, NY: St. Vladimir's Press, 1997.

Zizioulas, John D. *Communion and Otherness: Further Studies in Personhood and the Church.* London: T&T Clark, 2006.

Author Index

Classic
Apollinaris 6
Arius 58, 64, 84
Athanasius 8, 58–9, 64–80, 83–5, 88, 121–2, 125, 132, 142
Augustine 24, 28, 50, 76–7, 98, 105–9

Basil of Caesarea 82–4

Calvin, John 31, 138 n.85
Chemnitz, Martin 121–32, 141, 148
Crellius, John 134–5
Cyril of Alexandria 6, 84–9, 121–2, 125, 130, 132, 142

Epiphanius 103
Eutyches 6–7

Gregory of Nazianzus (Nazianzen) 76–7, 82–3
Gregory of Nyssa 108

Ignatius of Antioch 10–11
Irenaeus of Lyons 30, 43 n.46, 58–64, 66, 69–71, 74–5, 78–80, 89
Irving, Edward 141–6

John Chrysostom 83–4, 86
John of Damascus 76–7, 122 n.26
Justin Martyr 2–5, 33, 45, 66, 135, 173

Luther, Martin 94–6, 129

Nestorius 6–7, 84–7, 125 n.35

Owen, John 133–41

Tertullian 9–11, 76–7
Theodore of Mopsuestia 83, 86–8, 174

Contemporary
Alfaro, Sammy 29, 153–7
Ayres, Lewis 7–9, 173

Barth, Karl 17–18, 95, 145–7
Bobrinskoy, Boris 82–4, 86, 89–90, 174
Bryant, Herschel Odell 58–9
Bulgakov, Sergius 25–6

Cantalamessa, Raniero 2–3, 60, 77–8, 80–1, 151–2
Coffey, David 27–8, 93–4, 104–13, 116 n.1
Congar, Yves 2, 108
Crisp, Oliver D. 138–9

Dabney, D. Lyle 94–7
Davidson, Ivor 160–1
Del Colle, Ralph 27–8, 110, 158–9
De la Potterie, Ignace 33–5
Dunn, James D. G. 36–42, 47, 144–6, 173

Gorman, Michael J. 51–5
Gunton, Colin 141–3

Habets, Myk 116, 133–41, 146–7
Haight, Roger 12–17
Hawthorne, Gerald F. 42–8

Jenkins, Skip 29–30, 116, 141–9

Kasper, Walter 19–20
Keating, Daniel A. 87–8

Ladaria, Luis F. 111 n.87, 116 n.1
Lampe, G. W. H. 13 nn.35, 38; 13–14 n.39; 14 nn.40, 41
Laytham, D. Brent 49–50

Macchia, Frank 29
McCormack, Bruce L. 138 n.85, 140–1 n.92, 146 n.118
Moltmann, Jürgen 93–104, 112, 174–5
Mühlen, Heribert 23–4

Orbe, Antonio 60–1, 68 n.48, 70 n.52, 81

Peppiatt, Lucy 157–64
Pinnock, Clark H. 30–2

Rahner, Karl 17–20, 110
Rogers, Eugene F. 18, 20

Sánchez M., Leopoldo A. 50, 116, 121–32, 141, 146–9, 164–72
Schoonenberg, P. J. A. M. 118–19
Simonetti, Manlio 74
Snavely, Andréa 29
Spence, Alan 137–8

van der Kooi, Cornelis 16–17, 117–21
Vanhoye, A. 34–5, 45

Weinandy, Thomas G. 27, 116 n.1, 159–60

Zizioulas, John D. 24–5

Subject Index

Adam, last Adam 25, 30–2, 43, 60–4, 71, 74 n.74, 88–9, 132, 142–4
adoptionism 13, 15–16, 64–5, 88 n.115
Alexandrian Christology 69, 76, 84–5, 90, 121–2, 124, 174
Alexandrian Spirit Christology 82–3, 85, 87–9, 122, 174
  (*see also* Antiochene Spirit Christology)
anhypostasis 118
  (*see also* enhypostasis)
anointing of Jesus, views of
  active and passive significance 78, 81
  baptism (*see* baptism, of Jesus)
  cosmic 5, 63
  ecclesial, exemplary 77, 80–1
  incarnational 67–9, 75–7, 122
  king, prophet, priest 152
  revelatory 77–8
  three anointings (Irving) 144
Antiochene Spirit Christology 83, 86–8
  (*see also* Alexandrian Spirit Christology)
Apollinarianism 6, 130, 139–40
appropriation 109–10
Arianism 2–3, 6, 58, 60, 64–71, 83–4, 108, 169
atonement 30–2, 130–1 n.58

baptism, Christian 18, 24–5, 62, 77, 80–1, 85–6
baptism, of Jesus 3–5, 22–5, 33–4, 38–9, 44, 60–6, 75–80, 87 n.111, 88 n.115, 89, 105–6, 151

Christ (*see* Jesus Christ; *see* Jesus Christ, life and work)
communicatio idiomatum
  (communication of attributes) 123, 140
communio naturarum (communion of natures) 140 n.92

deification 60–1, 64–6, 69–70, 72, 84, 88
docetism 118–20, 133, 139, 141 n.92, 161

ecumenical councils
  Nicaea I (AD 325) 6–9
  Constantinople I (AD 381) 6, 8
  Ephesus (AD 431) 6, 85 n.103, 87 n.111, 125 n.35
  Chalcedon (AD 451) 6
  Constantinople II (AD 553) 87 nn.110–11
  Constantinople III (AD 680–1) 124
enhypostasis 118–19, 161
  (*see also* anhypostasis)
Eutychianism 6–7, 140 n.91

filioque ("and the Son") (*see* Trinity, models of, *filioque*)

genera (sing. *genus*), types of (Chemnitz) 123–6
  definition 123
  genus apotelesmaticum 124–5
  genus idiomaticum 123–4

Subject Index

genus maiestaticum 125–6
genus pneumatikon, genus habitualis (Sánchez) 126–32
Gnosticism 52–3, 58–66, 70–1
gratia habitualis (*see* Jesus Christ, habitual grace, gifts)

holiness (*see* sanctification, of Jesus; *see* sanctification, of saints)
Holy Spirit (*see* Spirit)

impassibility, divine 64, 84, 87–8, 95, 99, 113, 147
(*see also* kenosis)
in spiritu ("in the Spirit") (*see* Trinity, models of, *in spiritu*)

Jesus Christ
assumption of fallen flesh (Irving) 29–30, 116, 141–6, 160
Christology from above 121, 174
Christology from below 40, 173–4
Christology of inspiration 40–1
consciousness of eschatological power 37–9
consciousness of sonship 37, 40
Divine Companion (*Divino Compañero*) (Alfaro) 156
grace of union 127
habitual grace, gifts 23, 111 n.87, 127–8, 130, 137 n.79, 148
kenotic Christology 42–8, 68
obedience (*see* sanctification, of Jesus)
receiver, bearer, and giver of the Spirit (*see* Spirit Christology, compared to Logos Christology; *see also* Spirit Christology, varieties of)
sanctification (*see* sanctification, of Jesus)
sinlessness 106, 129, 142, 145, 148
Wisdom 12–13, 70

wisdom, growth in 43, 47, 90, 122–3, 128–9, 136, 137 n.79
Jesus Christ, life and work of
anointing (*see* anointing of Jesus, views of)
atonement (*see* atonement)
baptism (*see* baptism, of Jesus)
conception, birth 3, 19, 21–2, 43, 75, 77, 81, 129, 136, 142–4, 148–9
death 26, 34–5, 45–6, 96–9
exorcisms 25, 38, 45, 49
glorification 22, 26, 50, 53, 55, 87 n.111, 89, 119
healings, miracles 25, 38, 45, 83, 87 n.111, 130
infancy and youth 42–3
prayer 15, 26, 36–7, 39, 49–50, 152
(*see also* prayer)
preaching, proclamation 38, 45, 152
resurrection 3, 25–7, 46, 67, 74, 89, 103, 145, 155
temptation, testing 38, 44, 49–50
Transfiguration 25, 100
Justin's burden 2–5, 33, 45, 66, 135, 173

kenosis (*see* Jesus Christ, kenotic Christology; *see* Spirit, kenosis; *see also* impassibility, divine)

Logos (two-natures) Christology 58–9, 106, 118–21, 123–7, 130–1, 138–9, 169 (*see also* Spirit Christology, compared to Logos Christology; *see also* Spirit Christology, varieties of)
Lord's Prayer 49–50

modalism 15, 59 n.6
monothelitism 124 n.31

Nestorianism 6–7, 84, 138 n.85
Nicene faith, logic 7–9, 14, 173

Pentecostalism, rise of 28–30
perichoresis
　in Christ 125–6
　in the Trinity 27–8, 99–104, 112–13, 160, 174–5
pneumatology of the cross 55, 94–100, 104 (*see* Spirit, kenosis)
prayer 25, 36–7, 49–50, 159–60, 168, 170–1
　(*see also* Jesus, life and work of, prayer)
pro-Nicene theology (*see* Nicene faith, logic)

recapitulation 30, 43 n.46, 61–4, 88–9

sanctification, of Jesus 19, 23, 28, 30, 41–3, 66–8, 75–6, 79–82, 90, 110, 111 n.87, 122 n.26, 127, 129, 131, 133–4, 136–8, 141–6, 148–9, 160
sanctification, of saints 15, 19, 22 n.77, 23, 28, 30, 67–8, 72, 76, 79–81, 84, 110–11, 131, 144, 146, 160, 164–72
scholastic (neo-scholastic) theology 28, 109–10, 122, 127, 130
Second Vatican Council 20–4, 26–8
self-communication, divine 18–19, 109
Socianism 133–5
Spirit
　bond of love 23–4, 28, 98
　　(*see also* Trinity, mutual love theory)
　divine substance (*see* Spirit Christology, varieties of, pre-Nicene (pre-Chalcedonian))
　glorifying 99–104
　kenosis 26, 96–9 (*see* pneumatology of the cross)
　indwelling, of Jesus 20, 82–4, 98, 122, 128–9, 143 (*see* sanctification, of Jesus)
　indwelling, of saints 20, 67, 88, 103, 110–11, 163 (*see* sanctification, of saints)
　immediate agent of assumed humanity (Owen) 134–8, 144
　Pentecost 26, 29, 90
　person (hypostasis) 9–10, 13, 69–73, 94, 102, 107–10, 119, 128
　proprium (proper mission, work) 19, 27–8, 42–3, 75, 78, 90, 110–11, 135–6
　third article of the creed 1, 8, 18 n.56, 22, 95, 102, 145 n.116
　Wisdom 70–1, 119
Spirit Christology, compared to Logos Christology
　alternative to (parallel to) 118–19
　complementary to 119–21 (*see* Spirit Christology, varieties of, Nicene (Chalcedonian))
　replacement (substitute) for 117 (*see* Spirit Christology, varieties of, post-Nicene (post-Chalcedonian))
Spirit Christology, varieties of
　Johannine 50–5
　Lutheran 126–32
　Nicene (Chalcedonian) 5–10
　North American spirituality context 170–2
　Orthodox 24–6, 82–4, 89–90
　Pentecostal 28–30, 141–6
　pneumatic incarnation (*see* Spirit Christology, varieties of, pre-Nicene (pre-Chalcedonian))
　pneumatic inspiration (*see* Arianism, *see* Gnosticism)
　pneumatic mediation (*see* Spirit Christology, varieties of, Nicene (Chalcedonian))
　post-Christendom European context 157–64
　post-Nicene (post-Chalcedonian) 12–17, 117, 173
　pre-Nicene (pre-Chalcedonian) 10–11, 34, 58, 73–5, 122

Reformed 136–46
Roman Catholic 12–16, 18–24, 26–8, 104–11
US Latino/a context 153–7

Theological interpretation of Scripture 35, 48–55, 86–9
Trinity, models of
  bestowal (*see* Trinity, models of, return)
  doxological, Trinity in glorification 100–3, 112, 174
  eucharistic 103–4, 112
  filioque ("and the Son") 102–4
  in spiritu ("in the Spirit") 27, 67, 72, 103, 106, 112, 147, 175
  mission 105, 159, 174
    (*see also* Trinity, models of, procession)
  monarchical, Trinity in sending 27, 100–4, 112
  mutual love theory 28, 105–9, 111–13
    (*see also* Spirit, bond of love)
  per filium ("through the Son") 27, 100, 108 n.78, 112, 160, 174–5
  perichoretic, social (*see perichoresis*, in the Trinity)
  procession 27, 94, 102, 104–5, 108–10, 116 n.1, 174–5
  return 105–9, 111–12, 159

Scripture Index

Old Testament

Genesis
2:7	53, 88, 89 n.117

Psalms
2:6–7	21 n.76
2:7	4
33:6	70
45:7	5, 122 n.26
45:7–8	64
68:18	132

Isaiah
11:1–2	23
11:1–3	3
12	50
42:1	106
61	53
61:1–2	38, 62, 63 n.23
61:1–3	52

Ezekiel
34–39	52
37:9–10	53
47	50

Zechariah
14	50

New Testament

Matthew
1:18–25	106
3:16	62
4	49
11:27	36–7
12:28	38, 49
26:38	26

Mark
1:9–11	105
14:32–42	36
15:34	31

Luke
1:35	11, 74, 76, 122 n.26, 137 n.79
1:26–38	106
2:40	128–9
2:52	122, 128
4:14	75
4:18–19	38
11:20	38
24:49	75

John
1:1–3	74
1:1–3, 14	15
1:16	22
1:25–7, 29–36	52
1:32–3	22, 53
1:33	50, 86 n.107
2:19–22	46
3:34	22, 52, 106, 132, 137 n.79
4:14	50
5:26	125
6:27	125

6:48–58	141 n.92	15:45, 49	41
7:37–9	107 n. 71		
7:38–9	50, 53, 55, 106	Galatians	
7:39	87–8	4:6	37, 41
8:58	15	5:22	41
9	52		
9–10	53	Ephesians	
10:17–18	46	4:15	21
14:16–17	52	5:30	132
14–16	53		
15:26	71, 102, 105, 108	Philippians	
16:13–15	11	2:7	146 n.118
16:14–15	103 n.53	2:9–10	64
17:5	15		
19:30, 34	50, 55, 107 n.71	1 Timothy	
19:30, 34–5	106	3:16	46
20:21–2	50		
20:22	53, 88, 89 n.117	Hebrews	
20:28	15	2:11 ff.	132
		2:17	35
Acts		4:15	35
1:8	75	7:16	98
2:4 ff.	132	7:26	137 n.79
10:38	21, 75	9:12, 15	34
		9:14	31, 34, 45, 98, 107
Romans		9:24	35
1:1–4	10, 46, 74	10:4–10	35
3:25	31	10:10	34
8:3–11	31, 46	10:14–16	35
8:14–17	27, 37, 41, 159		
12:6	132	1 John	
		1:1	124
1 Corinthians		1:7	141 n.92
1:24	75	2:20, 27	21
6:14	46		
12:3	41	Revelation	
13:4–7	41	5:12	132